WITHDRAWN

DATE DUE

D0142397

WITHDRAWN

The
Magician
the Witch
and the Law

The Middle Ages

a
series
edited by

EDWARD PETERS
Henry C. Lea, Associate Professor of Medieval History
University of Pennsylvania

The Magician the Witch and the Law

EDWARD
PETERS

University of Pennsylvania Press

1978

Copyright © 1978 by Edward Peters

All rights reserved

Printed in the United States of America

Library of Congress Cataloging in Publication Data

Peters, Edward, 1936–
    The magician, the witch, and the law.

    (The Middle Ages)
    Include index.
        1.   Magic—History.   2.   Witchcraft—History.
I.   Title.   II.   Series.
BF1593.P42   133.4′094   78-51341
ISBN 0-8122-7746-5 (cloth)
        0-8122-1101-4 (paper)

Composition by Deputy Crown, Inc.

To my mother
Marjorie Corcoran Peters

in memory of my father
Edward Murray Peters

Contents

	Preface	ix
	Introduction: Magic in Medieval Culture	xi
1.	The Transformations of the *Magus*	1
2.	Rhetoric and Magic in the Eleventh and Twelfth Centuries	21
3.	Learning and Magic in the Twelfth and Thirteenth Centuries	63
4.	The Systematic Condemnation of Magic in the Thirteenth Century	85
5.	The Sorcerer's Apprentice	110
6.	The Magician, the Witch, and the Law	138
	Appendix 1. *Res fragilis*: Torture in Early European Law	183
	Appendix 2. Nicholas Eymeric: On Heresy, Magic, and the Inquisitor	196
	Appendix 3. The Magician, the Witch and the Historians	203
	Index	213

Preface

This book is a study of medieval conceptions of, and attitudes toward *maleficium*, especially in those instances when *maleficium* served as a generic term to designate both magic and witchcraft. Its focus is primarily upon the ways by which theologians, moralists, and jurists defined *maleficium* and condemned it. It began as a development of my earlier work on witchcraft, but it soon broadened to include magic as well, a subject whose relation to witchcraft has not generally received much attention. The completion of this study has been greatly aided by several opportunities to present aspects of my work to colleagues and various learned, and interested, audiences. A grant from the Penrose Travel Fund of the American Philosophical Society enabled me to begin to survey much manuscript and early printed literature; the generosity of the University of Pennsylvania Press helped me to complete the work and prepare it for publication.

Early versions of portions of the present work have been given as talks to the following conferences and institutions: the Fourth International Congress of Medieval Canon Law at Toronto in 1972; the Medieval House of the University of Rochester; the Faculty Research Club of the University of Pennsylvania; the 1902 Lecture Series at Bryn Mawr College; Swarthmore College; the 1976 Western Michigan Medieval Conference at Kalamazoo. These generous occasions allowed me to present ongoing research—often in an unfinished and unpolished state—to critical and helpful audiences. Professor Alan C. Kors of the University of Pennsylvania, ever since we collaborated on our documentary collection *Witchcraft in Europe,* has been an intelligent and critical adviser. Several colleagues at the Department of History of the University of Pennsylvania have helped me frame my argument and improve it. I am also personally grateful to Professor William Jones of the University of New Hampshire, Dr. Thomas Waldman of Philadelphia, and to Professor James M. Muldoon of Rutgers University, Camden, for having helped me with parts of this book when they were still only in conversational form. These individuals, institutions, and occasions have contributed greatly to whatever value my work has, and not at all to its shortcomings.

My family has, as usual, gone without me for long and unconscionable periods of time, both during the preliminary studies and research and during the final preparation of the manuscript. My gratitude to them is greatest of all. I also acknowledge the contribution of the many students at the University of Pennsylvania who have taken History 532, Topics in Medieval History, when, as they often did, those topics turned out to be heresy, dissent, magic, and witchcraft.

Modern historical literature on the subjects of magic and witchcraft is both extensive and diverse. The bibliographical essay in Appendix 3, below, attempts to describe the most important modern studies and to indicate the best and most recent bibliographical guides through it. Since these subjects are not of interest to medievalists alone, I have tried to provide translations of the major texts discussed, to give their locations in the original languages in footnotes, and to suggest in the footnotes the best scholarly guides to particular topics. Neither pretends to be exhaustive; both pretend to efficiency of reference.

Historians perforce write about chronological change in a past whose future they already know. This book attempts to put the great witchcraft persecutions of the sixteenth and seventeenth centuries and the contemporary concern over learned magic well into the remote future of the writers whose attitudes toward magic it analyses. In doing so, I hope that I have been able to particularize in sharper relief than usual the actual concerns of thinkers between the ninth and the sixteenth centuries and thereby to have contributed a chapter on some neglected aspects of the condemnation of *maleficium* to the history of the religious culture of early Europe.

Philadelphia, 1978

Introduction

Magic in Medieval Culture

Cornelius Agrippa von Nettesheim, a sixteenth-century humanist, critic of witch-trials, and eager student of natural magic, once remarked that magic, a *sublimis, sacraque disciplina,* honored by the greatest thinkers of antiquity, had been unjustly condemned by the early Fathers of the Church. Until his own age, this condemnation had resulted in a very deficient sort of magic, not only in the corrupt and uncomprehending practices of necromancers and witches, but in the *deliramenta* and *superstitiones* of no less formidable medieval thinkers than Roger Bacon and Arnald of Villanova. Agrippa's conception of a learned and high magic, "not witchcraft, not superstition, not demonolatry, but wise, priestly and prophetic," is the matter of another book than this, although it is necessary to point out that it was not as far removed from the thought, and the period, of Roger Bacon and Arnald of Villanova as Agrippa professed to think. The claims made by Agrippa and others in the fifteenth and sixteenth centuries for a pristine natural magic did not go unchallenged, however, and more than one practitioner of high magic found himself charged with necromancy and, *superstitio,* the very traits Agrippa and others had restricted to the lesser castes of the magic profession.

Agrippa's magic had to free itself of such charges because until it was announced by Pico and Ficino in the fifteenth century, no court or confessor recognized any form of magic but that which had been condemned by the Church Fathers and repeatedly denounced in all sources until the fifteenth century. As a historian of magic Agrippa was generally right.

The place of magic in the organization of knowledge of the Greek, Hellenistic and Roman worlds, never entirely free of opprobrium, came under new attacks in the first and second centuries A.D. from Christian writers and later from Roman emperors. After its last flowering in the fourth and fifth centuries, most of the learned magic of the world of late antiquity disappeared into manuscripts or into thin air, where much of it remained, completely inaccessible to those who might have wished to seek it out, until the recovery of much classical literature in the fifteenth and sixteenth centuries. Renaissance humanism, with its passionate and indiscriminate zest for classical information retrieval, also revived much of ancient magic and made for some of it the claims enunciated by Agrippa in his eloquent and fruitless defense of *prisca magia.*

The high Neoplatonic magic of the Renaissance might indeed be condemned as the old demonological magic in new dress, but it had about it the pretense and dress of learning—and it had influential patrons. Its practitioners never ran quite the risk of systematic condemnation and persecution as did those necromancers and witches of whom Agrippa so scornfully spoke. By the beginning of the seventeenth century, Shakespeare's Prospero could renounce his magic, drown his books, and step back into the normal Christian world of Milan. Others, however, paid heavier prices for engaging in what Agrippa had called the corrupted and uncomprehending magic of the Middle Ages and the early Renaissance. They were tried, convicted, and burned as *malefici,* and their circumstances have concerned historians from the early nineteenth century until the present.

Of the two, the witch has received by far the most attention. For epistemological reasons, some of which are discussed below in the bibliographical essay in Appendix 3, the phenomenon of witchcraft and witch persecutions in early modern Europe has attracted the attention of some of the best—and some of the worst—modern historians. The high learned magic so eloquently praised by Agrippa has also attracted the attention of historians. The third group, however, Agrippa's "necromancers," has received far less attention. Its members have either been discussed under the broad heading of learned magic or as an undifferentiated part of the category of witches. The formal character of learned magic, on the one hand, and the failure among historians to discriminate clearly among types variously categorized as witches, are two reasons for the infrequency of scholarly discussion of the figure of the magician in medieval history. A third reason may be the extraordinarily literary context in which the best-known medieval magicians—Merlin, Faust, and Simon Magus—are to be found. The air of faerie that surrounds Merlin, at least, is not readily amenable to serious historical analysis.

Yet Agrippa's ignorant necromancers, and not the Renaissance *magus* or the witch, were the object of most theological, moral, and legal condemnation from the fifth to the fifteenth centuries. The nature of that condemnation and the conception of the *crimen magiae* in literary and legal sources colored both the suspicion of the later learned *magus* and the fear and prosecution of the witch. In addition, the actual occurence of magicians at different times and places between the fifth and the sixteenth centuries also influenced both traditional and novel forms of condemnation. Finally, the nature of the sources that discuss the crime of magic, the *crimen magiae,* must also be taken into account if one wishes to obtain a historical sense of precisely what medieval writers thought magicians were.

This book began, in part, as the study of some questions that had arisen when I collaborated with Professor Alan C. Kors of the University of Pennsylvania on the anthology of texts in translation, *Witchcraft in Europe.* Those questions originally clustered around the figure of the witch and her medieval antecedents. Among those antecedents, I found the magician, Agrippa's necromancer rather than his learned *magus.* The magician has intruded himself into the history of witchcraft condemnations and persecutions on the basis of his occurence in the source materials of medieval and Renaissance ideas of deviance and dissent. *Maleficium,* the term that all sources down to the eighteenth century employed to designate witchcraft, originally meant generally injurious crime and, specifically within that category, magic. Witches were prosecuted in the sixteenth and seventeenth centuries in part, at least, because they, like the magicians, employed a kind of *maleficium.* Like the magician and the heretic, they ran afoul of specific laws that had their roots in Roman and canonical legal traditions and Christian theology. Thus, the purpose of this book is to explore some of the links among the magician, the witch, and the law within the context of medieval culture and the specific character of medieval historical sources.

The first chapter deals with the transformations of the *magus,* that is, with the process by which the learned magic of the ancient world was transformed in late antique and early medieval sources into the demonic magic known to most medieval thinkers and linked by them to certain forms of heresy, blasphemy, and superstition, particularly to idolatry. Thereafter, the progression is roughly chronological. The final chapter treats the problem of magician and witch, suggesting that the final transformation of the *magus* was caused in part by the thought of fifteenth-century theologians and lawyers, a new literalness in reading the legal parts of the Old Testament, a sharper idea of pact with the demon, a large literature on magic, and a new sense of sacramental responsibility principally on the part of secular magistrates rather than inquisitors.

More than heresy or magic specifically, however, such terms as *super-*

stitio and *idolatria* acquired new sharpness. These are the theological offenses of magician, heretic, and witch alike. There are other terms that are not treated as extensively as these but are as important; some I intend to pursue at a later date. The chief among these is *curiositas*, "the passion for knowing unnecessary things." It was the shape of legitimate knowledge in medieval society that defined, by excluding them, the magician, the heretic, and the witch. Others are *latria* and *dulia*, the technical names for the veneration magicians and witches paid to demons. Finally, magic, like heresy, was a political offense. Spiritual and temporal powers were both vulnerable to heresy, but magic looms large as a social and political weapon in the fourteenth and fifteenth centuries. Attempts of learned magicians and some philosophers to separate "good" and "bad" magic, "learned" and "unlearned" magic, "philosophical" from "bestial" magic, never wholly succeeded. Whether it pleased him or not, a magician like Agrippa von Nettesheim was closer to the victims of witch-trials than he knew, or cared to acknowledge.

Some of the most familiar elements in the history of witchcraft are virtually omitted from the following study. Rather than account for the particulars of night-flight, sabbats, cannibalism, infanticide, and weather-magic, I have tried to look at a broader area, that of *superstitio* and *idolatria*. Within that broader area, the nature of *maleficium* clearly expands to include the magician as well as the witch. Both figures, in addition, took on some of their coloration from antique and medieval traditions of invective against heresy and heretics. The studies of Jeffrey Russell and Norman Cohn deal extensively with the forms of invective; those dealing with accusations of cannibalism, orgy, and ritual secrecy offer important dimensions to many of the materials dealt with in this book. If I have treated these problems with less thoroughness than they deserve, it is because the treatments of Russell and Cohn already offer substantial commentary and analysis, and I have profited from them greatly. Some movements, notably Catharism, the most violently attacked heresy of the Middle Ages, shared the brunt of much of this sort of invective, although Catharism is relatively lightly treated in the following pages.

This book is a study of the ways by which the writers of different kinds of texts conceptualized the phenomenon of magic and created the forms of invective that crossed genre limits and helped to shape the common image of the heretic, magician, and witch alike. It traces something of a high road in this process, relying on new information that may be obtained from some well-known texts by emphasizing the contexts in which those works were produced.

The contextual circumstances of invective against magic are essential to consider, because, as later chapters of this book will argue, it was largely by lifting the portrait of the magician and the traits attributed to him out of their original contexts and placing them in new contexts that the sixteenth-century onslaught against magic and witchcraft was accomplished. From their diverse origins, the traits of the magician were shaped into a commonly understood image by the end of the thirteenth century. To whatever extent they may have disagreed about other aspects of magic, sixteenth-century apologists like Agrippa and earlier medieval theologians and moralists shared the same view of demonological magic. Indeed, to make any defense of high magic at all in the sixteenth and seventeenth centuries, any apologist had to condemn demonological magic in virtually the same breath. The critics of high and low magic alike were less discriminating. Not only such well-known critics as Jean Bodin, but otherwise cautious and sceptical thinkers like Johann Weyer agreed on the nature and necessity of the condemnation of magicians. Early modern Europe knew several different kinds of magic, but most of its thinkers, regardless of their individual reasons, uniformly condemned the magic of the Middle Ages and thus, in their distinctive ways, helped to maintain the prosecution of magicians and witches both through the seventeenth century.

The first chapter of Keith Thomas' massive study of *Religion and the Decline of Magic* is entitled "The Magic of the Medieval Church." In it, Thomas examines one pole of medieval awareness of "Magic," that at which the powers of sacrament, saint, and priest tended toward debasement in the realm of popular, including clerical, attitudes toward the invocation of divine powers to ameliorate the circumstances of earthly life. At the other pole, of course, there was another kind of what modern thinkers might be inclined to call magic, the blinding power of miracle, authentic sacrament, or direct divine intervention. At the latter extreme, there is no magic at all, since the chief feature of magic is its power of compelling, rather than beseeching, supernatural forces. The closer that medieval beliefs veered toward the automatic power of compulsion over spirits, whether beneficient or evil, the closer it came to magic. Churchmen were not unaware of this dilemma, and late medieval attacks on *superstitio* included both those beliefs that were condemned outright and those beliefs that, while strictly still within the realm of orthodoxy, nevertheless suggested too great a dependence upon the compulsive powers of sacraments and sacramentals. Moreover, this condemnation of beliefs in the compulsive power of the Church's sacraments and other elements of the Christian cult was not the only basis for the attack on magical beliefs. Magicians and, later, witches could also invoke and beseech the demons, and this element of invocation, of offering them those forms of veneration, *latria* and *dulia*, that were strictly reserved for God and the saints, seemed certainly more blasphemous, if not more dangerous, than

the belief in the compulsive powers of ritual magic itself. Thus, as both
a perversion of proper forms of devotion and as an art that claimed or
was accused of claiming to enable its practitioners to compel supernatural forces, magic in all of its variations was savagely condemned
by churchmen.

To medieval thinkers, magic was the earliest and most illicit form of
human commerce with demons. Heresy was another, and the images of
the magician and the heretic were shaped by the same kind of fear and
revulsion. Moreover, magic could be learned, and the medieval organization of legitimate knowledge was one of the weapons that medieval
thinkers used consistently to attack magical practices. Not only was
magic a form of false religion, but it was also a form of forbidden knowledge. Finally, magic, although its critics accused it of working wonders
(*mira*) rather than miracles (*miracula*), caused injury, and therefore was
punishable under criminal law as well as under ecclesiastical strictures.
Thus, the full force of ecclesiastical condemnation was available to secular magistrates from an early date, and late medieval writers on magic
rarely failed to mention the civil, as well as the spiritual liability of the
crimen magiae.

To search for witches alone in medieval sources is to narrow the limits
of a legitimate historical question. Just as the concept of *maleficium* in
law covered many offenses, so did the concept of *superstitio*. Any historian
concerned with the history of magic and witchcraft as cultural phenomena
has to consider the specific cultural contexts of those offenses. Having
started out in search of the witch, I found that the sources I encountered,
when broken down into genres and analyzed as texts of particular kinds,
revealed less and less about medieval "witchcraft" and more and more
about other areas which few writers had discussed. The rule of looking
at what the sources *say* is one of two rules that I have followed throughout. The other is to consider ideas and documents *in context*. If one puts
the image of the sixteenth-century witch out of one's mind for a while,
one finds something very different in the medieval sources. Except for a
very few pages at the end, this book does not address the sixteenth and
seventeenth centuries. It begins with the history of the one figure that I
(and Cohn) have discovered in the sources, the magician. In dealing with
this figure, I have fleshed out in antiquity and the early Middle Ages his
emergence in the Christian world-view and his importance in theology,
particularly in patristic literature. This treatment may also help to supplement and clarify some of Cohn's findings.

Second, this book deals very carefully with words. As a colleague once
suggested to me, the English language permits one to speak of sorcerers
and witches chiefly because the English language derives from Romance
and Germanic roots. In Latin, the same word was used for both magician

and witch, *maleficus(a)*. The word *sorcier(e)* describes both in French. *Zauberei* means 'magic' in German, and *Hexe* means 'witch,' but *Hexe* is a late development. Thus, this study focuses upon *maleficium* in whatever form it is found, and it rarely uses the word witch to apply to any person before 1450 or so. For the image of the witch in the fifteenth and sixteenth centuries is derived from that of the magician, the idolater, the *superstitiosus*. The word *magici* is much more accurate when applied to occult practices of any kind before the middle of the fifteenth century.

Third, this study attempts to deal with the rhetorical traditions that shaped the picture of the magician, the heretic, and the witch. One of the skills of the rhetorician generally was his mastery over forms of chaos, violence, and the supernatural. The rhetorical learning of the Middle Ages contributed to the depiction of those social types whom most people detested. In addition to the rhetoric of the sources, I have paid most attention to the genre of the sources. Thus, for example, when a monastic writer in the twelfth century describes heretics' activities, a magician, or extreme violence, he does so in part because of the demands of his genre, and in part because of his view of the lay world generally. Both these elements have to be taken into account in analyzing the place of his remarks, not only in his own world, but as they appeared to later people who did not view them in the same context. Finally, I have paid close attention to the milieu of the source. A legal tract addresses different questions from a sermon, and the ideas in both, while they may be related, are not identical. In some cases, notably that of John of Salisbury's *Policraticus* discussed in Chapter 2, I have argued that the book's genre, in this case a moral treatise for courtiers, must be considered when interpreting the texts.

Fourth, I have attempted to delineate some of the social contexts in which the magician is most likely to be found. One of the dilemmas of the historian of witchcraft is that, outside of accusations, trial records, and theoretical treatises, it is hard to find witches that correspond to the best-known ideal type of the sixteenth century. It is easy to find heretics. It is also easy to find magicians, and the sources where magicians are found, with real magic books and real attempts to alter the lives of human beings, help to explain why the ideas about them took shape and how they circulated. I have focused upon the court as the political center, rather than the law-court, because it seems from the documents that the court life and the nature of courtiers' attitudes toward security, incertitude, ambition, and fear—as well as the personnel in the court and their life style—help to explain the fourteenth-century phenomenon of trials for political sorcery, so badly understood by most political historians. I have also investigated the texts that would have been best known to different kinds of people in different social circumstances. Thus, to discuss theologians' ideas of magician and witch, it is important to know the kinds of books theologians got their information from, as it is for lawyers, preachers, and inquisitors. The generic relationships of texts to ideas is similar to the relationship of institutions like the court to the character of belief in, and fear of, magic.

This book, then, deals with a number of topics that have been treated by other historians of witchcraft, but its focus on the history of the magician, the social reality of magic, and the interrelations among the ideas of *magic, maleficia, idolatria,* and *superstitio* makes it an addition to and clarification of certain ideas in modern scholarship, and not a repetition of them. It is philosophcally closest to Cohn's *Europe's Inner Demons,* but it has benefitted from the work of most of the historians mentioned above, particularly Russell. Although I disagree with Russell about a number of points on the medieval history of the magician, in developing my own approach, I often found that an encounter with *Witchcraft in the Middle Ages* was stimulating and helped to focus my own work; without it this book would have been much longer.

The nature of the sources for such a discussion of magic in medieval culture as this book contains is not the same as that for later studies of witchcraft or learned magic. The vast evidence for popular beliefs upon which Thomas built the monumental *Religion and the Decline of Magic* is lacking, as is the vast mass of archival data that characterizes the internal history of individual witchcraft persecutions in the work of MacFarlane and Midelfort. Medieval sources permit one, rather, to observe the learned tradition that depicted the figure of the magician and the process by which the learned tradition was applied by spiritual and temporal magistrates to particular figures. The existence by the thirteenth century of the *type* of demonological magician enabled theologians and magistrates to deal with diverse cases of magic that came before them. The creation of the type is the history that this book attempts to describe, for it lay behind the learned magus of the Renaissance as well as the necromancers and witches that even the defenders of learned magic condemned.

1

The Transformations
of the *Magus*

The Hellenic world, as it set about its task of organizing and systematizing knowledge, recognized and defined magic and the figure of the
magos. The term *magos* first appeared in Greek as a designation of the
Persian astrologer-priests who, Herodotus tells us, accompanied the army
of Xerxes into Greece.[1] From its first Greek use, the term shared much
of the opprobrium of other things Persian and generally oriental that so
characterizes subsequent Greek intellectual life. The association of the
magoi with hated Persia and the unfamiliar sight and sound of their
practices perhaps helped to add the meaning "trickster" or "quack" to the
original sense of *magos*, an extension noted as early as the fifth century
B.C. After the fifth century the Persian origin of the *magos* ceased to be
emphasized, and the term displaced older Greek designations of practitioners of magic. A *magos* became a practitioner (or pretended practitioner) of arts that elicited the aid of gods or *daimones* for his own
benefit or for that of his clients, usually for criminal purposes. Plato, in
The Laws, is explicit in his condemnation of *magoi* and their practices:

As for those who add the character of a beast of prey to their atheism or belief
in divine indifference or venality, those who in their contempt of mankind
bewitch so many of the living by the pretense of evoking the dead and the
promise of winning over the gods by the supposed sorceries of prayer, sacrifice
and incantations and thus do their best for lucre to ruin individuals, whole
families, and communities, the law shall direct the court to sentence a culprit
convicted of belonging to this class to incarceration in the central prison,

1

where no free citizen shall have access to him. . . . At death he shall be cast out beyond the borders without burial, and if any free citizen has a hand in his burial, he shall be liable to a prosecution for impiety at the suit of any who cares to take proceedings.[2]

In Plato's view the *magos* committed a crime so deadly in the eyes of the community and the gods that it rivalled that of Polynices in the eyes of Creon, and violation of the prohibition of burial was, of course, the great offense of Sophocles' Antigone.

Arthur Darby Nock suggests a succinct definition of the Greek and later Roman concept of *mageia*:

The profession by private individuals of the possession of technical ability enabling them to supply recipes or perform rites to help their clients or damage their clients' enemies; the use by such clients or by others of such proceedings to damage enemies; and—corresponding to the vague modern use already mentioned—the religions belonging to aliens or on any general ground disapproved.[3]

The older Greek term for magic, *goeteia*, gave way before *mageia*, the individual *goes* before *magos*, and *goeteia* became a kind of species of magic. According to some philosophers it was the kind of magic that used evil *daimones*, whereas *mageia* employed only good *daimones*. The association of the *magos* with *daimones*, good or bad, was in part a development of the Platonic theory that *daimones* were intermediaries between the divine and the human realms. The *magoi*, therefore, were those who could by their art or pretense consult and sometimes command the *daimones*. Such professional, or technical contact with the *daimones*, however, was rarely looked upon with equanimity in Greek law. In spite of the claims of some *magoi* that they employed a legitimate and divinely approved *techne*, or *ars*, and in spite of the claim of some later religious philosophers that there were permitted, as well as forbidden forms of *mageia*, hostility more often than not characterized the Greek and later the Roman attitude toward magical practices and practitioners. That hostility was compounded of various measures of scorn and fear, for although the *magoi* may have been hated and distrusted, there was also widespread belief that their arts did indeed pose a considerable threat to the well-being of the Greek and Roman community.[4]

Although Plato was harsh in his condemnation of magicians, the laws of Greece and Rome were harsher. They contained stiff penalties for the practice of magic, especially when that magic could be proved to have caused injury or loss. Besides its alleged impiety, magic also attracted the hostility of philosophers because it appeared to conflict with the ethical character of legitimate intellectual inquiry since it was sometimes considered to be a form of aimless erudition, *curiositas,* which was attacked in other forms as well. The ethical bent of the later Hellenistic world harbored little good-will toward magicians who professed to be able to command or compel the *daimones,* especially if such powers hinted at impiety, caused human injury, or deflected the magician from the proper path of philosophical inquiry. Well before the advent of Christianity, therefore, the figure of the *magos* and the nature of his art had been a powerful concern for philosophers and lawgivers as well. One of the first tasks of Christians was not to condemn the *magos* on any particularly original ground, but to prove that they themselves were not *magoi.*

Greeks and Romans were not the only people who defined, feared, and condemned magical practices. The Septuagint version of Old Testament used the Greek word *magos* freely to condemn those magicians of Pharaoh depicted in Exodus 7:8, as well as the practices condemned at length in the legal portions of Leviticus and Deuteronomy. The later Latin translations of the Bible translated *magos* by *magus,* because it had come to have a similar meaning in the Roman world to its meaning in the Greek world. Again and again in the Old Testament, Jews were warned against practicing magic or consulting magicians. Such prohibitions, however, did not stop these practices, and Greeks, Romans, Jews, and early Christians alike appear to have persisted in consulting magicians well into the fifth and sixth centuries A.D., and probably long after.[5]

Among the first and most important episodes in the encounter of Christianity with pagan magic is the story, recounted in Acts 13:6–12, of the meeting of St. Paul with the Jewish magician Elymas, in the entourage of a sympathetic Roman proconsul, Sergius Paulus:

. . . an intelligent man, who had sent for Barnabas and Saul and wanted to hear the word of God. This Elymas the sorcerer [*magus*] (for that is how his name may be understood) seeking to turn the proconsul away from the faith, resisted them. Saul, however, also known as Paul, filled with the Holy Spirit, looked upon him and said: "O you who are full of fraud and all falsehood, son of the devil, enemy to all justice, will you never stop trying to subvert the just ways of the Lord. And now behold, the hand of God is upon thee, and you will be blind, and for a time will not see the sun." And immediately mist and shadows came over him, and he groped about for someone to take his hand and lead him.[6]

At its very outset, in a simple version of what would later become a common rhetorical tradition, Christianity set itself sharply against the practice of magic in the person of one of its earliest and most influential figures, St. Paul himself. To pagans, of course, such a contest might have seemed to be a contention of magicians to see who was stronger (also a literary theme), and indeed Christians were accused by their critics of practicing magic themselves. But in this story, Elymas's *daimones* never appear, and the hand of God was something that even mildly curious pagans like Sergius Paulus could recognize.

Early Christianity attacked other aspects of the pagan world besides its magic, principally its learned culture, and often the denunciation of pagan literature and philosophy took the form of including and even identifying them with magic, thus further insulting the pagans who themselves never identified the two. Tertullian's famous taunt, "What has Athens to do with Jerusalem," was taken by many Christians to include all aspects of pagan thought.[7] The writings of Tertullian condemn both magic and that vain erudition that "is able to study nature without caring for him who created it and governs it: they only trouble themselves in a great emptiness."[8] Indeed, it is as a subspecies of *curiositas* that Tertullian denounces magic, and he denounces less the practice itself than the mental attitude that to him pervades all papan philosophy, the passion for knowledge that does not recognize the final end of all true knowledge, the knowledge of God. As the gods of the pagans became demons in Christian eyes, pagan ethics, religion, and philosophy joined pagan magic as condemned. For Tertullian, the magicians' nefarious practices, pagan consultations of oracles, and other forms of divination were all performed with the aid of demons. Early Christian demonology at its outset identified the magical arts with the power of the devil.

In the search for a form of Christian culture that might retain the acceptable aspects of pagan letters while discarding the dangerous and damnable, a search that extended from Tertullian through St. Augustine's *De doctrina christiana*, many Church Fathers found it impossible to conceive of a Christianity that was not based upon Latin culture. Tertullian himself reproached his fellow Christians with their ignorance of the faith, which made them prone to diversion from it. Between his richly exploited vein of contempt for the pagan philosophers (which he derived from pagan antiphilosophical literary traditions) and his genuine concern over Christian ignorance, Tertullian was the first of many Christian thinkers to come to terms with pagan antique culture without falling prey to the errors in it that they equally denounced.

In many respects, the search for a Christian accomodation to pagan culture ended with St. Augustine's *De doctrina christiana* between 396 and 427.[9] This treatise, enormously influential in its own time, continued to inspire thinkers for many centuries to come, down into the nineteenth and twentieth centuries. In the *De doctrina christiana*, Augustine lays out those elements of pagan literary culture that are helpful for the understanding of scripture, and those that are not. In book 2, Augustine takes up the definition of superstitious practices, and it is here that he makes his ordered, coherent denunciation of magic, linking it to idolatry and superstition, and banishing it from God's world altogether. Book 2 of the *De doctrina* includes a discussion of the understanding of signs and the ignorance which prevents a proper understanding of them. In considering the value of studying pagan literature, Augustine insists that:

Every good and true Christian should understand that, wherever he may find truth, it is his Lord's. And confessing and acknowledging this truth also in the sacred writings, he will repudiate superstitious imaginings and will deplore and guard against men who, "When they knew God have not glorified Him as God, or given thanks; but became vain in their thoughts, and their foolish heart was darkened. For professing themselves to be wise, they became fools. And they changed the glory of the incorruptible God into the likeness of the image of a corruptible man, and of birds, and of four-footed beasts, and of creeping things."[10]

Augustine's quotation from St. Paul (Romans 1:22–23) echoes the imagery of the story of Elymas in Acts, and the whole passage is a continuation of Tertullian, as well as an important chapter in the search for a Christian wisdom that so marked the patristic age.

Augustine then goes on in book 2, chapters 19-24, to discuss the content of pagan superstition, which he casts wholly in terms of *superstitio* and various forms of *magia*. Chapter 20 is a catalogue of what Augustine calls "the magical arts," and in this catalogue, he includes virtually all the forms of idol-worship, particularly in the casual habits of everyday life: pacts with demons, haruspicy, augury, medical magic, and the observance of omens and signs. Chapter 21 adds astrology, as does chapter 22, also adding a discussion of the *genethliaci*, those who predict a person's future from the study of birthdays. Chapter 23 sums up the reason for his condemnation of pagan superstition:

For it is brought about as if by a certain secret judgement of God that men who desire evil things are subjected to illusion and deception as a reward for their desires, being mocked and deceived by those fallen angels to whom, according to the most beautiful ordering of things, the lowest part of this world is subject by the law of Divine Providence.

Even if the image of the dead Samuel told the truth to King Saul, says Augustine, the means by which the spirit was called up were nevertheless to be condemned:

Therefore, all arts pertaining to a trifling or noxious superstition constituted on the basis of a pestiferous association of men and demons as if through a pact of faithless and decitful friendship should be completely repudiated and avoided by the Christian . . .

Such practices "all imply a pestiferous curiosity, an excruciating solicitude, and a mortal slavery." By the beginning of the fifth century, when Augustine wrote, *magia* was already cast away no longer regarded as a legitimate part of Christian knowledge. And Augustine used the term *magia* to include the whole panoply of magic as practised in the pagan and early Christian worlds. Nowhere is this attitude more strongly expressed than in the *De civitate Dei*, especially in books 10, 18, and 19.

In chapter 9 of book 10, Augustine distinguishes between the true sacrifices offered to God and the worship of idols and demons. Miracles, Augustine says, were intended to support the worship of the true God, and they were performed by simple faith and confidence:

. . . not by spells and charms composed according to the rules of criminal superstition, the craft which is called magic or sorcery . . . a detestable name, or by the more honorable title of theurgy. For people attempt to make some sort of distinction between practitioners of evil arts, who are to be condemned, classing these as "sorcerers" (the popular name for which is necromancy) and others whom they are prepared to regard as praiseworthy, attributing to them the practice of theurgy. In fact, both types are engaged in the fraudulent rites of demons, wrongly called angels.[11]

Chapters 17 and 18 of book 18 deny the reality of humans who change their shapes. Book 19, chapter 9, again takes up the theme of the deceit of the demons. In these and other passages throughout his writings, Augustine gathers up what had indeed been discrete magical practices, classes them all under the heading of *superstitio*, and condemns them emphatically, blaming the deceit of the demons and the undisciplined *curiositas* of ignorant humans.

Augustine thus links two of the most important strands of early Christian culture: the separation of a Christian learning from the many disciplines of pagan antiquity, and the growth of Christian demonology. In the new organization of legitimate knowledge, everything pertaining to magic, astrology, and divination is rejected as *superstitio* and therefore made a deception of the devil.

The history of late Jewish and early Christian demonology has produced an extensive literature that can only be summed up here.[12] Jewish demonology has been attributed to the popularity of apocalyptic literature which, with conversion, also became the intellectual property of the early Christian community. The apocryphal *Book of Enoch* treated good and wicked angels, unclean spirits, divine punishment through the medium of Satan, and idolatry. To this demonology the early Fathers, from Justin Martyr to St. Ambrose and St. Augustine, made their own distinctive contributions. Justin particularly gave shape and identity to the demons and explained their powers over humans:

They afterwards subdued the human race to themselves partly by magical writings, and partly by fears and the punishments they occasioned, and partly by teaching them to offer sacrifices and incense and libations, of which things they stood in need after they were enslaved by lustful passions.[13]

Here the magical arts, already under attack on other grounds by early Christian writers, are explicitly identified as one of the means by which demons extended their power over humans.

The human race, therefore, was particularly prone to demonic interference, deceit, and temptation, and in early Christian baptisms dissociation of the catechumen from the world of demons was dramatically underlined and emphasized. In addition to this theoretical and practical demonology, other aspects of early Christian life also contributed both to the concept of Satan and to the condemnation of magic. The idea of the Antichrist, a human born either of Satan's union with a human woman or from a human union presided over by Satan, appears in the *Didache apostolorum* and in the writings of a number of Fathers, including St. Ambrose.[14] The association of the Antichrist with Satan is parallelled by his association with *magia*. However the Antichrist is to be born, all writers agree that he will be raised by magicians and use their deceits to attract other humans to him. The legend of Antichrist was rooted in apocalyptic writings, including the *Book of Revelations*, but, as Norman Cohn and others have shown, it received its fullest development in the Sybilline writings, particularly the *Tiburtina* and the *Pseudo-Methodius.*[15] These traditions were conveyed to later medieval Europe in Adso's *Libellus de Antichristo*, written around the middle of the tenth century:

Antichrist will have magicians, criminals, soothsayers, and wizards, who, with the devil's inspiration, will bring him up and instruct him in every iniquity, trickery, and wicked art. And evil spirits will be his leaders and eternal friends and inseparable comrades.[16]

Antichrist's illusions and deceits specifically will make people believe that he is their leader. The association of the figure of Antichrist of with those of the magicians contributed to reinforcing the uniform hostility of early Christianity to what was universally denounced as magic.

The figure of Simon Magus also played a prominent role in the shaping of Christian attitudes toward magic. In some ways, he is the classic test figure for the Christian sense of the difference between the powers of the pagan gods and the power of the true God. Simon, a *magus* himself, converted to Christianity and asked to purchase the magical powers of the Apostles for his own benefit. Although he later became the archheretic in the reform movements of the eleventh and twelfth centuries

and as the "St. Simon" of later medieval anticlerical satire, his career
and its end offer a sharp picture of the Christian sense of the difference
between real miracles and the deceits and demonic connections of the
magi. Justin Martyr makes it clear that Simon performed his magical
feats through the power of the demon operating in him. In the apocryphal
Acts of Peter, Simon Magus confronts St. Peter and proves the power of
his gods by flying (which the commentators all agree was done by the
power of the demons). By invoking the name of God against the demons
who support Simon Magus, St. Peter makes him fall to the ground de-
feated. There is perhaps no better example in early Christian literature
of the Christian distinction between true miracles and the magical arts
practiced by those deceived by Satan. Like the encounter between St.
Paul and Elymas, that between St. Peter and Simon Magus was, in part
at least, a Christian attempt to distinguish between the demonic magic
that enveloped the pagan world (and of which Christians themselves
had been accused) and the true power of the Christian god, revealed
through his humble, simple, pious servants, not through wicked magicians.

With magic excluded from the legitimate sciences and associated with
devil worship and *superstitio,* Christians by the fourth century were able
to employ all the pagan literature that condemned magic on behalf of
their own cause. Augustine so uses Porphyry's letter to the Egyptian
priest Anebo in book 10 of the *De civitate Dei,* and the antimagical
writings of the Roman satirists (Horace, for example) could enter the
vocabulary of Christian invective.[17] Christians now could, and in the
Christian Empire did, sack pagan houses in search of magic books, and
they could invoke the full hostility of Roman law against magic.[18] As
Apuleius had once said (in his own defense against a charge of magic):
Calumniam magiae quae facilius infamatur quam probatur. Apuleius's
Apologia offers, in fact, an excellent survey of the magical ideas of the
second century A.D., and it is precisely this tissue of beliefs that came
under intense and unremitting Christian condemnation.[19]

But it was not the Christians alone who provided the most effective
condemnation of magic. The Roman state, in its laws from the Twelve
Tables to the *Corpus Iuris Civilis* of Justinian in the sixth century, condemned magic and its practitioners as vigorously as they were denounced
by Tertullian, Augustine, or Ambrose. The pagan distinction between
theurgia and *goeteia/magia,* ridiculed by Tertullian and Augustine, was
taken no more seriously by the Roman emperors. The distinction, in fact,
seems to have had more reality for philosophers than for their opponents—or even for the magicians themselves—since several historians
have pointed out that there was no visible difference between the
theurgia practiced by the "learned" magicians and the *goeteia* practiced
by the "low" magicians.

The best and most recent study of the position of magic in the fourth and fifth century Roman Empire is Peter Brown's essay, "Sorcery, Demons, and the Rise of Christianity: From Late Antiquity to the Middle Ages."[20] The great virtue of Brown's study is that it deals with the accusations of magic and the condemnation of magical practices in this period in a persuasive and well-documented social context, and thereby avoids focusing upon the literary sources and bringing to bear upon them the mentality of nineteenth- or twentieth-century rationalist scholars. "A precise *malaise* in the structure of the governing classes of the Roman Empire (especially in its eastern, Greek-speaking half) forced the ubiquitous sorcery beliefs of ancient man to a flash-point of accusations in the mid-fourth century A.D." They were produced by uncertainty, political instability, and conflict among the governing classes of the Empire, and they subsided when political and social stability was restored, by the end of the sixth century A.D. Brown describes the dilemma of the fourth and fifth centuries in anthropological terms:

This is when *two systems of power* are sensed to clash within the one society. On the one hand, there is *articulate* power, power defined and agreed upon by everyone (and especially by its holders): authority vested in precise persons; admiration and success gained by recognized channels. Running counter to this may be other forms of influence less easy to pin down . . . *inarticulate* power: the disturbing intangibles of social life; the imponderable advantages of certain groups; personal skills that succeed in a way that is unacceptable or difficult to understand. Where these two systems overlap, we may expect to find the sorcerer.

In such a world, as Brown goes on to describe it, the servants of the emperor, the representatives of *articulate* power par excellence (as, by analogy, the Christian missionaries and bishops would be, several centuries later in a totally Christianized society) became the most frequent accusers. Those who have recourse to any source of power outside the imperial scheme are the accused. Brown's great virtue in this argument is to attack the common victims' (and historian's) view that these charges were cynical or were "smears." At least once again, many centuries later, a similar spate of charges of political sorcery was launched against courtiers of kings and popes in fourteenth-century France and Avignon. As will be suggested below, Brown's model also offers a dimension for investigating these later medieval charges of political sorcery. Barred from organized political opposition to an increasingly autocratic emperor, the emperor's enemies, or even those who maintained their power and position without specific imperial favor, were charged with resorting to sorcery. Political and constitutional history, its rules and methods set down by rationalist institutional historians in the nineteenth

and twentieth centuries, has made no place for the problem of magic
and politics, nor for the intimate, ambiguous, hot-house atmosphere of
the court. Just as heresy is the sin against the Church par excellence, so
is magic the sin against the temporal ruler, or indeed against the spiritual
ruler seen as a private individual. And the court is its laboratory. "When
we see them in this light, we can appreciate how the sorcery accusations
of the fourth century mark a stage of conflict on the way to a greater
definition of the secular governing class of the Eastern Empire as an
aristocracy of service, formed under the emperor by divine right." The
emperor's servants, chiefly Christians, of course had the added support
of the Christian view that pagan gods were demons and that the pagan
traditional aristocracy must of necessity have engaged in commerce
with demons. As the early fourteenth century saw, the charges would
work the opposite way as well: traditional "feudal" aristocrats, the king's
"natural" advisers, brought charges of sorcery against upstart parvenu
royal servants and favorites, in an age precisely when the royal power
veered between the traditional limited personal authority of a king surrounded by aristocrats and the ambitious centralizing tendencies of late
medieval kings and their low-born, but loyal and ruthless servants. Brown
also argues that the sorcerer had affiliations with the *demimonde*, important but socially ill-defined figures who wielded great power and favor:
the rhetor, the charioteer (thinking of Theodora, one might add the
actress and indeed *histriones* in general), and the holy man. For "un-
controlled religious power," too, threatened the regimentation of the
single authority of the state, and only the slow process of totally Chris-
tianizing the Empire relieved the tension in the relations between the
court and the holy man. The developing notion of Christian sanctity
must have saved others besides those great imperial opponents St.
Athanasius and St. Ambrose.

Brown traces the role of Christianity in these accusations and their
demise first to the universal Christian explanation for all misfortune, the
fallen character of the human race and God's anger against it. In the
works of Augustine, Brown sees a sense of identity that is flexible and
capacious enough to accomodate misfortune, ambiguity, and unpre-
dictability as predictable parts of the natural human condition:

This situation changed as Late Roman society became more fixed. The stabiliza-
tion of the local Christian communities and the elaboration of a finely-
articulated penitential system placed boundaries on Augustine's sense of the
unidentifiable guilt of a bottomless identity. The idea of ill-defined guilt
hardened into a sense of exposure to misfortune through the neglect of
prescribed actions. . . . The Church was the community for whom Satan had
been bound: his limitless powers had been bridled to permit the triumph of
the Gospel; more immediately, the practising Christian gained immunity from
sorcery.

The confrontation directly between the demon and the saint or God became more important than that between the sorcerer and his victim. Sorcerers either continue to serve the pagan gods (who are really demons) or work in Christian society through the power of the demon. They no longer have any *ars* that is dependent upon knowledge and professional skill; they no longer command the gods, but work under the illusion with which the devil has deceived them; the efficacy of sorcery itself is denied. Demonic power confronts the saint and the churchman and, in the great duel between them—an exemplary duel in which the devil is often turned to ridicule and occasionally to human service—the power of God is made manifest. This is the subject of early medieval hagiography, sermons, and miracle stories such as the *Dialogues* of Gregory the Great.

Brown also points out that the idea that God acts to eradicate horrendous evils directly, a version of what some historians have called the theory of immanent justice, tended to diminish the figure of the sorcerer after the sixth century. This notion contains great implications for the period between the sixth and the twelfth centuries because, as later chapters will argue, it is precisely in the eleventh and twelfth centuries that the theory of immanent justice—both divine immanence in law courts and in the phenomenal world in the shape of direct intervention—begins to weaken, and human agents once again have to take up the burdens of correcting the errors of human society. By the end of the fourth century, writers as different as Lactantius and John Cassian agreed that the magical arts, *magi*, and *malefici* were all created by the devil. In the fifth century Pope Leo I wrote that magic was simply one of the many *astutia* of the devil, through which he subdues the greater part of humanity with his *superstitiones*.

The universal condemnation of the magicians by early Christian writers was colored by elements of the Christian experience both before and after the conversion of the emperors to Christianity. Roman invective against religions that they found distasteful or even criminal was highly developed by the first century A.D. Roman hostility to certain mystery cults, to the Jews, and to the Druids and their human sacrifices helped to shape this invective, and regional hostilities throughout the Empire carried it even further. In his study *Europe's Inner Demons*, Norman Cohn traces this invective as what he calls the "prelude in antiquity" to the accusations made much later against heretics and magicians and witches in the medieval Christian world.[27] Acts of idolatry, cannibalism, sexual promiscuity, infanticide, and unspeakable rites were levelled at Christians (and are found in the work of the Christian apologists) from the fund of social invective that the Romans reserved for a number of categories of infamous people, including political conspirators. Cohn argues that, "In each case the murder and the cannibalistic feast form part of a ritual by which a group of conspirators affirms its solidarity."

By assimilating the Christian *agape,* or love feast, to the pagan Bacchanalia, the stereotypical association of political conspirators, pagan writers succeeded in depicting Christians as enemies of the state in terms familiar to Romans through their earlier political associations. The Christian denial of the values of the pagan world (Tacitus had said that Christians possessed an *odium humani generis,* a hatred for human nature) did not prevent Christians from borrowing forms of pagan invective.

These anti-Christian injunctions, Cohn argues, were adopted by Christians themselves in their attacks on heterodoxy from the third century on. Indeed, although there is no space to summarize it here, Christian orthodox invective against heterodoxy in the fourth and fifth centuries constituted a bitter and violent indictment of religious deviance.[21a] As Cohn has suggested, some of the elements of this attack came from traditional Roman invective, but the attacks on the heretics had other sources as well. Apocalyptic prophecies were pressed into service, with their invective against the enemies of God, and the literature thus created entered the patristic tradition, to be returned to again and again when religious dissent became a problem. As noted above, the prevalence of heresy was not a major problem before the eleventh century. It is in the context of eleventh-century antiheretical literature, most of which was produced by monastic writers familiar with patristic invective, that these traits were assumed to be those of eleventh- and twelfth-century heretics. Thus patristic antiheretical invective came to color the descriptions of later heretics, magicians, and witches. This literary tradition is important to emphasize. The great prestige of the Fathers in later centuries and the twelfth-century idea that contemporary heresies were old heresies renewed justified the use of this traditional invective.

The Christian condemnation of magic, the association of magicians with the figure of Antichrist, the fear of heresy, and the borrowing of traditional forms of Roman invective to condemn both magicians and heretics constituted the foundation of the Christian attitude toward both magic and heresy. As the foregoing discussion has suggested, *both* magicians and heretics were condemned, and the terms of their denunciation were similar, having roots in classical pagan forms of invective. Another source of Christian invective contributed to the rhetorical coloration of both. To the Christian, the one person who possessed an *odium humani generis* was the Jew. Along with the heretic and the magician, the Jew was also considered to be a child of Satan, from the first anti-Jewish polemics in the New Testament to the raging antisemitism of the sixteenth century. Such texts as John 8:44 call the Devil the father of the Jews, and the first mention of a "synagogue of Satan," an epithet frequently launched against later heretical groups and witches' assemblies, occurs in Revelation 2:9 and 3:9.[22] Church fathers accused Jews of worshipping Satan and charged them with idolatry (the crime of the magicians), giving their children to the demons. The magician encountered by St. Paul in the retinue of Sergius Paulus was the Jew Elymas. Jewish magicians, probably an extremely small group in the late antique world, loomed large in Christian rhetoric. Jews were associated with the triumph of Antichrist. Jews had been accused of widespread practice of magic and possession of magic lore in the Roman world before Christians made those charges their own, and the fondness of non-Jewish magicians for Hebrew lore and their use of the Hebrew language helped perpetuate the Jews' reputation as sorcerers down through the Middle Ages. From Origen on, the Jew as sorcerer remained a learned and popular motif. The charge of sorcery, by the fourth century fixed in association with that of diabolism, increased Christian hated and fear of the Jew, and the association of Jews with sorcery enhanced the diabolic attributes of all magic. Jewish magicians, necromancers, poisoners, and servants of the devil through magical arts populate medieval European literary sources and aided in the general condemnation of magic by associating it with an especially hated people.

As Joshua Trachtenberg has noted, late medieval lawbooks often listed the crime of sorcery among laws pertaining to the restriction of Jews. The legend of Theophilus, one of the most influential sources for later Christian ideas of pact with the devil and its requirement for magical practices, was written in Byzantium early in the seventh century. In it the priest Theophilus is guided by a Jewish magician and is given magical powers in return for his apostasy. This early literal association of a Jewish magician with pact with the devil—anticipated in the story of the magician, the devil, and the Senator Proterius in the fifth century—remained familiar in Byzantium and was later adopted by medieval storytellers, the most notable of whom was Rutebeuf in the thirteenth century.[23] The popularity of the story lent several of the most important motifs to the later story of Faust. Historians have generally left the case of Faust out of the discussion of magic, heresy, and witchcraft, but the story clearly draws upon elements that were commonplace beliefs as early as the end of the sixth century. The tale of Faust is not as removed from the burning of witches and the condemnation of even learned magic in the sixteenth century as many historians indicate.

Many of the ideas from various sources described above made their way into the *Etymologies* of Isidore of Seville, written early in the seventh century.[24] Isidore's *Etymologies* became an immensely popular reference work for later medieval writers, and his views on magic remained influential down to the twelfth century, when, as we shall see, they were taken up vigorously by Hugh of St. Victor and thus passed into scholastic theology and philosophy. Isidore's pompous pretentions to learning and his heavy reliance on earlier encyclopedists did not prevent him from vehemently condemning magic in all its forms. Like St. Augustine, Isidore was willing to recognize distinctions among different kinds of magic, but he too condemned all of these as damnable.

The strictures against magical practices in Roman law in the Theodosian Code were passed on to later European society in the form of Germanic law codes. Sometimes, as in the case of the *Breviarium Alarici,* they were embellished with additional comments. Such, for example, was the case of the text in *Theodosian Code 9.16.3:*

The science of those who are equipped with magic arts and who are revealed to have worked against the safety of men or to have turned virtuous minds to lust shall be punished and deservedly avenged by the most severe laws.

The *Breviarium* added (perhaps not for the first time) the injunction:

Magicians, enchanters, conjurors of storms, or those who, through the invocation of demons throw into confusion the minds of men shall be punished with every kind of penalty.

Although some historians of witchcraft have made much of the injunctions against the magical arts in the Germanic laws, seeing a new infusion of magic in the folk customs of the Germanic peoples, the Latin terminology and consistency of these laws with earlier Roman law and patristic literature makes any uniquely Germanic folk practices hard to distinguish. If there were traditional folk practices condemned in the Visigothic and Frankish laws, they were condemned in the same tone and for the same reasons that magic had been condemned earlier. The bulk of pagan beliefs and new superstitions occasioned by them were treated in the *indiculi superstitionum* published by many Church councils between the sixth and the tenth centuries and in the treatises *De superstitionibus rusticorum* written by ecclesiastics during the same period. This literature has been widely surveyed by folklorists and religious and literary historians. Some of it contains elements dealing with the older beliefs of the new European peoples, and these are integrated into Christianity through the sources mentioned above and the penitentials written in the eighth and ninth centuries. In many respects the most complete of these penitentials (which includes many of the materials considered by councils and individual writers) is book 5 of Burchard of Worms' *Decretum,* an early eleventh-century compendium of old beliefs systematically set out within the context of the developing canon law.[25] Such writers as Russell and Lea have summarized the elements of these beliefs that appear to contribute to later ideas of witches, but it seems to me that, in law at least, these ideas virtually disappear from view after the compendium of Burchard. As will be discussed in Chapter 3, the analytical lawbooks of the twelfth and thirteenth centuries rely far more on patristic materials than upon the host of early medieval pagan and Christian popular beliefs that these sources display. Although these beliefs and the cultures that produced them play an important role in the cultural history of Europe, they did not play a particularly important part in the lawyers' and theologians' consideration of magic—and later, witchcraft—in the twelfth, thirteenth, and fourteenth centuries, except insofar as one or two of them, notably those described in the *Canon Episcopi*, were transmitted by the learned lawyers and theologians of this period. During the fifteenth century, to be sure, popular beliefs once again fell under the purview of learned theologians, but they responded to these with the learned materials of the twelfth and thirteenth centuries. They did not return to the old penitentials and excavate primitive tribal beliefs in order to check them against the practices they observed in their own time; they turned instead to the traditional learned legal and theological literature, and there was in this virtually no reference to earlier beliefs and customs, pagan or Christian. What worried later theologians and lawyers was what worried their patristic and later sources: evidence of practices that had been condemned from the days of Tertullian and Justin Martyr as sinful magic. The inquisitors and their colleagues on secular benches responded to fifteenth and sixteenth century phenomena with the intellectual resources of fifteenth and sixteenth century lawyers and theologians. The problem of witchcraft persecutions looms large enough in this period without tracing either its inspiration or the response to it from the materials included in *indiculi superstitionum*, tracts *De superstitione rusticorum*, penitentials that no one read, or the encyclopedic and often astonishing collections of popular beliefs assembled and displayed by the tireless energy of Burchard of Worms.

The Carolingian renaissance, which performed the first stage of that renewal of early Christian learning that was vigorously continued by eleventh and twelfth century scholars, also helped to revive some of the patristic strictures against magic. In the work of its most important representatives, Alcuin and the authors of the capitularies, it is possible to see a renewed concern for many forms of deviance, often a singularly learned concern based upon a reading of the texts of Augustine and others. In the work of Hincmar of Reims and Hrabanus Maurus in the ninth century, we see a revival of the patristic interest in and concern about learned magic. It is learned magic that occupied the greatest minds of the ninth century, a *superstitio* that derived not from *ignorantia* or *simplicitas*, but from an *ars*—one that fascinated, even as it repelled, those ninth century scholars who dealt with it.

It has been said of the court of Louis the Pious, son of Charlemagne, that every great man at it had his own personal astrologer. The texture of Carolingian court life suggests the plausibility of this remark, because in the heady atmosphere of transforming an Iron Age assembly of warbands and settlers into an ideal Christian kingdom, the Carolingian Empire often presents (as it did to itself) the image of a composite of late Roman imperial and barbarian Germanic styles of life and thought. The classical works that Carolingian scholars discovered, edited, and circulated among themselves were the very ones that managed to preserve much antiquarianism along with Christian piety. The religious basis of Charlemagne's and Louis's *renovatio* has long been recognized. What has often not been recognized as fully is how much of the old learned world of late antiquity came with the Christian materials. In the sophisticated, learned, violent, and self-serving Carolingian court world those who had access to, and even a rudimentary understanding of, learned magic could easily find employers. No residual pagan superstitions or folk beliefs were necessary. The Carolingian aristocrats knew how to value learned magicians as it valued learned chroniclers, holy men, astrologers, wandering Irish scholar monks, and any other successful means of making their way through the rapidly changing post-tribal world of Charlemagne's renewed Roman Empire and Louis's rapidly deteriorating Christian kingdom.[26]

In his treatise *De divortio Lotharii*, Hincmar of Reims took up the question of whether or not a man could be enchanted and thereby lose his potency. In his consideration of the divorce case of the emperor Lothar, Hincmar argued that *maleficium* could indeed prevent a man from consummating his marriage, although in the case at hand he accused the emperor's mistress of having performed the act of *maleficium*. Hincmar's text became quite influential, since it was cited on many other occasions and was included in Gratian's *Decretum*, the first modern book of canon law, in 1140.

Far more important, however, was the work of Hrabanus Maurus of Fulda. In his early work on Christian learning, the *De institutione clericorum*, Hrabanus defended the study of pagan literature, but advisedly:

There are two kinds of doctrines which were exercised among the gentiles: one dealt with those things which were instituted by men . . . the other instituted by divinity. That which was instituted by men was partly superstition and partly not. Superstitiosum est quidquid institutum est ab hominibus ad facienda et colenda pertinens, vel colendum sicut Deum creaturam, vel partem illam creaturae, vel ad consultationes et pacta quaedam significationem cum daemonibus placita atque foederata, qualia sunt molimina magicarum artium quae quidem commemorare potius quam docere assolent poetae.[27]

These magical arts, the product of superstitious human institutions and involving pact with the demon, should be avoided. Hrabanus's treatise *De magicis artibus,* opens with a long series of biblical citations against all forms of magic and then lists all the varieties of magic known to the Church Fathers.[28] Although the actions of the magicians sometimes work, Hrabanus says, they do so only because the magicians have made a pact with Satan and because God in his wisdom permits the demons to accomplish what the magicians think they accomplish. *Curiositas* and *cupiditas* urge the magicians to admire the demons, especially the prophecies that the demons make and the *mira* (not *miracula*) they perform. Hrabanus appears to know in surprising detail of what he speaks, and this store of knowledge on the part of an abbot of Fulda and archbishop of Mainz who died in 857 is a clear reflection of the familiarity of Carolingian clerics with the tradition of magical arts. Perhaps most of Hrabanus's knowledge was acquired through scripture and the works of St. Augustine, but much of his commentary has a personal and knowledgeable ring to it. In fact, Hrabanus concludes his tract with the plea that the kingdom of God, that is now spreading over the whole world, not be destroyed by human vanity, demonic illusions, and the magic arts. The kings and prelates of his own age are addressed and urged to obliterate these practices, lest the wrath of God fall upon them as it fell upon Ahab and Ochozias. Far more than popular superstitions and folklore, Hrabanus treats the same kind of learned practices that Augustine had dealt with, and he does not do so as an antiquarian.

The dislike of magic found in Hincmar and Hrabanus suggests that the Carolingian period witnessed a revival (or continuation) of learned magic. By the beginning of the tenth century, a number of writers (including the canonist Regino of Prüm) described in legal collections and penitentials, practices that were partly folk-beliefs and partly the residuum of learned magic. By preserving the texts of an earlier age and adding to them, the Carolingian writers transmitted to later centuries not the traditional folk beliefs of the penitentials, but the definition of, hostility toward, and condemnation of learned magic, both from the Fathers and from their own works. Hrabanus knew well the associations with heresy found in earlier writers: in commenting on Exodus 22:18, *Maleficos non patieris vivere,* he remarks:

Typologically, we may understand *maleficos* as meaning heretics, instigated not by the spirit of God but by the wicked spirit; they introduce perverse sects in order to deceive men, which the law of God orders to be abolished, that is, separated and anathematised from the community of the faithful who live a true life in God, so that *maleficium,* which is error, shall be extinguished.[29]

As we will see below, this figurative interpretation of a text that was later taken with appalling literalness by the instigators of the witch persecutions in the fifteenth and sixteenth centuries, continued to be understood figuratively through the twelfth century. But the description and denunciation of magic, the association of *maleficium* with heresy, and the details of pact and charges of *idolatria* and *superstitio,* reflected considerable concern for the presence and danger of magic. The great Carolingian heresies remained, for the most part, the property of monks in monasteries; but magic pervaded the court and, as far as Hrabanus was concerned, most of the world. Heretical magicians were a real and pressing danger; the *magos* of Xerxes, turned quack, philosopher, theurgist, *maleficus,* and servant of the devil, plagued the fears of Greeks and Romans, Jews and Christians, and the newly Christianized inhabitants of Germanic Europe. Idolater and heretic, he was finally transformed in patristic literature into God's human enemy and an enemy of mankind itself. Teacher of Antichrist, with his books, charms, and demonic power, he entered the consciousness of later medieval Europe. Invective against magicians tainted Jews and heretics. It is found first in the rhetorical language of eleventh- and twelfth-century writers.

NOTES

1. Aside from the standard reference encyclopedias, see Walter Burkert, "ΓΟΗΣ: zum griechischen Schamanismus," *Rhenisches Museum* 105 (1962): 36-55. See also Arthur Darby Nock, *Essays on Religion and Magic in the Ancient World,* ed. Zeph Stewart, 2 vols. (Cambridge, Mass., 1972), 1: 15, "Paul and the Magus," pp. 308-30; 2: 30, "Greeks and Magi," pp. 516-26; Lynn Thorndike, *History of Magic and Experimental Science,* 8 vols. (New York, 1923-1958), 1: 41-181.

2. Plato *The Laws* 10.909b; 11.933a-e; cf. *Republic* 364b. See also Jacqueline de Romilly, *Magic and Rhetoric in Ancient Greece* (Cambridge, Mass., 1975), pp. 25-43.

3. Nock, "Paul and the Magus," p. 315.

4. The reputation of Apuleius as a magician and the interest in and fear of magic in his romance *Metamorphoses* is described by Adam Abt, *Die Apologie des Apuleius von Madaura und die antike Zauberei,* Religionsgeschichtliche Versuche und Vorarbeiten, Bd. 4 (Giessen, 1908); Antonie Wlosok, "Zur Einheit der Metamorphosen des Apuleius," *Philologus* 113 (1969): 66-84, and Horst Rüdiger, "Curiositas und Magie," *Wort und Text. Festschrift für Fritz Schalk* (Frankfurt, 1963): 57-82. See the more general survey by A. A. Barb, "The Survival of the Magic Arts," in *The Conflict Between Paganism and Christianity in the Fourth Century,* ed. A. Momigliano (Oxford, 1963), pp. 100-125; Clyde Pharr, "The Interdiction of Magic in Roman Law," *Transac-*

tions of the American Philological Association 63 (1932): 269-95, and especially the study of Peter Brown, cited below, n. 18.

5. A good brief introduction is H. A. Kelly, *The Devil, Demonology and Witchcraft* (New York, 1974). See also Nock, "Paul and the Magus"; L. Gardette, "Magie," *Dictionnaire de théologie catholique,* vol. 9, cols. 1510-50; J. Annequin, *Recherches sur l'action magique et ses representations (Ier et Ième siècles après J.C.)* (Paris, 1973). For magic in Jewish life, see Judah Goldin, "The Magic of Magic and Superstition," in *Aspects of Religious Propaganda in Judaism and Early Christianity,* ed. Elisabeth Schüssler Fiorenze (Notre Dame, Ind., 1976), pp. 115-48, and below, n. 22.

6. Nock, "Paul and the Magus," passim. See also Morton Smith, *Clement of Alexandria and a Secret Gospel of Mark* (Cambridge, Mass., 1973), pp. 229-37.

7. Jean-Claude Fredouille, *Tertullien et la conversion de la culture antique* (Paris, 1972), pp. 412-42.

8. *Ad nationes* 2.4.19; Fredouille, *Tertullien,* p. 415.

9. Augustine, *De doctrina christiana,* ed. W. M. Green (Vienna, 1963), and Augustine, *On Christian Doctrine,* trans. with introduction by D. W. Robertson, Jr. (Indianapolis, 1958).

10. Augustine *On Christian Doctrine* 2.18.28 (Robertson trans. p. 54). On divination, see Robert La Roche, *La Divination* (Washington, 1957), pp. 1-213.

11. Augustine, *Concerning the City of God Against the Pagans,* trans. Henry Bettenson (Baltimore, 1972), p. 383.

12. See Kelly, *Devil, Demonology, and Witchcraft*; Thorndike, *History* 1: 340-522; Joshua Trachtenberg, *Jewish Magic and Superstition* (reprint ed.; New York, 1970).

13. Kelly, *Devil, Demonology, and Witchcraft,* pp. 28-31; for the following pages, see especially Otto Böcher, *Dämonenfurcht und Dämonenabwehr* (Stuttgart–Berlin, 1970).

14. See Michael McHugh, "Satan in St. Ambrose," *Classical Folia* 26 (1972): 94-103.

15. Norman Cohn, *The Pursuit of the Millennium* (New York, 1970); Paul J. Alexander, "Medieval Apocalypses as Historical Sources," *American Historical Review* 73 (1968): 997-1018; Joshua Trachtenberg, *The Devil and the Jew* (New Haven, 1943), pp. 32-43.

16. John Wright, trans., *The Play of Antichrist* (Toronto, 1967), pp. 103-10. Medieval listeners would recognize the inverted parallel between Antichrist and Jesus. The former was raised and taught by magicians, but at Christ's birth the Magi gave up their arts.

17. See the discussion in Julio Caro Baroja, *The World of the Witches,* trans. O. N. V. Glendinning (Chicago, 1965), pp. 17-57.

18. Peter Brown, "Sorcery, Demons and the Rise of Christianity: from Late Antiquity to the Middle Ages," in *Religion and Society in the Age of Saint Augustine,* ed. P. Brown (New York, 1972), pp. 119-46, n. 6 on p. 126. See also Campbell Bonner, "Witchcraft in The Lecture Room of Libanius," *Transactions of The American Philological Association* 43 (1932): 34-44.

19. The best discussion of Apuleius's *Apologia* and of magic generally in

second-century Rome is still Adam Abt, *Die Apologie des Apuleius von Madaura und die antike Zauberei,* Religionsgeschichtliche Versuche und Vorarbeiten, Bd. 4 (Giessen, 1908). See above, n. 4.

20. See Brown, "Sorcery." This immensely important study contrasts sharply with the earlier study of Barb, "Survival of the Magic Arts."

21. Norman Cohn, *Europe's Inner Demons: An Enquiry Inspired by the Great Witch-Hunt* (New York, 1975), pp. 1-15. Of all recent books on the subject, Cohn's seems to me among the freshest and most accurate, although it is marred by many typographical and editorial errors.

22. The standard work is Trachtenberg's *The Devil and the Jew.* See also Bernard Blumenkranz, *Juifs et Chrétiens dans le monde occidental, 430-1096* (Paris, 1960), and Brown, "Sorcery," pp. 140-42. More recent, although not as comprehensive, is Venetia Newall, "The Jew as Witch-Figure," in *The Witch Figure,* ed. V. Newall (London, 1973), pp. 95-124. See also Leon Poliakov, "Le diable et les Juifs," in *Entretiens sur l'homme et le diable,* ed. Max Milner (Paris, 1965), pp. 189-212.

23. L. Radermacher, "Griechische Quellen zur Faustsage," *Sitzungsberichte der Wiener Akademie der Wissenschaften* 206 (1927); Carl Kiesewetter, *Faust in der Geschichte und Tradition* (reprinted.; Hildesheim, 1963), pp. 114-18; Jeffrey Russell, *Witchcraft in the Middle Ages* (Ithaca, 1972), p. 61. See also Henry Chadwick, *Priscillian of Avila* (Oxford, 1976), esp. pp. 51-56.

24. W. M. Lindsay, ed., *Isidori Hispalensis Episcopi Etymologiarum,* 2 vols. (Oxford, 1911), VIII, ix, 1 ff. *De Magis;* IX, 2, 43; XIV, 3, 12; XIV, 8, 17. Cf. Hans Philipp, *Die historisch-geographischen Quellen in den Etymologiae des Isidorus von Sevilla* (Berlin, 1912); J. Fontaine, *Isidore de Seville et la culture classique dans l'Espagne wisigothique,* 2 vols. (Paris, 1959). For Hugh of St. Victor, see below, Chapter 3.

25. *Patrologia Latina* 140, cols. 537-1090. See also John T. McNeill and Helena M. Gamer, *Medieval Handbooks of Penance* (New York, 1930); John T. McNeill, "Folk-Paganism in the Penitentials," *Journal of Religion* 13 (1933): 450-66; Cyrille Vogel, "Pratiques superstitieuses au début du IXe siècle d'après le *Corrector sive Medicus* de Burchard, évêque de Worms (965–1025)," in *Études de civilization médiévale (IXe - XIIe siècles). Mélanges offerts à Edmond-René Labande* (Poitiers, 1974), pp. 751-61. See also Henry Charles Lea, *Materials Toward a History of Witchcraft,* ed. and comp. Arthur Howland (Philadelphia, 1938), passim; Russell, *Witchcraft,* pp. 63-100.

26. Pierre Riché, "La magie carolingienne," *Académie des Inscriptions et Belles-Lettres, Comptes Rendus des Séances de l'année 1973, Janvier-Mars,* pp. 127-38, is a comprehensive survey with good bibliographical references, and Raoul Manselli, "Simbolismo e magia nell'alto medioevo," in *Simboli e simbologia nell'alto Medioevo* (Spoleto, 1976), pp. 293-348.

27. *PL* 107, col. 392.

28. *PL* 110, cols. 1095-1108.

29. *PL* 108, col. 121. See the brief discussion in Lea, *Materials,* 1:205. On the use of this important interpretation in the twelfth-century *glossa ordinaria* to the Bible, see below, Chapter 3.

2

Rhetoric and Magic in the
Eleventh and Twelfth Centuries

DIATRIBE AND CHRONICLE

From the eighth to the late twelfth century, the literature which re-corded both heretical and magical practices came from a limited intellec-tual and institutional sphere. This literature was primarily monastic, drew heavily upon the authority of patristic literary traditions, and had the purpose of improving the moral character of its readers, not neces-sarily describing its subjects accurately for them. At the basis of this intellectual tradition lay the study of grammar and rhetoric, until the eleventh century the two chief subjects of the *trivium*, far outdistancing dialectic and the *quadrivium*, which only came into curricular prominence after 1100. Thus, in examining tenth- and eleventh-century literature on magic, witchcraft, and heresy, its rhetorical, exegetical, moral, and monastic basis must be kept in mind. As the next section of this chapter will suggest, much of the well-known association of heresy and magic and reports of the excesses of deviant behavior that mark the literature of the eleventh and twelfth centuries derive from this tradition. In this section I propose to examine the role of rhetoric in the preservation and transmission (and perhaps creation) of beliefs about magicians, witches, and heretics in the late tenth and eleventh centuries.

One of the true monstrosities of medieval literature is the *Rhetorima-chia*, written by Anselm of Besate around 1050.[1] As its most recent com-mentator remarks, "modern readers have thought well neither of the author nor of his work. Carl Erdmann called Anselm a *'bizarre Rhetoriker und extreme literat.'* For R. L. Poole, the *Rhetorimachia* was 'a master-piece of laborious futility.' While R. W. Southern finds it 'painful to read,' and refers to Anselm's 'absurd tirades.' It is impossible not to agree."[2] Yet the *Rhetorimachia,* although distasteful, is an important text in the history of beliefs in magic and witchcraft, not merely because it describes magical practices at tedious length and thus illuminates a hitherto obscure period in the history of magical beliefs, but particularly because it emphasizes the importance of the art of rhetoric as a vehicle for preserving and transmitting those beliefs.

Anselm was born at Besate around 1020, studied rhetoric and logic at Parma and Reggio, served in Henry III's Italian *scriptorium* between 1045 and 1047 and worked in Henry's German chancery in 1048 and 1049. He appears to have died in the service of the bishop of Hildesheim sometime in the 1060's. Although he studied dialectic, he appears never to have been a successful dialectician, and he based his fame on his expertise in rhetoric. The *Rhetorimachia,* produced between 1047 and 1050, was his *chef d'oeuvre,* although a modest one. Anselm is, among other things, an interesting example of an ambitious, aristocratic eleventh-century cleric with intellectual pretensions who attempted to parlay his limited abilities into a successful ecclesiastical career under Henry III—and failed.

Among his many interests and alleged proficiencies, Anselm appears to have loved the classical Latin rhetoricians the most. His veneration for them, as H. E. J. Cowdrey points out, veers close to that of an earlier Italian, Vilgard of Ravenna, who was led by the appearance of Vergil, Horace, and Juvenal in a dream to believe in his own share in their immortality and to proclaim that their writings should be venerated as much as scripture.[3] Vilgard was burned for his heresy in 1000, and Anselm never went quite as far in his own veneration of his classical sources. One of the aims of the study of rhetoric was the art of persuasion, and another was the power of the rhetor to control the most disparate subjects through his command of language.[4] The *Rhetorimachia* fails in both these respects, but in his choice of a subject for the demonstration of his powers of persuasion and control, Anselm reveals one of the important roles of rhetoric—that of exercising the intellectual powers of the writer by describing particularly strange and unusual scenes as if they were true. As Cowdrey points out, quoting Cicero's *Rhetorica,* "non potius veritatem probat facultas rhetorica, sed verisimilitudinem."[5] As we will see, in the work of Anselm and other eleventh- and twelfth-century writers whose primary expertise was rhetorical, verisimilitude was indeed given to unlikely subjects, among them the practices of magicians and the behavior of heretics. In this sense, eleventh-century rhetoricians and their twelfth-century successors did precisely what engravers and painters of the sixteenth and seventeenth centuries did; they chose bizarre and often occult subjects for their art precisely because these subjects offered them an opportunity to demonstrate their talents upon subjects that were uncommon, fearsome, and unusual. What others might and did make of the images they thus ordered and gave verisimilitude to, was not their affair.

In the rhetorical tradition in which Anselm wrote, the object of the rhetor was to create and win a fictitious dispute, usually of a legal character. In order to maintain the interest of the reader, these disputes were intricately constructed, filled with picturesque detail, exaggerated, and, above all, cogently argued. They centered upon wholly fictitious situations (*controversiae*), and, as E. R. Curtius has pointed out, unusual elements and characters were often introduced "to make these imaginary situations more exciting."[6] Thus, Anselm the rhetorician created the *Rhetorimachia* according to the rules of late antique rhetoric and chose for the subject of his work the fictitious indictment of his cousin Rotiland as a magician and servant of the devil. Anselm's choice of a *controversia* is hardly an example of domestic loyalty (although we do not know for certain that he even had a cousin named Rotiland), and his ingenious accusations and descriptions of Rotiland's infernal practices have disgusted other historians besides Erdmann, Poole, and Southern. Yet in the *Rhetorimachia*, Anselm lays out a barrage of accusations that appear familiar to historians of later accusations of magic, heresy, and witchcraft. What may have been well within the limits of rhetorical exercise, and was understood in that way in the eleventh century, influenced later chroniclers and moralists in a setting in which the fictitious character of the work was ignored or forgotten and only the rhetorical concentration on the enormities of the magician, witch, and heretic remained. These, described no longer in *controversiae*, but in chronicle, moral story, and invective against heretics, contributed much to the image of the magician, the witch, and the heretic in the twelfth century and after. Historians of magic, heresy, and witchcraft have not customarily emphasized the importance of rhetoric in shaping, preserving, and transmitting many of the most conspicuous features of invective against ecclesiastical deviants to later writers who took them perfectly seriously and literally; but, as this section will suggest, that is very likely what happened between 1050 and 1250.[7]

Karl Manitius, the most recent editor and commentator upon the *Rhetorimachia*, has argued cogently that the treatise is a fictitious *controversia*, deriving much of the basis of its charges against the hapless Rotiland from Anselm's reading in classical and late-antique Latin courses. Manitius also notes, however, that some of the accusations against

Rotiland seem to have few, if any, classical precedents and may well be Anselm's versions of contemporary theories of magical practices.[8] Certainly the accusation that Rotiland is a servant of the devil, that his magical charms are in "Hebrew, or rather demonic language," and the indication that some of Rotiland's alleged practices derive from "folk-magic," indicate that Anselm was not merely a rhetorical servant of classical *topoi*. In all probability, Anselm's *Rhetorimachia*, for all its classical dress, admitted elements unknown to classical writers, and admitted them under the license all rhetoricians had to add color and drama to the *controversia*. What he added, however, probably did not come from the stock-in-trade figures of pirates, wizards, poisoners, and other exotic characters out of late-antique rhetoric, but figures already known to him and his audience out of the learned invective of his own time and place.

Anselm's inventions, then, lead us to the question often begged (or casually referred to and dropped) by many writers on the history of magic and witchcraft: to what extent did these writers, whether learned rhetoricians or monastic moralists, depict popular or folk customs of their own times? The question of folklore in a largely illiterate and highly localized society is naturally tempting to raise, and folklorists have contributed much to the history of popular beliefs of the Middle Ages and later.[9] There is, however, a danger in ascribing occult practices that appear to have no classical literary or patristic antecedents to folklore, since once these materials have passed through the literary mills of writers like Anselm, Peter Damian, or Guibert de Nogent, they are technically no longer folklore, but literary materials. C. S. Lewis and other literary historians have warned again and again against assuming a non-literary source for the marvelous when it is found described by literary figures of the eleventh and twelfth centuries.[10] As we have seen before and will see again, the surest indications of popular beliefs that seemed to run counter to those of Christianity are to be found in the penitentials and the *indiculi superstitionum* from ecclesiastical sources.[11] If the elements that Anselm denounces in Rotiland's magical repertoire did have some basis in popular or learned practices of the later eleventh century in northern Italy, it would be hard to identify them, since Anselm has worked over all of the materials he uses. One of the major problems of identifying popular ideas and practices in the writings of trained clerics (whether these are products of secular and cathedral schools like Anselm or monastic schools like Guibert de Nogent later in the century) is that the hand of the writer transmutes his materials as it touches them. At the core of an episode there may well once have been a popular practice, but in written form the "popular" elements have been transformed into a literary work, with emphasis, exaggeration, moralizing, and additions.

It is this finished literary presentation of magical and heretical beliefs and practices that most strongly influenced the theologians and lawyers of a later period. Although Anselm of Besate's work does not appear to have been widely read (it survives only in two manuscripts), his choice of subject matter, depiction of a magician, and introduction of a number of elements that later become common-place in describing witches and heretics, suggest that the rhetoricians' training and interests lie behind a number of depictions of the enormities of magicians, witches, and heretics, especially those that contain incongruous elements or depict practices that are wholly implausible.

Marie-Thérèse d'Alverny has observed of Anselm that, "The picturesque history that Anselm tells suggests that certain amateurs of occultism did not hesitate to organize such formidable ceremonies [as those of Rotiland] when love moved them."[12] D'Alverny goes on to suggest a certain continuity in the use of *libri nigromantie*, possibly from late antiquity, but certainly between the eleventh and the thirteenth centuries. William of Auvergne, bishop of Paris in the thirteenth century, once remarked that he had held these books in his own hands while a student at Paris in the later twelfth century. The final section of this chapter will deal with the attribution of magical practices to figures from tenth- and eleventh-century history.[13] It remains to analyze the *Rhetorimachia* and its shabby stock of demonological and magical indictments of the author's cousin Rotiland.

Anselm begins his work with two dedicatory letters, one an exaggerated panegyric of Henry III in which he compares Henry to Augustus and himself to Vergil, and a longer one (which clearly states the fictitious character of his work) to his former teacher Drogo of Parma. In the letter to Drogo, however, Anselm indicates that perhaps his interest in magic is not purely rhetorical. Some of his critics, he says, accuse him of being a demoniac.[14] His literary interest and perhaps, as R. L. Poole suggests, his unusual intellectual pursuits, may very well have drawn down upon him criticisms similar to those made against Vilgard of Ravenna.[15] It is impossible to say whether Anselm, because of his interest in classical literature and his apparent excessive fondness for topics such as that of the *Rhetorimachia*, did in fact have a local reputation for trafficing with demons. The remark may simply be an attempt to impugn his enemies' criticisms by exaggerating their content and thereby ridiculing them. As we will see below, however, Anselm was not the only tenth- or eleventh-century figure accused of commerce with demons.

The first book of the *Rhetorimachia* consists of Anselm's demonstration of his prowess as a rhetorician and logician by criticizing the competence and character of his cousin Rotiland. Twice in the first book, in chapters 13 and 15, Anselm accuses Rotiland of following the precepts of "your lord, Mammon, whose rules and precepts you cherish as you would sacred canons."[16] One of these precepts is an occult ritual for performing amatory magic by keeping vigil for three nights with a cock and a cat, which are then burned, producing a powder "that has great power over girls and married women." So great is Rotiland's evil that he would not resist the opportunity to use such magic and worse on his own mother and father: "Aut enim tuis malificiis incantacionibus diu egrotantes iam defecissent aut ipsis malifciis sani occidissent. Ut pro tanta incommoditate iam cibares matrem ipso pulmone rubete. . . ."[17]

It is in the second book, however, that Anselm's accusations against Rotiland are fully orchestrated. It begins with an account of Anselm's dream in which Robert, Rotiland's dead father, appears to Anselm and, after speaking briefly about the rest of their family, launches into a denunciation of his son Rotiland, "sceleratissimus . . . Qui cum omnes scelere et maleficio precellat, mirror, cur illum terra sustineat, et cum pro omnibus valeat in nequitia, cur iam illi non aperiatur terra."[18] Robertus then goes on to describe a particular example of Rotiland's *maleficium*. Once Rotiland left the city of Parma by night accompanied by a young boy. He buried the boy up to the waist in the earth, lit a fire around him, and forced him to suffer the acrid fumes all night while Rotiland chanted a love-charm, then uttered words in a language "either Hebraic or diabolic." The boy then stole Rotiland's magic book (*quaternio . . . nigromantie*), and Rotiland was forced to invoke the aid of a demon in order to recover it.[19]

In the second part of book 2, Anselm, having demonstrated his prowess as an accuser, shows his skill as a defender when Rotiland accuses him of similar offenses. Among the charges is that Anselm performed a magical abortion by the use of a mule's hoof.[20] Others include keeping the company of panderers and seducers, "perambulating Italy," and keeping improper vigils. Anselm refutes these changes easily, and the book ends with another denunciation of Rotiland as a *maleficus*.[21]

The third book of the *Rhetorimachia* consists of a sustained piece of invective directed against Rotiland as a seducer, a thief, a willing servant of the devil (including the detail of a formal pact), and finally as an accomplished magician who learned from a Saracen ("Now, thanks be to God, a Christian") the secret of cutting the hands off corpses by magic and then using these members to fulfill his own evil desires. Anselm ends the third book and the *Rhetorimachia* itself by denouncing Rotiland as living according to the same law as his master the devil.[22]

It is not surprising that historians of a period that saw the passionate stirrings of ecclesiastical and spiritual reform, the attacks of Peter Damian and Cardinal Humbert on clerical indiscipline, and the devotional genius of the new monastic movement throughout Europe, give short shrift to

Anselm and his peculiar world. H. E. J. Cowdrey summarizes this point effectively:

In the eyes of adherents of reform such a work [as the *Rhetorimachia*] stood condemned on many grounds: the delight in the devices of dialectic and rhetoric for their own sake; the air of free, worldly humanism; the preference for the classics over scripture and Christian authors; the savage diatribe, so far removed from either morality or justice; the pride of the old, unreformed Ambrosian church and the consequent approval of a married secular clergy. The winds of change which blew through later eleventh-century Italy swept Anselm's world away.[23]

It is also true that Anselm's work appears to have had little direct impact in its own time and left little influence behind it. I do not claim that the *Rhetorimachia* played any role in the later depictions of heretics and magicians.

There are, however, several elements of the work and the intellectual world it depicts that are important. First, Anselm used it (perhaps injudiciously) to obtain a lucrative and prestigious career for himself. It would be peculiar indeed if he did not think that his topic, as well as his rhetorical genius, would be of interest to his chosen readers. In spite of the echoes of Horace, Cicero, and other pagan classical writers, Anselm is not describing a nameless, first-century magician out of a Senecan *controversia*, but a Christian who has willingly made a pact with the devil. This Christian uses his occult powers to achieve perfectly comprehensible eleventh-century aims; he engages in actions that are not only revolting in the abstract, but were concerns of eleventh-century moralists as well; he uses books of magic; and he is associated not only with occult magic and theft, but also with lust and lasciviousness. Curtius, Manitius, and Cowdrey may argue legitimately that Anselm was working in a rhetorical vein that was purely literary, not influential, and known by all to be fictitious (Anselm admitted the fictitiousness of the charges against Rotiland himself). But the elements of the charges are not fictitious and they are in many instances strikingly similar to other, later charges made not in rhetorical flytings, but in serious descriptions of magicians, witches, and heretics. Anselm of Besate's work tells us little about the historical Rotiland, but it tells us a great deal about plausible accusations of magic and witchcraft in the eleventh century. For the point of the *Rhetorimachia*, according to its author, editor, and all subsequent commentators, is Cicero's observation: "*non potius veritatem probat facultas rhetorica, sed verisimilitudinem.*" Rotiland, historically, was not a magician. But the character Rotiland was indeed a magician and an accurate portrait—if Anselm lived up to Cicero's injunction—of what eleventh-century educated readers might be convinced from their own experience and knowledge *was* a magician. Like the charges of lasciviousness, theft, and other less occult crimes, the crime of magic had to be credible in the eyes of eleventh-century readers. Invective, to be effective, must bear some semblance to what people perceive to be possible. It is hard to escape the impression that, although the *Rhetorimachia* itself was (happily) without progeny, it affords a view of something more than rhetorical invention.

Anselm was not the only eleventh-century writer to comment on people who became servants of the devil and possessed magic books. Pope Sylvester II, the Aquitanian scholar Gerbert, became the subject of a series of legends about the search for knowledge of magic and encounters with supernatural phenomena.[24] Although it is difficult to date the beginnings of the Sylvester legends, the English chronicler William of Malmesbury has given the fullest version of the story.[25] Gerbert, who went to study magic in Toledo, stole a book of magic from his master, fled from Toledo, went to Reims where he became *grammaticus*, tutor to the future emperor Otto III, and later—pope. While pope, Sylvester was alleged to have made a pact with demons in return for magical powers and great knowledge. The legend of Sylvester was one of several that circulated around certain popes in the eleventh century. Gregory VII was accused by the Synod of Brixen in 1080 of having himself studied magic in Toledo and was denounced as a necromancer. The accusation goes on to mention a school of magic in Rome, founded by Sylvester II, at which no fewer than three other popes—Benedict IX, Gregory VI, and Gregory VII—had studied.[26]

It is possible that these accusations against popes were a kind of residuum of the sort of invective so freely exploited by Anselm of Besate in his treatise on rhetoric against Rotiland. They well may have been a part of Anselm's world that, as Cowdrey says, was "swept away" by the winds of change in the late eleventh century. They survived, if this is indeed the case, precisely as invective. It is not, in several senses, surprising that these stories should have survived in Italy. Many of them, particularly those told by Anselm of Besate, have a strong flavor of classical literature, particularly of satires and prose romances, and a degree of familiarity with this kind of literature survived in Italy longer than anywhere else in western Europe. Rumors of papal magic and legends concerning popes flourished as early as the seventh century, and the accusations against the eleventh-century popes cited above may have been, indeed, part of a longer tradition.

In the light of such eleventh-century invective, it is worthwhile to consider a passage found in the *Chronicle of the Kings of England*, written around 1142 by William of Malmesbury but showing evidence of use of some Italian materials from the preceding century. William's story of the witch of Berkeley was popular for a long time and was excerpted in later collections of *exempla*. The story shares to some extent several features of the literature discussed so far:

At the same time something similar occurred in England, not by divine miracle, but by infernal craft; which when I shall have related, the credit of the narrative will not be shaken, though the minds of the hearers should be incredulous; for I have heard it from a man of such character, who swore he had seen it, that I should blush to disbelieve. There resided at Berkeley a woman addicted to witchcraft, as it afterwards appeared, and skilled in ancient augury: she was excessively gluttonous, perfectly lascivious, setting no bounds to her debaucheries, as she was not old, though fast declining in life. On a certain day, as she was regaling, a jack-daw, which was a very great favourite, chattered a little more loudly than usual. On hearing which the woman's knife fell from her hand, her countenance grew pale, and deeply groaning, "This day," said she, "my plough has completed its last furrow; to-day I shall hear of, and suffer, some dreadful calamity." While yet speaking, the messenger of her misfortunes arrived; and being asked, why he approached with so distressed an air? "I bring news," said he, "from the village," naming the place, "of the death of your son, and of the whole family, by a sudden accident." At this intelligence, the woman, sorely afflicted, immediately took to her bed, and perceiving the disorder rapidly approaching the vitals, she summoned her surviving children, a monk, and a nun, by hasty letters; and, when they arrived, with faltering voice, addressed them thus: "Formerly, my children, I constantly administered to my wretched circumstances by demoniacal arts: I have been the sink of every vice, the teacher of every allurement: yet, while practising these crimes, I was accustomed to soothe my hapless soul with the hope of your piety. Despairing of myself, I rested my expectations on you; I advanced you as my defenders against evil spirits, my safeguards against my strongest foes. Now, since I have approached the end of my life, and shall have those eager to punish, who lured me to sin, I entreat you by your mother's breasts, if you have any regard, any affection, at least to endeavour to alleviate my torments; and, although you cannot revoke the sentence already passed upon my soul, yet you may, perhaps, rescue my body, by these means: sew up my corpse in the skin of a stag; lay it on its back in a stone coffin; fasten down the lid with lead and iron; on this lay a stone, bound round with three iron chains of enormous weight; let there be psalms sung for fifty nights, and masses said for an equal number of days, to allay the ferocious attacks of my adversaries. If I lie thus secure for three nights, on the fourth day bury your mother in the ground; although I fear, lest the earth, which has been so often burdened with my crimes, should refuse to receive and cherish me in her bosom." They did their utmost to comply with her injunctions: but alas! vain were pious tears, vows, or entreaties; so great was the woman's guilt, so great the devil's violence. For on the first two nights, while the choir of priests was singing psalms around the body, the devils, one by one, with the utmost ease bursting open the door of the church, though closed with an immense bolt, broke asunder the two outer chains; the middle one being more laboriously wrought, remained entire. On the third night, about cock-crow, the whole monastery seemed to be overthrown from its very foundation, by the clamour of the approaching enemy. One devil, more terrible in appearance than the rest, and of loftier stature, broke the gates to shivers by the violence of his attack. The priests grew motionless with fear; their hair stood on end, and they became speechless. He proceeded, as it appeared, with haughty step towards the coffin, and calling on the woman by name, commanded her to rise. She replying that she could not on account of the chains: "You shall be loosed," said he, "and to your cost:" and directly he broke the chain, which had mocked the ferocity of the others, with as little exertion as though it had been made of flax. He also beat down the cover of the coffin with his foot, and taking her by the hand, before them all, he dragged her out of the church. At the doors appeared a black horse, proudly neighing, with iron hooks projecting over his whole back; on which the wretched creature was placed, and, immediately, with the whole party, vanished from the eyes of the beholders; her pitiable cries, however, for assistance, were heard for nearly the space of four miles. No person will deem this incredible, who has read St. Gregory's Dialogues; who tells, in his fourth book, of a wicked man that had been buried in a church, and was cast out of doors again by devils. Among the French also, what I am about to relate is frequently mentioned. Charles Martel, a man of renowned valour, who obliged the Saracens, when they had invaded France, to retire to Spain, was, at his death, buried in the church of St. Denys; but as he had seized much of the property of almost all the monasteries in France for the purpose of paying his soldiers, he was visibly taken away from his tomb by evil spirits, and has nowhere been seen to his day. At length this was revealed to the bishop of Orleans, and by him publicly made known.[27]

William's chronicle contains many asides (author's digressions within a narrative) of this kind. The form that they take is that of a series of exemplary tales illustrating a point or a diversion made in the course of the history. The story of the witch of Berkeley, for example, occurs in the course of a long interruption of the English section of the chronicle dealing with events in 1065. William has just finished telling the story of the family of Godwin when he breaks his narrative in order "to record what, as I have learned from ancient men, happened at this time at Rome." William then goes on to narrate the pontificate of Gregory VI (1045–46) in considerable (and largely fictitious) detail. He ends the account with a description of Gregory's burial. His enemies had threatened to prevent the pope from being buried within the precincts of St. Peter's and had indeed blocked the entrance to the church. Gregory proposed to his companions that his body be carried to the church in any case so that God, not Gregory's enemies, might decide whether or not the pope should receive the traditional burial. The doors of the church, chained and bolted by Gregory's enemies, flew open at the approach of Gregory's funeral procession, and Gregory received proper papal burial.

The theme of supernatural intervention in the burial of a holy man suggests to William a story illustrating the opposite—the story of the witch of Berkeley and her inability to find a secure tomb. At the end of the story of the witch, William goes on to cite several shorter references—all references to impossible burials—from Gregory the Great and the legends surrounding the fate of Charles Martel.

William, having concluded his digressions, returned to Rome, this time for another story. This one concerned a young bridegroom who casually placed his wedding ring upon the finger of a statue of Venus, which refused to relinquish the ring and prevented the youth's consummation of his recent marriage. The youth in despair visited a priest named Palumbus, who was "very skilled in necromancy, could raise up magical figures, terrify devils, and impell them to do anything he chose." Palumbus instructed the youth to go to a crossroads where he would see a strange procession. He had to address the last figure in the procession and show him the letter Palumbus had given him. The youth did as instructed, and the demon to whom he showed the letter forced the statue of Venus to relinquish the ring and restore the youth to his bride. The unfortunate Palumbus, however, vexed the demon considerably, and the demon predicted his death, before which the priest-necromancer "confessed to the pope unheard of crimes."[28]

This story in turn is followed by an account of the discovery in Rome of the body of Pallas, Aeneas's companion. This is followed by an account of Siamese twins born in Normandy, which gives way to a reflection on the royal saints of Anglo-Saxon England, the story of the seven sleepers of Ephesus, and a consideration of the nature of portents. Only after this extremely long disgression, much of which is clearly based on non-English sources, does William return to the death of Edward and William's conquest in 1066. Thus, in its placing in the chronicle and in the texts that accompany it, William's story of the witch of Berkeley immediately raises suspicions as to its provenance and its relation to any sort of magical activity connected with eleventh- or twelfth-century England. Much the same observations may be made of William's famous account of the magical activities of Pope Sylvester II. This account follows a letter of Pope John XV, cited in order to establish peace between Richard of Normandy and Ethelraed of England. The quotation of the letter is followed by the famous account of the Sylvester/Gerbert legend, which is followed by the story of a magical Italian cave, filled with treasure and visited by an Aquitanian tourist, a "professor . . . who was said to know the unutterable name of God," and a "Jew-necromancer."[29] This story is followed by one concerning two Italian witches who pretend to transform a youth into an ass, a tale doubted by Pope Leo IX, but whose possibility was assured by no less a consultant than Peter Damian,

who cited Simon Magus as his authority.[30] William pauses after the story
of the two women to observe that "it is better to dilate on much matters
than to dwell on Ethelraed's indolence and calamities." He then goes on
to tell the tale of a group of young people condemned to dance for a
year in a cemetery in Cologne as punishment for having violated the
sanctity of the place. William then recounts the tale of the hideous bishop
of Cologne and another story of a nun ravished by a kidnapper. He then,
after this long digression, takes up the story of Ethelraed once more.

William's sources for these stories are varied. Several of them are
surely of Italian origin, perhaps connected with the traditions we have
seen at work in the writing of Anselm of Besate, papal polemics of the
eleventh century, and the late antique rhetorical interest in stories of
magic and fabulous adventures. Others seem to be moral tales based on
roughly contemporary events. These may be highly reworked versions of
popular tales. The story of the witch of Berkeley is the most obvious one
of this type, but this story, too, reveals the hand of the writer more than
the voice of popular narrative. The witch looks, at a closer glance, much
more like a classical Mediterranean witch. "Gluttonous, lascivious, and
skilled at ancient augury," she is emphatically not a rustic woman, of the
type later prosecuted for witchcraft. Her children, the monk and the
nun, and the elaborately dramatic scene of the devil bursting the church
doors and the locks on her coffin, ending in the wild ride, did enter folklore much later, appearing—among other places—in Olavus Magnus's
history of Scandinavia in the sixteenth century.[31] But the story as told by
William of Malmesbury is no longer (if it ever was) a popular tale out
of folklore. It is an *exemplum* illustrating the powers of God and the
demons to gain access to dead bodies. It is also, I suggest, part of that
literary tradition of stories of magicians and witches that seems to have
survived into the eleventh century in central and northern Italy, possessing strong classical antecedents and influences, and occupying a place
in satire and invective as well as moral tale and *exemplum.*

What is most striking about all the sources discussed in this section,
is their *literary* character. Anselm of Besate announces at the beginning
of his work that his charges against Rotiland are ficitious; yet he por-
trays a figure recognizeable to eleventh-century clerical readers as a
magician. The invective against tenth- and eleventh-century popes is also
literary, as are the episodes described by William of Malmesbury. Yet,
taken together, they contain virtually all of the elements for which later
heretics, magicians, and witches were punished. It is not sufficient to
say, as some historians have, that these accusations are simply conventional rhetoric. In spite of the extraordinary literary virtuosity of the
accusations levelled in these sources, the accusations themselves rarely,
if ever, led to ecclesiastical or temporal punishment. Much more serious

were the descriptions of heretical beliefs and activities that began to appear in the eleventh century and flourished in the twelfth. In these, which derived not from a literary tradition of the secular clergy, but from monastic sources and patristic antecedents, many of the accusations we have seen so far were applied directly to contemporary heretics and magicians, with very different results.

THE DESCRIPTION OF HERETICAL PRACTICES, 1050–1250

The various magical activities discussed, if not practiced, by Anselm of Besate, his cousin, and other magicians of the eleventh century suggest several common aspects of the beginnings of a new learned magic that grew stronger during the late eleventh, twelfth, and thirteenth centuries. First, those involved in or accused of magical practices were all either laymen or secular clergy. When they were seriously denounced, the denunciations came from monastic sources, most conspicuously St. Peter Damian, but from others as well. Second, the practices described derive wholly from literary sources, not from the philosophical and scientific treatises which, along with cabalism and astrology, became influential later in the twelfth century. It is important to note that these two traditions of learned magic—that deriving from literary sources and that deriving from scientific or philosophical sources—had different futures. The literary depictions influenced later descriptions of heretics, magicians, and witches; the formal, learned magic that appeared with the revival of interest in antiquity and Islamic learning after the early twelfth century made a partially respectable and protected place for itself in the learned university world of the twelfth and thirteenth centuries. The protected character and learned qualities of the latter tradition made it the true antecedent of the humanists' interests in natural magic in the fifteenth and sixteenth centuries, although the humanists themselves, as we have seen, professed considerable scorn for it. Third, the focus of these practices was less upon a pact with the devil than with the rhetorician's skill in describing and accusing his enemy of grotesque and unnatural, but only secondarily blasphemous, actions. In literary terms, the text of Anselm represents a flyting rather than a denunciation. The focus of these works seems to be the author's skill in controlling grotesquerie and *narratio fabulosa*, a traditional province of the trained rhetorician, rather than the inherent substance of the actions and practices described. On the other hand, monastic critics focus upon the actions and practices themselves. That these criticisms did not lead directly to harsh punishments, or at least an attempt to seek out and reform magicians, may be explained by the fact that they were perceived in such a way as to confirm the monastic belief that the world was full of horrors and temptations. Monastic writers denounced the evils of the world, but they usually made little effort to change them. Not until the Investiture Contest and the principles of Gregorian Reform did the practices of the world become the business of ecclesiastical judges and coercive powers.

One of the most influential currents of eleventh- and twelfth-century life for secular and monastic clergy alike, however, was the growth of various kinds of heresy: doctrinal in the monastic and later the secular and lay worlds, reformist in the secular clergy and among other lay-people.[32] It is the chronicles that first inform historians of the growth of heresy, and it is in the chronicles that the descriptions of heretical beliefs and practices are most graphically described. Too often, historians have taken chroniclers' and other ecclesiastical descriptions of heretical practices at face value, and even the truism that descriptions of magicians' and witches' practices grew out of descriptions of heretical practices usually is cited without the compelling question: out of what did the descriptions of heretics' practices come? Two answers that have gained the greatest currency are, first, that the practices described were real, that heretics did these things (for a variety of reasons), and that churchmen very naturally feared for their flocks because of them; second, that the practices described were the product of the fevered imaginations of church prosecutors and theologians, that they corresponded with nothing in reality, that they were simply a momentary form taken in the eternal duel of theology with "reason." The rhetorical character of Anselm of Besate's *Rhetorimachia* and the principles of rhetoric in general, however, suggest another interpretation: that the duty of clerical chroniclers was not simply to record, but to advocate reform and revulsion from the dangers of heresy. To do this, the particular details of heretical or magical practices were far less important than the horror they induced in the reading about them. Moreover, chroniclers were writers. Trained in grammar and rhetoric, they were proud of their command of rhetorical devices, not the least important of which was the rhetorician's ability to impose a narrative and stylistic order upon chaotic human behavior. In *Inferno,* canto 25, when Dante observes, "Let Lucan now be silent . . ." —for Dante's own description of the metamorphosis of the thieves out-does both Lucan and Ovid—the poet indicates the delight and pride of the rhetorician in controlling chaos and describing the indescribable. Twelfth- and thirteenth-century chroniclers, although there were few Dantes among them, nevertheless worked along similar lines. An examination of several familiar texts in the light of the rhetorical tradition and the moral aims of monastic chroniclers may suggest a reading somewhat different from the traditional ones.

As an exemplary text, we may consider a passage from the chronicle of Ralph, Abbot of the Cisterican monastery of Coggeshall in England, composed sometime in the last quarter of the twelfth century:

In the time of Louis, King of France, who fathered King Philip, while the error of certain heretics, who are called Publicans in the vernacular, was spreading through several of the provinces of France, a marvelous thing happened in the city of Rheims in connection with an old woman infected with that plague. For one day when Lord William, archbishop of that city and King Philip's uncle, was taking a canter with his clergy outside the city, one of his clerks, Master Gervais of Tilbury by name, noticed a girl walking alone in a vineyard. Urged by the curiosity of hot-blooded youth, he turned aside to her, as we later heard from his own lips when he was a canon. He greeted her and attentively inquired whose daughter she was and what she was doing there alone, and then, after admiring her beauty for a while, he at length in courtly fashion made her a proposal of wanton love. She was much abashed, and with eyes cast down, she answered him with simple gesture and a certain gravity of speech: "Good youth, the Lord does not desire me ever to be your friend or the friend of any man, for if ever I forsook my virginity and my body had once been defiled, I should most assuredly fall under eternal damnation without hope of recall."

As he heard this, Master Gervais at once realized that she was one of that most impious sect of Publicans, who at that time were everywhere being sought out and destroyed, especially by Philip, count of Flanders, who was harassing them pitilessly with righteous cruelty. Some of them, indeed, had come to England and were seized at Oxford, where by command of King Henry II they were shamefully branded on their foreheads with a red-hot key. While the aforesaid clerk was arguing with the girl to demonstrate the errors of such an answer, the archbishop approached with his retinue and, learning the cause of the argument, ordered the girl seized and brought with him to the city. When he addressed her in the presence of his clergy and advanced many scriptural passages and reasonable arguments to confute her error, she replied that she had not yet been well enough taught to demonstrate the falsity of such statements but she admitted that she had a mistress in the city who, by her arguments, would very easily refute everyone's objections. So, when the girl had disclosed the woman's name and abode, she was immediately sought out, found, and haled before the archbishop by his officials. When she was assailed from all sides by the archbishop himself and the clergy with many questions and with texts of the Holy Scriptures which might destroy such error, by perverse interpretation she so altered all the texts advanced that it became obvious to everyone that the spirit of all error spoke through her mouth. Indeed, to the texts and narratives of both the Old and New Testaments which they put to her, she answered as easily, as much by memory, as though she had mastered a knowledge of all the Scriptures and had been well trained in this kind of response, mixing the false with the true and mocking the true interpretation of our faith with a kind of perverted insight. Therefore, because it was impossible to recall the obstinate minds of both these persons from the error of their ways by threat or persuasion, or by any arguments or scriptural texts, they were placed in prison until the following day.

On the morrow they were recalled to the archepiscopal court, before the archbishop and all the clergy, and in the presence of the nobility were again confronted with many reasons for renouncing their error publicly. But since they yielded not at all to salutary admonitions but persisted stubbornly in error once adopted, it was unanimously decreed that they be delivered to the flames. When the fire had been lighted in the city and the officials were about to drag them to the punishment decreed, that mistress of vile error exclaimed, "O foolish and unjust judges, do you think now to burn me in your flames? I fear not your judgment, nor do I tremble at the waiting fire!" With these words, she suddenly pulled a ball of thread from her heaving bosom and threw it out of a large window, but keeping the end of the thread in her hands; then in a loud voice, audible to all, she said "Catch!" At the word, she was lifted from the earth before everyone's eyes and followed the ball out the window in rapid flight, sustained, we believe, by the ministry of the evil spirits who once caught Simon Magus up into the air. What became of that wicked woman, or whither she was transported, the onlookers could in no wise discover. But the girl had not yet become so deeply involved in the madness of that sect; and, since she still was present, yet could be recalled from the stubborn course upon which she had embarked neither by the inducement of reason nor by the promise of riches, she was burned. She caused a great deal of astonishment to many, for she emitted no sigh, not a tear, no groan, but endured all the agony of the conflagration steadfastly and eagerly, like a martyr of Christ. But for how different a cause from the Christian religion, for which they of the past were slaughtered by pagans! People of this wicked sect choose to die rather than be converted from error; but they have nothing in common with the constancy and steadfastness of martyrs for Christ, since it is piety which brings contempt for death to the latter, to the former it is hardness of heart.

These heretics allege that children should not be baptized until they reach the age of understanding; they add that prayers should not be offered for the dead, nor intercession asked of the saints. They condemn marriages; they preach virginity as a cover for their lasciviousness. They abhor milk and anything made thereof and all food which is the product of coition. They do not believe that purgatorial fire awaits one after death but that once the soul is released it goes immediately to rest or to damnation. They accept no scriptures as holy except the Gospels and the canonical letters. They are countryfolk and so cannot be overcome by rational argument, corrected by scriptural texts, or swayed by persuasions. They choose rather to die than to be converted from this most impious sect. Those who have delved into their secrets declare also that these persons do not believe that God administers human affairs or exercises any direction or control over earthly creatures. Instead, an apostate angel, whom they call Luzabel, presides over all the material creation, and all things on earth are done by his will. The body is shaped by the devil, the soul is created by God and infused into the body; whence it comes about that a persistent struggle is always being waged between body and soul. Some also say that in their subterranean haunts they perform execrable sacrifices to their Lucifer at stated times and that there they enact certain sacriligious infamies.[33]

Ralph's story deserves close attention, because what seems to the author a perfectly ordinary series of events can be broken down into very different categories and seen to derive from very different sources. At the end of our analysis, we will consider just how much of Ralph's account can be accepted as an accurate reflection of heretical beliefs and practices in late twelfth-century Reims. The first point to make is that of Ralph's source. He himself tells us that the story came from the experience of Gervais of Tilbury, at the time a clerk in the service of Archbishop William of Reims, later marshal of the Kingdom of Arles under Emperor Otto IV, and finally a canon regular in England, and the author of a famous book of stories and moralia, the *Otia Imperialia*. The next section of this chapter will discuss Gervais's work in greater detail; suffice it to say here that any story told by Gervais of Tilbury ought to be looked at with considerable scepticism, for he was a moralist and storyteller par excellence, a learned opportunist and skillful courtier who certainly would not have been above constructing a pious *exemplum* to suit the interests and talents of a credulous Cistercian chronicler. For, if indeed Gervais told the story to Ralph, pious construction is precisely what he engaged in.

The scene which opens the story—that of the clerk accosting a pretty young girl in the countryside and asking her to make love—is one familiar to literary critics, if not to historians proper: it is the opening of a *pastourelle*. The form is fixed: first the encounter, then the debate, then the man (or the woman) winning the argument and having his (or her) way. If there was a girl whose answer to Gervais's proposition triggered his recognition of the publican heresy, it is highly unlikely that she did so in the course of a routine response to the opening conversational gambit of a *pastourelle*. If one cannot accuse Gervais of sour grapes, one can clearly accuse him—and find him guilty—of dressing up his account in literary formula.

The fate of the young girl's teacher is also quite implausible. People may have escaped from the careful scrutiny of the archbishop of Reims, but they did not do so by flying out of his palace window attached to the end of a thrown ball of string. Such a story, beginning with a *pastourelle* and ending with an unacceptable disappearance, may have several grains of truth in it, but its construction is enough to warn the historian about the character of twelfth-century chroniclers and the different purposes of historians and chroniclers. That the diocese of Reims contained heretics of a dualist character is evident. Evident too, is the emphasis upon celibacy, the understanding of scriptures, and the relationship of the older woman as teacher to the younger. In his asides, in fact, Ralph seems to describe accurately the persecution of Publicans in Flanders and England and, at the end of the passage cited here, to summarize at least some of their beliefs accurately. The entire passage, however, must be considered neither accurate nor descriptive of the events of 1179. Whether the literary embellishment should be attributed to Gervais of Tilbury or to Ralph himself, it is clear that the chronicler's description of this episode must be regarded with extreme caution as evidence of anything but the chronicler's technique.

At the heart of the story, however, there are certain events that require consideration. In his muddled description of Publican beliefs at the end of the episode, Ralph presents a recognizable picture corroborated by other sources of some aspects of twelfth-century dualism; however, some elements of his description are clearly contradictory and are inspired not by accuracy, but by the traditional explanation of heretical behavior: Heretics' emphasis upon virginity is regarded as a cover for lasciviousness; heretics are rustics and cannot be reasoned with (although the girl and her mistress reside in Reims); they perform sacrifices to Lucifer; their heroism in the face of persecution comes from hardness of heart, rather than piety. These last elements are already familiar from the literature of the earlier twelfth century, and by the time Ralph wrote they had become almost a *topos* in describing heretics. Yet even these topical commonplaces do not exactly account for, or fit, the material in the story at Reims. The relationship between the older woman and the young girl, as between a teacher and a pupil, is not accounted for in Ralph's conventional summary of heretical beliefs. The older woman's knowledge of scripture (sufficient to hold her own with the learned and skillful *familia* of the archbishop of Reims) is not that of an ignorant or stubborn rustic who holds tenaciously to a few memorized precepts, but that of someone familiar with the Bible, skillful enough in debate to hold off the archbishop's clerks (in what language, one wonders), and possessing (even Ralph/Gervais is forced to admit it) intellectual powers formidable enough to be labelled by the horrified chronicler as "perverted insight." In sum, this episode, widely cited in many sources, is a tissue of literary and rhetorical embellishment filled out with generalized conventional descriptions of Publican beliefs and one or two verifiable facts, surrounding what may be an accurate story, but a story whose accuracy is very hard to distinguish from the presentation made by Ralph. It is impossible to determine whether the skillful storyteller Gervais—showing the inventiveness that marked the *Otia Imperialia*—recounted this episode to a credulous Cistercian chronicler, or whether Ralph used Gervais's story because it seemed appropriate and was memorable enough to strike revulsion into the young Cistercians who were the chronicle's audience. That the story as it stands is a rhetorical fabrication, however, cannot be doubted. Its greatest importance is precisely as an illustration of the manner, not the accuracy, in which the depiction of heretics was accepted in the late twelfth century.

Other stories of heretics also circulated around the court of Archbishop William of Reims. Walter Map, in the *De nugiis curialium,* remarks that William of Reims once told him personally the story of the knight who sprinkled blessed salt on food set before him by his nephew, the follower of an unnamed heretical sect that seems to have practiced deceptive magic. Once the salt was sprinkled on the food, "suddenly the fish disappeared and there on the dish was left some substance like pellets of hare dung." After failing to convince his nephew of the error of his ways, the knight enclosed the nephew and his teachers in a house and attempted unsuccessfully to burn it to the ground. Only when the bishop of Vienne performed a certain ritual upon the heretics/magicians, were they able to be consumed by the flames.[34]

Walter Map's accounts of heretics are no less inaccurate than Ralph of Coggeshall's, although they contain more plausible details. Nevertheless, the curious recurrence of William of Reims in these two stories from very different sources suggests that the prelate may have figured in a number of traditions describing heretics. In any case, Map's story is at least as literary as Ralph's, if not quite as artfully constructed. One indication, then, of the source of the activities and beliefs attributed by ecclesiastical writers to heretical and magical sects, is rhetorical. Walter Map, Gervais of Tilbury, and Ralph of Coggeshall all share the same aims: to arrest the attention of their readers, to heighten the reader's revulsion by setting their stories in skillful literary constructions, and to demonstrate the rhetorician's ability to control and display his repulsive materials in a manner strikingly similar to other aspects of Romanesque aesthetic ideas. It is to the depiction of magic and heresy in terms of that literary aesthetic that we must now turn.

What is common to the stories told by Ralph of Coggeshall and Walter Map is the element of embellishing what may be considered an accurate core account of heretical beliefs and practices (identifiable because they are in part corroborated by other, less literary sources) with literarily devised and clearly fictitious elements. A number of historians of heresy and witchcraft have commented upon the general character of medieval ecclesiastical invective and its unreliability in most areas an an illustration of actual behavior and belief. As others, too, have pointed out, the purpose of such accounts as Ralph's and Walter Map's was not to inform accurately, but to arouse within the pious reader the appropriate revulsion against the object being condemned. Hence, by analogy and by invoking different spheres of meaning, chroniclers consistently empha-

sized the personal depravity of heretics and witches, their physical de-
formities and illnesses, their sexual behavior, and their unalterable subjection to Satan. In addition, since the heresies and deviant practices
condemned were regarded as manifestations of the devil's eternal enmity
to Christians, descriptions of older heresies and condemnations of other
forms of deviant practice from the first centuries of Christian history were
often applied to the enemies of the twelfth and thirteenth centuries.
These practices were not, of course, conscious deception, nor were they
even manifestations of *fraus pia,* pious fraud. To excite the horror and
arouse the zealousness of contemporary Christians, writers like Ralph of
Coggeshall and Walter Map described their heretics in a manner perfectly consistent with the mentality of the twelfth century. They and
other writers like them were, in fact, faced by a serious problem. Before
the late eleventh century, reformist and learned heresies had largely
occurred within the precincts of the monastic cloister. Other deviant
beliefs were dealt with by councils, penitentials, sermons, occasional
treatises, and royal decrees, but they did not generate a conspicuous
literature, and the monastic literature of heresy was hardly appropriate to
describe the social, intellectual and spiritual ferment of the late eleventh-
and twelfth-century laity and clergy. Consequently, the task of describing heresy, warning orthodox Christians of its dangers, and alerting the
Christian public to the depravity of the heretics was a relatively new
one, even at the end of the twelfth century when Ralph and Walter
wrote. Like much other literature of the period, their works shared something of the Romanesque mentality. In some respects, although analogies
with the visual arts are always dangerous, the grotesqueries and literary
embellishments of the two stories cited above are analogous to the
visualization of the struggle between good and evil that occupies so much
of Romanesque art. Most of the activities that later would be attributed
to witches and magicians were already present in the invective against
spiritual deviancy developed by twelfth-century theologians and chroniclers, except for certain traits that did not appear until much later and
seem to me to be far less important. The development of this invective
and its use in the twelfth and early thirteenth centuries have not yet
been investigated.

In their fine collection of documents on the history of heresy, Walter
Wakefield and A. P. Evans included the two passages discussed at the
beginning of this chapter under the general subtitle, "From Heresy to
Witchcraft."[35] In so designating these texts, Wakefield and Evans recognized the common elements in twelfth-century ideas of heretical conduct
and occult practices. It is worth pointing out that most of the embellished
invective describing heretics of the sort discussed above dates from the
twelfth century. During the thirteenth and fourteenth centuries, church-

men and laymen alike described heretical beliefs and behavior in much more accurate terms. Theologians and inquisitors produced accurate and usable descriptions of heretical beliefs, culminating in the handbooks for inquisitors, the best known of which is that of Bernard Gui.[36] Although some traditional invective lingered, particularly in the case of the Brethren of the Free Spirit, heresy became rationalized and its persecutors became astute in recognizing what heretics actually believed and did. The twelfth century, on the other hand, was the one century in which heretical beliefs and activities were described, not in accurate, but in symbolic terms.

The course for magicians and witches was somewhat different. As the next chapter will show, the survival of ancient magical practices was greatly transformed by the recovery of Greek and Arabic works, the sociology of the magicians, the developments in Latin theology, and the work of canon lawyers. As heretics became better, or at least more accurately understood, magicians and witches alone were left with the elements they once had shared with heretics in twelfth-century sources. These sources were preserved in collections of miracle stories, handbooks for instructing novices in religious orders, sermons, *exempla,* memoirs, and occasional treatises.[37] In short, the portrait of the heretic, magician, and witch which the twelfth century writers indiscriminately developed, remained applicable only to the last two of these after the early thirteenth century. Having once shared with heretics the picturesque invective of Ralph of Coggeshall, Walter Map, and Gervais of Tilbury, magicians and witches were virtually the only figures to whom it was applied between the late thirteenth and the eighteenth centuries. Therefore, the nature of twelfth-century invective becomes especially important, since it is the magicians and witches, and not the heretics, who bore most of its brunt during the next five centuries.

The sources of twelfth-century ecclesiastical invective are not at all certain. R. I. Moore and Norman Cohn have pointed out the similarity between many descriptions of twelfth-century heretical practices and those attributed to early Christians by their pagan opponents.[38] In one case at least, that of Guibert of Nogent, this kind of source may very well have been used. In his *Memoirs,* Guibert describes a heretical sect which supposedly held secret meetings, encouraged indiscriminate sexual coupling, communally burned the children born from such intercourse, and from the ashes of the children made a kind of bread which, when eaten, strengthened the heretical beliefs of the sect.[39] Guibert's source for at least part of this description appears to be Augustine's treatise on heresies and perhaps his reading in other early Church Fathers. A number of scholars have pointed out the similarities between Guibert's account of these "Manichean" rites and those condemned at the Synod of Orleans in 1022—particularly the magical food and the material from which it is made and the sexual license of the secret, nocturnal gatherings.[40] Whether Guibert modelled his own account on that of the Synod of Orleans, or whether both sources drew upon earlier ones, two conclusions may be reached concerning these and much other twelfth-century literature on heretics. First, especially in the case of Guibert, those who described heretical beliefs were more widely read than most of their predecessors, and they applied the fruits of their wide reading to the cases they judged or described. Second, perhaps out of late antique sources, these writers had by the early twelfth century created a distinctive form of invective against certain kinds of heretics. This invective—having part of its roots in Roman invective against magicians, objects of satire, Jews, and deviant Christians—was applied to both heretics and magicians in the twelfth century. Although heretics soon came under the scrutiny and authority of different sorts of thinkers and writers, the invective used against them in the early twelfth century occasionally remained, and certainly applied to groups such as magicians and witches long after it ceased to be applied generally to heretics.

Variant forms of the paradigm of the secret meetings of deviants existed in Christian literature at least as early as the first apologists, and many of them were preserved in the works of the Church Fathers, particularly St. Augustine. Augustine's description of Manichean and Montanist practices appears to have been the source, certainly of Guibert of Nogent's description, probably of the Synod of Orleans, and surely of other eleventh- and twelfth-century accounts such as those of Adhémar of Chabannes and Paul of St. Peire de Chartres. The new interest in such writings as Augustine's on the part of eleventh- and twelfth-century writers on heresy was probably a result of their generally increased familiarity with earlier patristic literature that characterizes so many other aspects of late eleventh- and early twelfth-century Christian thought.

In the Byzantine Empire, no such renewed acquaintance with patristic literature was needed because no break with earlier literature had ever taken place. In Michael Psellos's treatise *On the Operation of the Demons*, for example, descriptions of a heretical sect referred to as "Messalians" sound very similar to the passages in Augustine, the Synod of 1022 at Orleans, Guibert of Nogent, and Walter Map. There is little likelihood that Psellos knew Augustine or that the twelfth-century Latin writers knew Psellos; both kinds of writer, however, were able to draw upon an old tradition of patristic anti-heretical invective which, in their own minds, at least, remained valid for the eleventh and twelfth centuries because the ancient heresies themselves had survived "secretly" and the heresies represented by eleventh- and twelfth-century heretics were in fact these old heresies surfacing once again. What had been true when

Augustine and others wrote of Montanists and Manicheans was, in the twelfth-century monastic writer's view, equally true of those heretics he described.

Such a process does not depend exclusively upon what Jeffrey Russell has called "literary clichés." Guibert and other chroniclers believed that they witnessed the same heresies as Augustine, Justin, and other Church Fathers, and they described them similarly. It should be noted that virtually all of the twelfth-century descriptions of abominable heretical practices structurally serve as asides, author's digressions within a narrative. The heretics do not confess to them; indeed, the heretics' obstinacy, noted above in the ill-fitting observations of Ralph of Coggeshall, is assumed to be the reason for their failure to convert to orthodox Christianity or even to understand the questions asked of them. Thus, it is clearly the writer himself, or a particular informant, who adds the details derived from patristic and other sources. In Guibert's case, and certainly in that of others, the writer's own learning made him familiar with this literature. Since his purpose in writing was to inculcate moral virtues and warn the faithful against the dangers threatening them (the same danger that had threatened their ancestors in the early Church), his description of the heretics' practices and beliefs had to follow rhetorical and moral rules. Those rules were not the ones that usually guide the modern historian, but neither were they simply literary clichés or arbitrary embellishments. They were essential parts of the writer's business, and by omitting them he would have failed in his full purpose. These heretical beliefs, whether or not they applied to the particular twelfth-century heretics in question, nevertheless applied symbolically to all heretics, and the reader had to be informed of this. The appearance of the heretics, their apparent sanctity, their exalted moral conduct, their skill at argument, their persausiveness, and their attractiveness could not be ignored; but these very rules required that appearances be countered by the harsh, if symbolic, truth of their condition, and that truth had been stated by the Fathers. They were in this, as in all other fields, *auctoritates,* and their *auctoritas* extended in time as well as morality.

As stated above, it should also be emphasized that most of these writings came out of monastic circles, and they reflect the monastic literary dependence upon patristic sources as well as the dim monastic view of the life of laypeople. Moreover, many of them were written for monks, and the monastic audience looked for moral guidance—for, as it were, a higher kind of truth—rather than for a mere narrative of detail. Monastic historiography and other literature, particularly before the advent of scholastic thought and the growth of other kinds of intellectual communities, was distinctive and purposeful. Heavily dependent upon literary traditions and shaped by principles of literary exegesis, it was in part responsible for many characteristic features of Romanesque art and literature. Especially important in the light of the texts considered here is the enormous power to convey ideas graphically, both through descriptive writing and through the visual arts. The Romanesque monastic aim was to teach, and to employ dramatic, arresting images to drive its lessons home. The literary genres in which descriptions of heresies occur—histories, chronicles, and collections of moral stories—lent themselves perfectly to these requirements. For, after all, Guibert, Ralph of Coggeshall, and others were not writing collections of law; they were not, in the twelfth-century academic sense, theologians; they were certainly not formulating doctrine; they were teaching a community of Christians that, whether monastic or lay, was in great danger. And they invoked the most graphic sources they knew of to hammer home awareness of revulsion against that danger. That their works were later used by others who shared little of their world view and none of their mentality could hardly have been foreseen by them. These features, plus the wide circulation of this literature during the twelfth century and its later influence, have often prevented historians from seeing their literary productions in a measured light. Attacked by what they thought—in fact, were assured—were ancient heresies revived, they turned to their strongest *auctoritates*, the Fathers, to repel those heresies. In doing so they created a literature that had a long history and great influence. They influenced other, later writers who, like Walter Map, wrote for different audiences. It is, in fact, in the differences between their outlook and method and those of later writers that the transmission of invective against heretics and magicians took place.

Besides the details of heretical practices discussed above, another conspicuous feature of the literature which discusses twelfth-century heresy, is the emphasis on its secrecy. It may be too much to say that twelfth-century ecclesiastics had a pathological fear of secret teachings and meetings, but this element is certainly stressed again and again, even in descriptions of heretical practices that do not emphasize or even mention the grotesque details we have seen above. One of the motives behind Peter the Venerable's treatise *Against the Petrobrusians*, for example, is his astonishment at the growth of the heresy, local bishops' ignorance of that growth, and contemporary intellectuals' tendency to scorn it instead of attack it.[41] Petrobrusianism, Peter warns, is not preached and defended openly, but "whispered" from mouth to ear. The heretics at Orleans in 1022 also offered secret teachings to Heribert and Arefast, and Ralph of Coggeshall's old woman was, presumably, a secret teacher as well. This motif of secret, insidious teaching and outward normality became more and more important in attacks on heresy as the twelfth century wore on.

It was not merely against heretics and magicians that this twelfth-century concern with secret meetings and secret teachings was directed. In Peter Abelard's *Confessio fidei,* one of the accusations (based upon Proverbs 9:17) made against him was that he had taught secretly and differently from his open teaching in the schools; he had offered *acquas furtivas et panem absconditem.*[42] It is this accusation that Abelard passionately denies; he has never taught such things. Other masters of the schools were also accused of surreptitious teachings, sometimes verging on the heretical. Secret teaching and hidden books certainly played their part in the earlier world of Anselm of Besate, but in the twelfth century the fear of secrecy came into full force. In his sermon against heresy in 1144, St. Bernard (who may have levelled the original accusation at Abelard) holds forth on the verse of Canticles 2:15, "Catch us the little foxes that destroy the vines, for our vineyard hath flourished."[43] In this sermon Bernard launches a formidable attack, not on openly professed heretics, but upon those "who would rather injure than conquer and who do not even wish to disclose themselves, but prefer to slink about in the shadows." As it had in earlier commentaries on the Old Testament, the metaphor of the little foxes became commonplace in discussions of heretics and entered the vocabulary of papal letters as well as sermons and later biblical commentary.

As Jeffrey Russell has pointed out, these denunciations of heretics mingle accusations of magic and witchcraft with attacks upon heretical errors. Monastic chroniclers and moralists in the first half of the twelfth century made the first concerted attack upon ecclesiastical deviance by emphasizing the elements of secrecy, abasement before the demon, lasciviousness, cannibalism, magic food, and hypnotic attraction by feigning Christian virtues. The monastic view of the lay world, its dependence upon patristic literary authority, its belief in the eternity of ancient heresies, and its growing fear of secrecy, in the schools as well as the heretics' conventicles and "synagogues," thus gave shape to a paradigm of deviance that did not soon lose its power. The paradigm was itself also shaped by such rhetorical adventures as that of Anselm of Besate, discussed at the beginning of this chapter, and continued in a number of literary genres through the twelfth and thirteenth centuries. It is to these genres that we now turn.

COURTIERS' TRIFLES AND MAGIC, 1150–1220

Anselm of Besate represents a kind of formal rhetorical source for the history of ideas of magic. The monastic descriptions of the enormities of heretics' and magicians' conduct come from a second rhetorical tradition. A third category of rhetorical sources that helps to cast light on twelfth-

and thirteenth-century beliefs and magical practices is the literature influenced by and directed at the court. As early as the twelfth century,
moralists began to associate fear of magical practices with the court, the
newest and most potent source of power and wealth in twelfth-century
society.

Although the phenomenon of the court certainly antedates the middle
of the twelfth century, the first literature directed at couriers and their
masters appeared shortly after that date. This section will deal with three
works of this genre: John of Salisbury's *Policraticus* (1159), Walter
Map's *De nugiis curialium* (1181–93), and Gervais of Tilbury's *Otia
Imperialia* (1214–18). Although the authors of these works are English,
the works themselves should not be considered uniquely English, for
their authors derive their materials from many different kinds of sources,
including classical antiquity. Their citation here is for one reason; as
John of Salisbury put it, "I deal in part with the frivolities of court life,
bearing more heavily on those I find harder to tolerate."[44] Among the
frivolities noted by John of Salisbury, Walter Map, and Gervais of Tilbury
is the courtier's interest in and fear of magic. As will be argued from
legal materials in Chapter 4, the prevalence of magic at twelfth- and
thirteenth-century courts played an important role in the later persecution of magicians and witches. Indeed, it is commonly accepted that the
prosecution of witches grew out of the prosecution of heretics.[45] It will be
the contention of this book that in fact magicians and heretics had always
been associated, and that while the forms of legal prosecution of heretics
paved the way for similar actions taken against witches after the fifteenth
century, it was the fear of and actual prosecution of magicians in several
key trials of the later thirteenth through the fifteenth centuries that is the
real stage following the persecution of heretics, and the preliminary
stage in persecuting witches.

The magician—and, to a certain extent, the heretic—appears usually
in a few specific places in medieval society. The most frequent of these
is the court. A number of twelfth-century writers point out the presence
and fear of magicians among courtiers, although their work has not often
been cited in this connection.

John of Salisbury's *Policraticus*, the second book of which is devoted
to the varieties of magic known and feared in the twelfth century, consists of two parts.[46] The first is a description and indictment of the vices
of courtiers, and the second is a description of the principles of ethics
and religion required to assure good rule and just governance. Historians
usually concentrate upon book 4 through book 8, since these contain
most of John's political and ethical theory. Books 1 and 2, however,
based on John's observations during a long career around many courts,
shed considerable light upon those vices to which courtiers are particu-

larly prone. It is not too much to say that the *Policraticus* is a book of vices and virtues for rulers and their courtiers and assistants.[47] Book 1 of the *Policraticus* treats the courtiers' vices of fear of fortune, impropriety, hunting, gambling, music, actors, mimes, jugglers, and illusionists. John's discussion of *praestigium* leads him naturally into the next vice, that of consulting magicians of all sorts. From book 1, chapter 10 through book 2, John describes the danger of magic to the twelfth-century courtier.[48]

John of Salisbury's treatment of magic among twelfth-century courtiers, like his treatment of many other topics, including politics, is complex. Many of his references are to works of classical literature and patristic thought. His description of different types of magic follows the descriptions of Isidore of Seville, St. Augustine, and Hrabanus Maurus. Therefore, it may be objected that John is attacking the literary tradition of magic, not magic as twelfth-century courtiers knew it. Indeed, one historian has observed that it is never clear whether John is talking about the court of Henry II of England or that of Augustus.[49] The answer seems to be that John does both. In raising the question of magic among couriers, John is obliged to describe the conventional types of magic and magicians as these types existed in the tradition of Christian literature. On the other hand, it is also clear that John has personally observed courtiers consulting magicians and has known their interest in magic at first hand. So that within the literary encyclopedism that characterized John's treatment of magic at twelfth-century courts there lie a genuine alarm at its prevalence, first-hand experience of its interest, and a profound awareness of the dangers it posed to unwitting, ambitious, unlearned courtiers who need to be instructed in its varieties and dangers as well as castigated for the attention they pay to its particular twelfth-century forms.

In chapter 28 of book 2, John interrupts his discussion of crystal-gazing and other forms of divination and tells a story of his own experience. It is not a passage that has been widely noted before, but it does cast some light on little noticed practices in early twelfth-century England:

During my boyhood I was placed under the direction of a priest, to teach me psalms. As he practiced the art of crystal gazing, it chanced that he after preliminary magical rites made use of me and a boy somewhat older, as we sat at his feet, for his sacrilegious art, in order that what he was seeking by means of finger nails moistened with some sort of sacred oil of crism, or of the smooth polished surface of a basin, might be made manifest to him by information imparted by us.

And so after pronouncing names which by the horror they inspired seemed to me, child though I was, to belong to demons, and after administering oaths of which, at God's instance, I know nothing, my companion asserted that he saw certain misty figures, but dimly, while I was so blind to all this that nothing appeared to me except the nails or basin and the other objects I had seen there before.

As a consequence I was adjudged useless for such purposes, and, as though I impeded the sacrilegious practices, I was condemned to have nothing to do with such things, and as often as they decided to practice their art I was banished as if an obstacle to the whole procedure. So propitious was God to me even at that early age.

But as I grew older more and more did I abominate this wickedness, and my horror of it was strengthened because, though at the time I made the acquaintance of many practitioners of the art, all of them before they died were deprived of their sight, either as a result of physical defect or by the hand of God, not to mention other miseries with which in my plain view they were afflicted. There were two exceptions—the priest whom I have mentioned and a certain deacon; for they, seeing the affliction of the crystal gazers, fled (the one to the bosom of the collegiate church—the other to the refuge to the monastery of Cluny) and adopted holy garb. None of the less I am sorry to say that even they, in comparison to others in their congregations, suffered many afflictions afterward.[50]

The figure of the clerical magician—whether crystal-gazer or necro-mancer—appears frequently in twelfth- and thirteenth-century literature. Such people are common in the writing of Walter Map, Caesarius of Heisterbach, and William of Malmesbury, as well as in many other collections of tales and chronicles. In John of Salisbury's experience, such figures were not fictitious creations, but included an actual teacher of his and several clerics he knew later in life. The figure of the priest who knows how to call up the devil is, in fact, almost a commonplace of twelfth-century moral stories, and even if most of these are fictitious, the evidence from John of Salisbury and others indicates that the type itself, at least, was based not on a literary tradition, but on the first-hand knowledge of twelfth-century writers.[51]

When considered more closely, the figure of the magician is not surprising. The skills required, presumably, for invoking demons were learned skills, and aside from the type of the Jew and the Saracen, the learned people of Europe before the end of the twelfth century were clergy. The figure of the Saracens who taught Rotiland his magic and pursued the fleeing Gerbert, as well as that of the "Jew-necromancer" in William of Malmesbury's story of the Aquitanian and the Italian mountain of gold, are types of this kind. As the twelfth century wore on, the real impact of Arabic learning, including magical, learning, became clear, and the Moslem magician was transformed from a figure of legend into a genuine teacher whose doctrines troubled the literature of the eleventh and twelfth centuries.[52] Moreover, the priests who invoked demons and practiced other forms of magic were secular priests, rarely monks. The circles of Anselm of Besate, papal Rome, wandering scholars, and clerical teachers were precisely the circles in which these clerical magicians moved. John of Salisbury himself emerged from such a circle, and with the growth of schools and universities in the twelfth and thirteenth centuries, these too became centers where learning of all sorts, even occult learning, became prevalent. When traditional theologians attacked the new masters of the twelfth-century schools, charges of teaching secret and forbidden knowledge, including knowledge of magic, were among their weapons. Peter Abelard was among the first, but he was certainly not the last, to be accused of offering secret, dangerous teachings to his students.[53]

Secular clergy, learned magic, invoking of demons, and the perils and temptations of the court all combine in the work of John of Salisbury and others to shed new light upon what is often called the renaissance of the twelfth century.[54] Even before the schools were suspected of fostering magic teachings, the courts became the first setting for magic. The role of the court in the cultural life of the twelfth, thirteenth, and fourteenth centuries has not received a great deal of attention from historians, who have usually focused upon its administrative, dynastic, artistic, and political roles. Of the three great twelfth-century institutions that transformed the whole of European life, the court has been discussed the least. Cities and universities, perhaps because they have survived into the modern world, have undeservedly received far more attention. Indeed, it is not too much to say that some of the circumstances which Peter Brown ascribed to the spread of magic in fourth- and fifth-century Rome begin to recur only in the twelfth century, and first in the court.[55] It is in the court that great power and wealth are to be won, not necessarily by diligent service or high birth, but by favor. Favor may be ostensible and direct, a reward for skill or talent, but it may also be indirect, the product of cultivated patrons, courtiers, servants, and other informal but real sources of power. The indictment of court life by John of Salisbury and others is based, to be sure, in part upon the conventional moral ideals of the twelfth-century Church. In another aspect, John criticizes specific vices and faults to which the courtier is especially prone. It is no accident that John begins the *Policraticus* with an indictment against those who believe that random fortune bestows favors and disgraces arbitrarily. The insecurity of the courtier—his need to play upon many stages at once, his pragmatic conviction that favor may be won by public and private methods, and his search for any methods that will assure or at least promise success—make him especially prone to the vices of flattery, consulting magicians, and perhaps even instigating magical powers against his own enemies, real or imagined.[56] In the humanist courts of the late fifteenth century described by Castiglione in *Il Corteggiano*,

Lauro Martines has found the same characteristics: immense insecurity, pressure to please the lord in many different areas, and the fear of falling victim to Fortune. The process that shaped Castiglione's courtier was already at work in the twelfth century, and the *Policraticus* is one of the earliest attempts to criticize the moral world of the court as a new phenomenon.[57]

The courtier's success might have depended as easily upon love, persuasion, the removal of an enemy, or attracting the personal affection of his lord, as upon talent, skill, and proven experience; he might have been driven to desperation to learn what the future held in store; or he might have felt himself to be the victim of magic. Under these circumstances, he could very readily provide employment for at least some of the types of magicians and soothsayers whom John of Salisbury took such great pains and so many leaves of the *Policraticus* to denounce. As will be shown in Chapter 4, the association of the courtier and the magician was not exclusively a twelfth-century phenomenon. As the world of the court grew greater, more wealthy, and more crowded, the place of the individual courtier became even less secure. By the end of the thirteenth century in Paris and Rome and shortly afterward elsewhere, the daily fear of magic was a real—and punishable—offense.

Walter Map's *De nugiis curialium*, "Courtiers' Trifles," was written in the 1180's and probably completed by 1193.[58] The word *nuga*, which appears in the titles of both the *Policraticus* and the *De nugiis*, is commonly translated as "trifles," that is, distractions, trivial faults, amusements, or frivolities. *Nuga*, however, has another meaning in medieval Latin. Merely by virtue of its first meaning, it also carried a moral connotation, implying vices. Thomas Aquinas, for example, a century later, distinguished between two kinds of evil human practices. Some are *noxia*, some are *nugatoria*. Basing his distinction on St. Augustine's *De doctrina Christiana*, Aquinas distinguishes them thus:

Noxia autem superstitio dicitur quae aliquid manisfeste illicitum continent; sicut invocationes et sacrificia daemonum, vel quodcumque huiusmodi. Nugatorium autem dicitur quando aliquis utitur re aliqua ad quod virtus eius extendi non potest; hoc enim in vanum fieri videtur.[59]

Nugae, therefore, are also forms of vice, less harmful than *noxia* but certainly more than "trifles." Such a meaning is clearer in the *Policraticus* which is, in fact, a sort of moral guidebook for courtiers and their masters. In the work of Walter Map, however, there is no such systematic schema, and his stories, although they are clearly moral stories, cover a much wider range than the serious learning of John of Salisbury. Thus, the work is harder to use as a reflection of Map's own observations.

The first section of the *De nugiis* lays out a serious of complaints about the life of the court, disguising the difficulties in contemporary courts by recounting the labors of classical figures out of mythology. After a long description of his own court, Map tells one of his most famous stories, that of the wandering, enchanted King Herla.[60] The story derives equally from folktale and literary tradition, but Map uses it as a dramatic counterpoint to his own muddled, vice-ridden household. He then goes on to illustrate how even astute rulers may be deceived by wicked courtiers, and how even withdrawal from the world of the court into that of the monastery does not always guarantee spiritual security.[61] Map's descriptions of true and false orders of monks leads him to a discussion of new orders, and then of new heresies. In this context, he tells the story, already cited above, of the Paterines, "who have lurked among Christians everywhere from the days of our Lord's Passion, and continue to wander from the truth."[62] At nightly meetings in their "synagogues" they await the arrival of a mysterious black cat, turn out the lights, bestow upon it the *osculum infame,* and engage in indiscriminate sexual promiscuity. Map then recounts an even less likely story, also cited above, in which food prepared by heretics appears wholesome and appetizing until it is sprinkled with salt; then it turns into a noisome substance.[63] Map's first few stories in book 2 deal with genuine sanctity. He then produces a series of stories concerning the alleged customs of the Welsh, and it is in these tales that some of Map's most picturesque stories of magic are found, including the famous tale of Edric Wild.[64] Map's tales of the Welsh have long been well known since later storytellers and poets have used them. But it is clear that they are stories only, and in no way touch the material of this study.

More immediate is the story of the knight Eudo and his pact with the Devil.[65] The pact with Satan is made, not by a magician, but by a foolish knight who through it gained great powers and wealth, worked wonders but suffered great remorse, and was only saved by leaping into a fire in penance. Although the story is decorously amplified in Map's characteristic style, it is possible to see in it the twelfth-century resentment against the violent knight and lord, and the ease of association of violence with literal bondage to Satan. This theme introduces a series of stories, perhaps not unrelated to Map's extraordinary literary diatribe against marriage in book 4, chapter 3, all of which deal with a mortal male married to a dead woman, a demon, or a fairy. Having turned to the subject to demons' deceitfulness, Map, following William of Malmesbury, retells the story of Sylvester II and his magical arts, adding to them the story of Gerbert's seduction by a phantom woman.[66]

Map then tells a series of stories of prodigies and wonders from various sources. Book 4 concludes with the story of the shoemaker of Constantinople, a tale of necrophilia and magic that appears to have been one of the sources for later accusations against the Templars, the story of Nicholas Pipe, a Sicilian diver, and other tales. Book 5 deals with historical rulers of recent history, and the work concludes with a recapitulation of the opening, another warning to kings to watch hard for courtiers' vices. It is clear that Map's book too deals with both meanings of *nugae*—trifling amusements and minor vices. Less direct and less serious than John of Salisbury, Map is far more picturesque, willing to draw on a diversity of sources to illustrate his often diluted moral points. Thus, although Map's *De nugiis* contains a far wider variety of tales of magic and the supernatural, and although these tales are used for ostensibly the same purposes as those of John of Salisbury, they are more the products of a literary humanism, and less accurate reflections of Map's own observance. As we have seen, even Map's accounts of his personal encounters with heretics are modest enough descriptions. In a few stories, however, there is evidence of the same concern for magic and demons in the life of the court as one finds in John of Salisbury. Map argues that knights and courtiers are uniquely vulnerable to the temptations of demons and magicians. Less explicit than John of Salisbury's work, Map's *De nugiis* is nevertheless part of the literature of courtly criticism that began in the twelfth century and lasted until the eighteenth.

Written for and about the courtly ruling classes of twelfth-century Europe, the *Policraticus* and the *De nugiis curialium* are not conventional tracts on vices and virtues of the kind best known from monastic and clerical academic circles, and they are certainly far from the penitential literature of the eleventh and twelfth centuries. They are, nevertheless, important works that reflect the twelfth-century writer's awareness of the unique character of courtly life and the temptations that it patricularly offered. Especially in Walter Map's case—beneath the classical allusions, the disgressions, the biting satire against Cistercians and charlatans, and the curiosities that amused his readers—there is a level of concern for knightly behavior in what is clearly to him, as to John of Salisbury, a new center of lay and clerical activity. As John Baldwin has shown, the phenomenon of the court and its particular temptations also troubled the moral theologians at Paris during the second half of the twelfth and the beginning of the thirteenth centuries.[67] As Erich Köhler and other historians have shown, even the Arthurian literary romances, long considered the characteristic literary forms of courtly society, deal in large part with moral and psychological dilemmas unique to courtly life. The magic of the romances, however, seems to me to be quite removed from the subjects treated by John of Salisbury, Walter Map, and the Paris theologians and moral reformers. In the latter works, the moral dangers of magic and other vices to which courtiers are especially prone are not symbolically described, but openly denounced. The direct moral voices of these ecclesiastical courtly critics reveal that the concern about magic at the courts was widespread, well known, and worrisome. Like actors, mimes, flatterers, usurers, and traducers, the sorcerer's apprentices who divined, created love potions, and told the future at twelfth-century European courts were well known to moral critics. In the works discussed so far in this section, it is clear that the old injunctions of Isidore of Seville and Augustine, reiterated by Hrabanus Maurus and Hugh of St. Victor, underlay the basis of the hostility John of Salisbury and others to the idea and practice of magic in all forms. But the critics' hostility was not merely general and academic. They saw the magicians at court and denounced specifically the noble's and the courtier's vulnerability to them. A century later, more learned magicians attended other courts and they, too, aroused hostility and eventually repressive legislation.

This literature was written for the court, too, partly to warn courtiers and rulers about the temptations unique to their station and life-style, and partly to amuse them. John of Salisbury conveyed moral instruction and criticism along with pious, classical humanism; Walter Map wrote with an ornate Latin style, a powerful imagination, and a natural genius for story telling. These latter qualities have tended to make both the early books of the *Policraticus* and the whole of the *De nugiis curialium* somewhat remote from most scholarly discussions of the twelfth century. Seen in the light of their function as both instruction and amusement books aimed at the noble courtly class, however, both works (and others) reveal a considerable concern over the casual and hitherto generally unnoticed use of various kinds of magic in the courts of twelfth-century Europe.

A third work of a similar kind is the *Otia Imperialia* of Gervais of Tilbury,[68] Gervais was born in the early 1150s, perhaps at Tilbury in the western part of Essex. He probably received a clerical education, possibly continuing it on the continent, for he was known to be at Rome in 1166 and at Bologna, where he studied and taught canon law, by 1170. After 1180 he was in the service of Henry II of England; then, in that of Henry's son (Henry the young king). After attending the courts of Archbishop William of Reims and King William II of Sicily, he moved on to Arles, where he married well and was finally made marshal of the kingdom by Otto IV. After Otto's defeat at Bouvines in 1214 and his death in 1218, Gervais appears to have returned to England and entered a house of canons regular. He died sometime in the 1220s. His major work, the *Otia Imperialia*, was probably begun in the household of Henry the young king and completed for Otto IV sometime between 1214 and 1218. The work has been called a commonplace book, a compilation from earlier authors, Christian and classical, dealing with history, political geography, and "marvels," aimed at soothing and instructing the ruler during his few moments of leisure.

The work opens with a description of the *regnum* and *sacerdotium* in which, not surprisingly, the authority of the *sacerdotium* is exalted and that of the *regnum* subordinated to it. But good rulers work tirelessly, says Gervais, and they need the restorative powers of their few moments of leisure:

Enim vero in dilucidis intervallis imperialis maiestas nonunquam sono citharae David, vexationem, in Saule a Spiritu perturbante factam, amotam sentit, aut emollitam. Quia ergo optimum naturae fatigatae remedium est amare novitates et gaudere variis, nec decet tam sacras spiritu mimorum fallaci ventilari, dignum duxi aliquid auribus vestris ingerere, quo humana geretur recuperare.[69]

The first two of the three *divisiones* of the work treat the history and geography of the world down to the thirteenth century. The third *divisio* deals with *mirabilia*. This is an extremely broad heading under which Gervais includes both brief and extensive passages describing pagan and Christian mythology and legend, natural wonders, legendary anthropology, animal allegory, natural phenomena, and stories of phantoms, *lamiae* and *larvae nocturnae*.[70] In all, the third *divisio* is an interesting example of the kind of general information thought suitable to inform and divert a thirteenth-century prince during his leisure, and in this sense it can be regarded as a book of instruction, moral teaching, and entertainment.

Although historians of magic and witchcraft have given considerable attention to Gervais's stories of *lamiae, larvae nocturnae,* and supernatural flight, fewer have considered his portrait of an English magician at the court of Roger II of Sicily:

In the time of King Roger of Sicily there came a certain master of English origin asking the king of his bounty to make him a gift. Now the king, who was distinguished alike by birth and breeding, thought that some substantial favour would be demanded of him and he replied: 'Ask whatever gift you wish, and I will give it to you.' But the petitioner, a man of great learning, skilled and subtle in both the trivium and the quadrivium, experienced in physics and eminent in astronomy, told the king that he did not seek temporal rewards but rather what men might deem worthless, namely Vergil's bones, wherever they might be found within the confines of his kingdom. The king granted his request and, armed with a royal warrant, the master came to Naples, where Vergil had displayed his genius in many ways. After he had produced his warrant, the people, though ignorant of the place of sepulture, accorded their obedience and readily promised what, to the best of their belief, was an impossibility. In the end, however, the master, guided in the right direction by his art, located the bones within a tomb in the mountainside, although no sign of an opening could be discerned. The spot was excavated and after prolonged labour a tomb was exposed wherein was found the body of Vergil, not yet dissolved, and at his head a book. In this book the notary art was inscribed together with other diagrams relating to his science. After the dust and bones had been removed, the book was taken by the master. Then, however, the people of Naples remembered the particular affection that Vergil had for their city and feared lest it should be exposed to harm if the bones were taken away. They decided, therefore, to disregard the king's mandate rather than by obedience to be the cause of the destruction of the town. Vergil, it was thought, had himself placed the tomb in the bowels of the mountain, opining that the removal of his bones would bring his artifices to naught. The master of the knights, therefore, with a crowd of citizens, gathered the bones together again and, placing them in a leather bag, took them to a castle surrounded by the sea on the borders of the city, where they are shown through an iron grille to those wishing to see them.

When the master was asked what he had intended to do with the bones, he replied that, by his incantations, he would have so contrived that in answer to his questions the bones would have revealed to him the whole of Vergil's art and that he would have been satisfied if they had been given to him in their entirety for the space of forty days. Taking therefore, only the book with him, the master departed. We have ourselves seen extracts from this very book, made by the venerable cardinal John of Naples in the time of Pope Alexander, and by conducting experiments we have proved their truth.[71]

In his short study of Gervais, H. G. Richardson has contributed much toward unravelling the mixture of the fabulous and the actual elements that comprise the story. As Thorndike and others have shown, the appearance of books of the "notary art" in the twelfth and thirteenth centuries was also historical, and the transcription of some of the passages from there by John of Naples is not inconsistent with other clerical interest displayed in such works throughout the twelfth and thirteenth centuries. In short, Gervais, like John of Salisbury and Walter Map, addressed a courtly audience and assumed that his material on what may very generally be termed the occult was an appropriate part of the court's interest. Less a moralist than his two predecessors, Gervais was also a better storyteller, and his strong secular outlook reflects upon a life spent in courts in England, Normandy, Sicily and Arles. His observations represent a distinctive stage in identifying and appealing to the interests of temporal and ecclesiastical courts in their common function as courts. The story he is alleged to have told to Ralph of Coggeshall and the story of the English magician quoted above contain both literary and substantive embellishments that suggest a notable courtly interest in such matters.

To call these remarks, as Lea does, "popular beliefs accepted by churchmen," is to raise, in the case of Gervais at least, serious doubts.[72] First, as we have seen, Gervais was not yet a "churchman" in Lea's sense.

Second, he was writing a courtier's commonplace book, including a section on *mirabilia*, from which these extracts have been taken. Thus, they are, for Gervais, "wonders." Third, Gervais cites as his authorities St. Augustine, Apuleius, Plato, and Humbert, Archbishop of Arles—hardly representatives of "popular beliefs." If there is a core of "popular tale" among these stories, that core is quickly overlaid with learning and classical and patristic references. Moreover, Gervais is not writing law or history. He is writing to instruct and interest a ruler in his leisure hours. Otto IV, or indeed any other member of the vast, cosmopolitan family of twelfth- and thirteenth-century rulers of the Latin west, was expected to know of and to show some interest in these stories. The wonders of the world, like its geography and history, were fitting subjects for the leisure reading of a mighty prince.

The story of the English master contains other elements besides stories of flying women and night visitors. Here, too, we see the magician at court, this time seeking permission to remove the bones of an even greater magician, Vergil. The magic book, the power of the poet-magician's bones, and the incantations known to the English master all hark back to the stories told by Anselm of Besate, William of Malmesbury, and Walter Map. The learned magician (about whom Gervais is singularly neutral, even somewhat approving) is not condemned outright as he was in the *Policraticus*, but Gervais's approach to moral matters in the *Otia imperialia* seems to have been confined to the relations between *regnum* and *sacerdotium* in any case.

To sum up: different kinds of literary sources between the mid-eleventh and the early thirteenth century discussed magic in many forms. All of them derived their material from a literary tradition, all of them aimed at specific audiences, and none of them shared the theological or legal views of the late twelfth and early thirteenth centuries. Uniformly, they all denounced magic, proclaimed its reality, and associated it particularly with certain intellectual circles, heretics, courts, or Jews; and all reveal a strong literary influence from classical and patristic authors. In this sense, they all agree with the uniform condemnation of all forms of magic launched by the Fathers of the early church, codified by Isidore of Seville, and forcibly reiterated by Hugh of St. Victor in the *Didascalicon*. Both the heretic and the magician in these sources are colored in much the same terms. Both possessed secret books, and both used them. As we have also seen, there was a general fear of secret knowledge and secret teaching in other twelfth-century circles. Finally, all of the writers considered here, whatever their ultimate purpose, derived their method of depicting heretics and magicians and their accusations from a literary tradition. Two of them, at least, Anselm and Walter Map, eagerly demonstrated their rhetorical command of unusual and bizarre materials in their work. In doing so, they placed the figures of the magician and the heretic prominently in the consciousness of twelfth- and thirteenth-century literary audiences. The magicians and heretics themselves (the former probably guilty of at least some of the accusations charged by John of Salisbury, the latter probably not guilty of those practices that can be proven to derive from earlier literary traditions) became the objects of fear and revulsion, particularly to the worlds of the court and the monastery, to which most of the literature considered in this chapter was directed. Except for the English master described by Gervais of Tilbury and some of the popes described by William of Malmesbury, however, the content of the books of magic remained vague, and the charges of lascivious and magical practices among heretics remained unproven. Some of these characteristics were changed in the century between 1150 and 1250, not in literary works of the kind considered here, but in more formal works of learning and in the thought of theologians and lawyers.

NOTES

1. For Anselm, see the standard edition of his work: K. Manitius, ed., *Gunzo Epistola ad Augienses und Anselm von Besate Rhetorimachia, Monumenta Germaniae Historica,* Quellen zur Geistesgeschichte des Mittelalters, vol. 2 (Weimar, 1958). See also K. Manitius, "Magie und Rhetorik bei Anselm von Besate," *Deutsches Archiv* 12 (1956): 52-72; H. E. J. Cowdrey, "Anselm of Besate and Some North-Italian Scholars of the Eleventh Century," *Journal of Ecclesiastical History* 23 (1972): 115-24; Marie-Thérèse d'Alverny, "La survivance de la magie antique," in *Miscellanea Medievalia, I: Antike und Orient im Mittelalter,* ed. P. Wilpert (Berlin, 1962), pp. 154-78. I am grateful to my former student Michael Panitz for some of his own work on Anselm and eleventh-century magic.

2. Cowdrey, "Anselm of Besate," p. 116. See also R. L. Poole, *Illustrations of the History of Medieval Thought and Learning* (London, 1920), pp. 69-79.

3. Radulfus Glaber, *Les cinq livres de ses histoires,* ed. M. Prou (Paris, 1886), p. 50.

4. See E. R. Curtius, *European Literature in the Latin Middle Ages,* trans. W. R. Trask (Princeton, 1953), pp. 62-79, 154-59, with further references.

5. See Manitius, "Magie und Rhetorik," p. 53, nn. 1, 3; p. 71, n. 121 cites the essential texts from Cicero: *De oratore* 2, 59, 241; *De officiis* 2, 14, 51; *De inventione* 1, 21, 29. See also *Rhetorimachia,* p. 103; Cowdrey, "Anselm of Besate," p. 115.

6. Curtius, *Latin Middle Ages,* pp. 154-59.

7. There is no body of scholarly literature devoted to the relationship be-

tween rhetorical devices and later medieval thought. In the case of magic and heresy especially, however, it seems clear that the rhetorical character of eleventh- and twelfth-century sources was later forgotten, but the details contained in the rhetorical accounts were retained and illustrated in later thought.

8. *Rhetorimachia,* pp. 61-94; Manitius, "Magie und Rhetorik," *passim.*

9. The subject is exhaustively treated by Jeffrey Russell, *Witchcraft in the Middle Ages* (Ithaca, 1972), and by Julio Caro Baroja, *The World of the Witches,* trans. O. N. V. Glendinning (Chicago, 1965) and *Vidas magias y inquisición* (Madrid, 1967). See also Keith Thomas, *Religion and the Decline of Magic* (New York, 1971). Most of these works contain references to other studies. In general, the literary character of eleventh- and twelfth-century sources is so marked that it seems to me very misleading to attribute specific beliefs and practices to "folklore" when they are found in such sources. In general, the *indiculi superstitionum* and the penitentials up to the twelfth century seem to be more reliable sources for folk practices.

10. C. S. Lewis, *The Discarded Image* (Cambridge, England, 1964).

11. See, most recently, Cyrille Vogel, "Pratiques superstitieuses au debut du XIe siècle d'après le *Corrector sive medicus* de Burchard, évêque de Worms (965–1025)," in *Études de Civilization Mediévale (IXe–Xiie siècles) Mélanges offerts à Edmond-René Labande* (Poitiers, 1976), pp. 751-61, with further references.

12. d'Alverny, "La survivance de la magie antique," p. 178.

13. Ibid., pp. 163-64, 169-70. See below, Chapter 3, for William of Auvergne.

14. *Rhetorimachia,* p. 103.

15. Poole, *History of Medieval Thought and Learning,* pp. 71-72.

16. *Rhetorimachia,* pp. 124, 129-30.

17. Ibid., p. 130.

18. Ibid., pp. 142-43.

19. Ibid. p. 145. On the *quaterniones nigromantie* of the eleventh and twelfth centuries, see d'Alverny, "La survivance de la magie antique," pp. 154-78; Lynn Thorndike, *History of Magic and Experimental Science* (New York, 1923-58) 2:214-29; Manitius, "Magie und Rhetorik," p. 60.

20. *Rhetorimachia,* pp. 154-56. Like love potions, abortifacients were among the best-known products of the magical arts between the eleventh and the seventeenth centuries.

21. *Rhetorimachia,* pp. 169-80.

22. Ibid., pp. 160-62.

23. Cowdrey, "Anselm of Besate," p. 122.

24. On the origins of the Gerbert legend, see J. J. Döllinger, *Die Papstfabeln des Mittelalters* (Munich, 1863), pp. 155-59; F. Picavet, *Gerbert* (Paris, 1897); F. Eichengrün, *Gerbert als Persönlichkeit* (Leipzig, 1928).

25. *Patrologia Latina* 179, cols. 1137-44.

26. See references in Joseph Hansen, *Zauberwahn, Inquisition und Hexenprozess* (Munich, 1900), p. 96, and Döllinger, *Papstfabeln,* pp. 151-59. The charges of magic against eleventh-century popes have not, in general, attracted

the attention of modern scholars, except for the famous and fabulous case of Gerbert.

27. *PL* 179, cols. 1188-90.

28. Ibid., cols. 1190-91.

29. Ibid., cols. 1142-44.

30. Ibid., cols. 1144-45. I have not been able to discover any reference to this episode in the works of Peter Damian.

31. Olavus Magnus, *Historia de gentibus septentrionalibus* (Basel, 1567), book 3, chap. 21, pp. 119-20. Olavus cites Vincent of Beauvais as his source. The story is also cited in the thirteenth-century *Speculum Laicorum,* ed. J. Th. Welter (Paris, 1914), p. 104. The story also became a popular source of sixteenth-century illustrations. Besides the woodcut in Olavus Magnus, p. 119, see also Conrad Lycosthenus, *Prodigiorum ac Ostentorum Chronicon* (Basel, 1577). The story, as did many others like it, appears to have appealed to writers on popular devotion and penance in the fourteenth and fifteenth centuries. See G. R. Owst, *The Destructorium Viciorum of Alexander Carpenter* (London, S.P.C.K., 1952), pp. 32-37, and Owst, "*Sortilegium* in English Homiletic Literature of the Fourteenth Century," in *Studies Presented to Sir Hilary Jenkinson,* ed. J. Conway Davies (London, 1957), pp. 272-303.

32. I adopt the general categories of Jeffrey B. Russell, especially as described in his *Witchcraft in the Middle Ages* and his *Dissent and Reform in the Early Middle Ages* (Berkeley and Los Angeles, 1965) as well as his article "Interpretations of the Origins of Medieval Heresy," *Medieval Studies* 25 (1963): 26-53. More recently, the following works have offered some important modifications to Russell's thesis: R. I. Moore, "The Origins of Medieval Heresy," *History,* n. s. 55 (1970): 21-36; Walter Wakefield and A. P. Evans, *Heresies of the High Middle Ages* (New York, 1968); R. I. Moore, *The Birth of Popular Heresy* (New York, 1965); Janet L. Nelson, "Society, Theodicy and the Origins of Heresy: Towards a Reassessment of the Medieval Evidence," in *Schism, Heresy and Religious Protest, Studies in Church History,* vol. 9, ed. Derek Baker (Cambridge, England, 1972), pp. 65-77. On the relation to popular religion, see R. Manselli, *La religion populaire au moyen age* (Montreal and Paris, 1975) and the monumental work of Herbert Grundmann, *Religiöse Bewegungen im Mittelalter* (Hildesheim, 1961). Among other ongoing publications of current research, the numbers of the *Cahiers de Fanjeaux* usually contain important studies.

33. J. Stevenson, ed., *Radulphi de Coggeshall Chronicon Anglicanum,* (London, 1875), 121-25; translation in W. Wakefield and A. P. Evans, *Heresies,* pp. 251-54.

34. Walter Map, *De nugiis curialium,* ed. M. R. James (Oxford, 1914). See also below, p. 51.

35. Wakefield and Evans, *Heresies,* pp. 249-56.

36. See below, Chapter 6.

37. Especially the works of Caesarius of Heisterbach, Thomas of Cantimpré, Etienne de Bourbon, and Vincent of Beauvais.

38. Moore, *The Birth of Popular Heresy;* Norman Cohn. *Europe's Inner*

Demons: An Enquiry Inspired by the Great Witch-Hunt (New York, 1975), pp. 1-16.

39. Georges Bourguin, *Guibert de Nogent: Histoire de sa vie* (Paris, 1907); John F. Benton, *Self and Society in Medieval France* (New York, 1970), pp. 212-14.

40. *Gesta synodi aurelianensis,* in M. Bouquet, *Receuils des historiens des Gaules et de la France,* vol. 10 (Paris, 1738-86) pp. 536-39; Russell, *Dissent and Reform,* pp. 276-77. As Russell and Cohn have emphasized, early Christian invective against Gnostics, Manichaeans, and other heretics influenced later Christian depictions of Cathars and other heretics.

41. See James Fearns, "Peter von Bruis und die religiöse Bewegung des 12. Jahrhunderts," *Archiv für Kulturgeschichte* 48 (1966): 311-35; idem, *Petri Venerabilis Contra Petrobrusianos hereticos* (Turnhout, 1968); Jean Châtillon, "Pierre le Vénérable et les Pétrobrusiens," in *Pierre Abélard, Pierre le Vénérable, Colloques Internationaux du C. N. R. S.* (Paris, 1975), pp. 165-79.

42. Peter Abelard, *Ethica* c. 5, PL 178, col. 648. See also *Peter Abelard's Ethics,* ed. D. E. Luscombe (Oxford, 1971), and Leif Grane, *Peter Abelard* (New York, 1970), pp. 148, 183.

43. Jean Leclerq, *et al., Sancti Bernardi Sermones super Cantica Canticorum,* (Rome, 1957-58), vol. 2, sermon 65, pp. 172-77.

44. *Ioannis Saresberiensis episcopi Carnotensis Policratici,* ed. C. C. I. Webb, 2 vols. (Oxford, 1909), 1:14. All further references to the work will be to *Policraticus,* book, chapter, and page number in vol. 1 of Webb's edition.

45. In works from traditions as diverse as those which influenced Henry Charles Lea and Jeffrey Russell, the importance of prosecution of heresy for the later prosecution of witches is virtually taken for granted.

46. The best guide to the work, aside from Webb's introduction, is Hans Liebeschütz, *Medieval Humanism in the Life and Writings of John of Salisbury* (London, 1950), pp. 23-34.

47. Aside from some eleventh-century invective against couriers, such as that of Adalbero of Laon, the work of John of Salisbury is the first major moral treatise to recognize the unique structure of the twelfth-century court and to treat it as other twelfth-century writers treated the vices and virtues of other parts of traditional society.

48. *Policraticus,* book 1, chap. 10–book 2, *passim,* pp. 49-169.

49. Helen Waddell, *The Wandering Scholars* (reprint ed., London, 1968), p. xiii. It should be noted, however, that John is writing of the vices of powerful figures and addresses his book to Thomas Becket, then chancellor of Henry II, who himself was several times accused of resorting to the very practices that John condemns. It is not, therefore, surprising that John should cast his condemnation of twelfth-century courtiers' magic in classical and patristic terms.

50. *Policraticus,* book 2, chap. 28, pp. 164-65. On this episode and others similar to it, see Liebeschütz, *John of Salisbury,* pp. 26-27, 76-77, and Barbara Helbling-Gloor, *Natur und Aberglaube im Policraticus des Johannes von Salisbury* (Zurich, 1956).

51. See the figure discussed by Gervais of Tilbury, below, pp. 54-55, and in Chapter 4.

52. See Thorndyke, 2:14-304.

53. Above, p. 44; see also M.-D. Chenu, *Nature, Man, and Society in the Twelfth Century* trans. J. Taylor and L. K. Little (Chicago, 1968) pp. 270-309.

54. Notably by C. H. Haskins, *The Renaissance of the Twelfth Century* (Cambridge, Mass., 1927) and by many scholars since, the most recent of whom is Christopher Brooke, *The Twelfth-Century Renaissance* (New York, 1969). Few twelfth-century scholars, however, appear to have taken such criticisms as those of John of Salisbury seriously or to have paid much attention to the darker side of the twelfth century, the prevalence of magic, the rise of heresy, and the new emotionally charged anti-Jewish literature of the period. The dark side of the twelfth century renaissance has yet to find its historian.

55. See Peter Brown, "Sorcery, Demons, and the Rise of Christianity: from Late Antiquity to the Middle Ages," in *Religion and Society in the Age of Saint Augustine*, ed. P. Brown (New York, 1972).

56. It is in the life of those in late Roman imperial society whose careers were insecure and depended upon fortune and favor that Brown has found the greatest practice of magic in the fourth and fifth centuries. See Chapter 1, above, and Chapter 4, below, for thirteenth- and fourteenth-century courts.

57. Among other scholars, Erich Köhler has also noted the bearing of real social pressures upon courtiers. See also W. J. Schroder, *Der Ritter zwischen Welt und Gott* (Weimar, 1952).

58. Walter Map, *De nugiis curialium,* ed. M. R. James (Oxford, 1914). See also the English translation by F. Tupper and M. B. Ogle, *Master Walter Map's Book De Nugis Curialium (Courtiers' Trifles)* (New York, 1924), and James Hinton, "*De Nugis Curialium:* Its Plan and Composition," *PMLA* 32 (1917): 81-132.

59. Thomas Aquinas, *De Sortibus ad Dominum Jacobum de Tolongo,* in Aquinas, *Opuscula* (Paris, 1927), pp. 144-62; see also Charles E. Hopkin, *The Share of Thomas Aquinas in the Growth of the Witchcraft Delusion* (Philadelphia, 1940), pp. 87-88, n. 10.

60. Map, *De nugis curialium* 1, xi. See also Hinton, "*De Nugis Curialium*," p. 75, and Helaine Newstead, "Some Observations on King Herla and the Herlething," in *Medieval Literature and Folklore Studies: Essays in Honor of Francis Lee Utley,* eds. J. Mandel and B. A. Rosenberg (New Brunswick, 1970), pp. 105-10.

61. Map, *De nugis curialium* 1, xii-xiv.

62. Ibid. 1, xxix-xxxi.

63. The theme of illusory food and its association with heretics and, later, witches, suggests one aspect of the use of rhetorical commonplaces in the genre of invective against theological deviants.

64. Ibid. 2, viii-xxxii.

65. Ibid. 3, vi. This story has not often been associated with the peace movement of the eleventh and twelfth centuries, but it appears to me to derive from the invective against violent nobles that became common during this period.

66. Ibid., 4, xi.

67. John W. Baldwin, *Masters, Princes and Merchants: The Social Views of Peter the Chanter and His Circle,* 2 vols. (Princeton, 1970) 1:198-204. Peter

the Chanter identified *magicis* and *histriones* in the *Verbum Abbreviatum, PL* 205, cols. 153-56.

68. G. W. Leibnitz, ed., *Scriptores rerum brunsvicensium,* vol. 1 (Hanover, 1707), pp. 881-1005, and R. Pauli, ed., *MGH, Scriptores* xxvii, pp. 358-94.

69. *Script. rer. bruns.,* 1:883.

70. Ibid., 1:960-1005. Some of Gervais's stories have been widely cited in histories of witchcraft. See Henry Charles Lea, *Materials Toward a History of Witchcraft,* ed. and Comp. Arthur Howland (Philadelphia, 1938), 1:170-98; Hansen, *Zauberwahn,* p. 138; Russell, *Witchcraft in the Middle Ages,* pp. 117-18.

71. H. G. Richardson, "Gervase of Tilbury," *History* 46 (1961), reprinted in Sylvia Thrupp, ed., *Change in Medieval Society* (New York, 1964), pp. 89-102, with full bibliography.

72. Lea, *Materials,* 1:170-98.

3

Learning and Magic in the Twelfth and Thirteenth Centuries

THE PLACE OF MAGIC IN THE ORGANIZATION OF KNOWLEDGE

During the course of the twelfth century, European learning was greatly altered both by the increased absorption of Greek and Arabic scientific and philosophical works and by the articulation and influence of the scholastic method. In the process of acquainting itself with Arabic learning, however, western European culture also encountered an impressively large body of formal, learned magic, the most conspicuous and appealing of which was probably astrology, but alchemy and other forms of magic were also included. This influx of new knowledge, appealing to the scholastic method, greatly transformed the character of European learning and added considerable substance to the hitherto inchoate concept of learned magic. The casual references on the part of Anselm of Besate and others to books of necromancy and to the picturesque and terrifying, but not specific, denunciations of magic practices by moralists could be applied to a specific and available body of knowledge after the mid-twelfth century. The best place to begin to assess the significance of the new materials and methods for the history of the magician is to consider the history of the place of magic in the formal organization of knowledge, a topic that greatly interested intellectuals from the early twelfth century on.[1]

Shortly after his conversion to Christianity in 1106, the Spanish Jew

Pedro Alfonso produced a collection of stories called the *Disciplina clericalis,* "The Scholar's Guide," as its latest translators have christened it.² This work, which derives from the oriental traditions of learned storytelling, contains a brief discussion of the seven liberal arts. The narrator notes here that some scholars allow "necromancy" to be considered one of the arts, while others dispute about the competing claims of natural science and grammar. The whole passage is as follows:

> One of his pupils spoke to a teacher and said to him, "I would like for you to enumerate the seven arts, seven principles and seven gentlemanly pursuits in order."
> The teacher answered, "I will enumerate them for you. These are the arts: dialectics, arithmetic, geometry, physics, music, and astronomy. Concerning the seventh, many diverse opinions exist. The philosophers who do not believe in prognostication say that necromancy is the seventh; others among them, namely those who believe in prognostication and in philosophy, think that it should be a science which encompasses all natural matters and mundane elements. Those who do not devote themselves to philosophy say that it is grammar. These are the gentlemanly pursuits: riding, swimming, archery, boxing, fowling, chess, and poetry. The principles are the avoidance of gluttony, drunkenness, lust, violence, lying, avariciousness, and evil conversation."
> The pupil said, "I believe that in these times no one with these qualities exists."³

Pedro Alfonso's speculative division of the liberal arts undoubtedly derives from Arabic sources which treated the *trivium* and *quadrivium* with considerably greater freedom than Latins, possessing as they did a much wider acquaintance with sources for magic, the natural sciences, and letters. There is no evidence that any western writer unfamiliar with the sources and traditions that informed the *Disciplina clericalis* ever considered the seven liberal arts to consist of any but the traditionally accepted subjects of the *trivium* and *quadrivium*: grammar, rhetoric, dialectic, arithmetic, music, astronomy, and geometry.

There were, however, other divisions of knowledge in the twelfth century that did afford a place, not for "necromancy," as Latin literary usage understood the term, but for formal magic generally. A scheme of organizing the sciences, once falsely attributed to William of Conches, placed the sciences of "Magic" (astrology, sorcery, divination, augury, and illusion) parallel to the "Mechanical" arts; the two categories together constituted the larger classification of Practical Sciences. The three evils that plagued the human condition were Ignorance, Concupiscence, and Infirmity; and the Practical Sciences were considered the remedy for Infirmity. The school of Abelard adapted the scheme of the practical sciences devised by the first group into a new schema in which the Practical Sciences (including the "magical" and "mechanical" arts) were paralleled with Wisdom (divided into "eloquence" and "philosophy") as part of the natural means of human salvation.[4]

Around 1140 the archdeacon of Toledo, Gundissalinus, produced a work called *De divisione philosophiae*, in which he—probably closer to the Arabic sources of Pedro Alfonso than the twelfth-century thinkers mentioned above—gave a legitimate place to magic, not as a true science or as a virtue, but as worldly vanities that are neither to be praised nor condemned.[5]

By the middle of the twelfth century, then, the place of magic had obtained a foothold in the divisions of knowledge that derived either from Arabic sources (Pedro Alfonso and Gundissalinus) or from the philosophical and logical studies of the schools of northern France. Although Pedro Alfonso included magic as "necromancy," it is very likely that he had in mind the various forms of divination, including astrology and augury, rather than divining by means of corpses, the literal meaning of *necromantia* (later *nigromantia*).[6] Certainly, Gundissalinus gives his greatest attention to the divinatory sciences rather than to the full panoply of practices that could be labelled as magic in the twelfth century. The sciences designated as magic in the organization of knowledge by the school of William of Conches are probably similar. They consist of philosophical disciplines of the kind attributed to Gerbert and other popes in legend, the less diabolical practices of Rotiland in the *Rhetorimachia*, and the manipulation of natural forces by means of a variety of kinds of superior knowledge, perhaps not excluding the activities of the priest who tried to turn the young John of Salisbury into a medium. In the Arabic world, of course, these studies, particularly astrology, were considerably better developed than in western Europe, and they retained a respectable place in Islamic culture. In western Europe, however, the new twelfth-century interest in logic and philosophical learning borrowed slowly from these Arabic traditions, while coloring magic with some of the rhetorical descriptions we have seen in the literary sources of the eleventh and twelfth centuries. Not parallel at the beginning of the twelfth century, the Arabic and Latin divisions of the sciences drew closer together from the mid-twelfth century on. In spite of the growing familiarity in the west with Arabic philosophy and science, however, magic did not survive among the legitimate sciences, chiefly through the opposition and influence of Hugh of St. Victor.

In his *Didascalicon*, written around 1141, Hugh included a powerful denunciation of all forms of magic:

Magic is not accepted as a part of philosophy, but stands with a false claim outside it: the mistress of every form of iniquity and malice, lying about the truth and truly infecting men's minds, it seduces them from divine religion, prompts them from the cult of demons, fosters corruption of morals, and impels the minds of its devotees to every wicked and criminal indulgence. . . . Sorcerers are those who, with demonic incantations or amulets or any other execrable types of remedies, by the cooperation of the devils and by evil instinct, perform wicked things. Performers of illusions are those who with their demonic art make sport of human senses through imaginative illusions about one thing's being turned into another.[7]

Drawing heavily from late patristic and Carolingian strictures against magic, notably from the works of Isidore of Seville and Hrabanus Maurus, Hugh's blanket condemnation of all magic as demonic and sinful exerted considerable influence throughout the twelfth and thirteenth centuries. It drove magic from the tables of the organization of legitimate knowledge, in spite of the interest of twelfth century philosophers and the growing familiarity with and respect for Arabic astrology. In Robert Kilwardby's *De ortu sive divisione scientiarum,* written in the second half of the thirteenth century, Hugh's stricture against the place of magic among the legitimate sciences is repeated.[8] Somewhat earlier than Kilwardby, William of Auvergne, bishop of Paris, issued similar strictures, although William goes into much greater detail concerning the circulation of books of Arabic astrology and books of magic, *libri magorum atque maleficorum,* in Paris during his own student days.[9] The strictures of Hugh of St. Victor generally held, in spite of the survival of older books of magic, the preservation of charms and incantations in individual manuscripts during the twelfth century, the growing familiarity with, and interest in Arabic science (especially astrology), and the strong claims made by astrologers and, later, philosophers and natural scientists, that there was a legitimate place for at least certain kinds of magic during the late twelfth and thirteenth centuries. Repeated by William of Auvergne and Robert Kilwardby, Hugh's strictures were also echoed by other theologians and lawyers.[10] Even on those occasions when theologians had to admit that astrology seemed to be a legitimate science and could in theory advise human beings of the future, there seems to have been no case of any individual astrologer being able completely to escape the charges of being a magician or sorcerer. To a very slight extent, astrology alone seems to have acquired a certain degree of legitimacy in spite of the strictures of Hugh of St. Victor and his followers. But astrology is the only occult science that did, and in most individual cases particular astrologers were always liable to charges of dealing in forbidden magic.[11]

Other testimonies to the enduring influence of Hugh's exclusion of all forms of magic from legitimate knowledge are those of Roger Bacon and Arnald of Villanova late in the thirteenth century.[12] In spite of their own personal reputations as magicians (derived from the Victorine stricture), both writers condemned most forms of magic as diabolical. Even into the sixteenth and seventeenth centuries, those writers who defended the legitimacy of astrology, hermetic magic, or other forms of magic felt compelled to denounce the remaining forms as diabolic and damnable.[13] Thus, in spite of a number of forces favorable to the legitimate study of some forms of magic that proved formidable in the twelfth century, and even reappeared in the fifteenth and sixteenth centuries, the old patristic condemnation of magic outright, restated by Hugh of St. Victor early in the twelfth century and firmly a part of scholastic theology by the mid-thirteenth century, remained a virtually impassable obstacle. All types of magic were equally condemned by it and, more important, many practices formerly regarded merely as harmful superstitions could be condemned as magic. In a sense, the rhetorical tradition, represented by Anselm of Besate, the monastic depicters of heretical practices, and the courtier literature of Walter Map and Gervais of Tilbury, won the day at an important moment of the twelfth century, through the work of Hugh of St. Victor. In spite of the growing attractiveness and claims to legitimacy of several forms of magic, the Arabic divisions of the sciences represented by Pedro Alfonso and Gundissalinus, as well as the divisions of the sciences represented by the schools of William of Conches and Abelard, failed to give a place in the schemes of legitimate human knowledge to any form of magic except astrology. Moreover, as magical practices began to take on a new substance through the revival of Arabic and Greek philosophy, the content of magic changed. The actual practice was taken more seriously, the dangers it posed feared more intensely, and the strictures against it reiterated more frequently. The remaining sections of this chapter will trace the influence of Hugh of St. Victor and the growing explicitness and fear of magic through the work of theologians, canon lawyers, and philosophers during the twelfth and thirteenth centuries.

MAGIC AND THEOLOGY IN THE TWELFTH CENTURY

The work of Hugh of St. Victor on the place of magic among the legitimate sciences drew upon a patristic and twelfth-century theological tradition, and biblical study and the development of the science of theology continued to condemn magic in all its forms. Still, for the most part, twelfth-century biblical scholarship did not, any more than Hugh, do more than condemn witchcraft, heresy, and magic. No theologian appears to have advocated the more rigorous prosecution of these offenses that became characteristic of many churchmen, scholars and prelates during the thirteenth century, and few theologians elaborated upon the nature and content of magic.

Of the passages in scripture that dealt with magic, perhaps the most frequently cited text in the later medieval and early modern period was Exodus 22:18, "*Maleficos non patieris vivere*: "Thou shalt not suffer a [witch] to live." This text, frequently cited by later theologians and witch-hunters alike in its literal sense, was not in the twelfth century regarded as condemning the magician to death. The very term *maleficus* in the twelfth century indicated sorcerers generically—not, of course, the later type of witch or magician designated by the terms *malefica* or *maleficus* in the better-known witchcraft literature of a later period. The *glossa ordinaria* of the Bible, completed in the course of the early twelfth century, is explicit on this meaning:

Maleficos non patieris vivere. Qui praestigiis magicae artis et diabolicis figmentis agunt, haereticos intellige, qui a consortio fidelium qui vere vivunt, excommunicandi sunt, donec maleficium erroris in eis moriatur.[14]

That is, *maleficii* are those who use the illusions of the magic art and of the devil. They are heretics. They should be separated from the community of the faithful, which is true life. They are to be excommunicated so that their error will die with them.

This citation is important because of its threefold character: First, *maleficii* are associated with the devil; second, they are clearly identified as heretics; third, they are not to be killed, but excommunicated from the community of believers. In the last instance, *vivere* is clearly interpreted figuratively, not literally. The *glossa ordinaria*, earlier than most texts cited by historians, clearly identifies magic with heresy, long before those theologians of the thirteenth century who are alleged to have been the first to do so.

Other biblical texts also deal with magicians, and although few of them are as explicit as the gloss to Exodus 22:18, they systematically note that all forms of magic are forbidden. The episode described in Exodus 7–11, the defeat of Pharoah's magicians by Moses and Aaron and the ten plagues upon Egypt, was treated in highly figurative terms by the *glossa ordinaria*, partly as an anticipation of the coming of Christ, and partly as a figurative denunciation of the wisdom of the pagans.[15] The gloss to Exodus 8:18, for example, explains the plague of blood as the doctrines of the philosophers, the frogs as the images (*figmenta*) of the poets, and the maggots as the *sophismata* of the dialecticians, "which deceive the whole world." That section of the gloss to Exodus 8:19 attributed to Strabo notes, "Note that by the third sign the *magi* are overcome, since all worldly wisdom, evils, and philosophy are conquered by the Trinity."[16] That the gloss represents a traditional theological view is suggested by its similarity to St. Augustine's own treatment of the same text in the second book of his *Quaestionum in Heptateuchum*.[17]

The injunctions of Leviticus 19:31–20:6 also drew some comment from the glossators. The gloss to Leviticus 19:31, *neque ab ariolis*, states: "Veneficis, qui daemonum scilicet nomina invocant, et aliquando corpus curant, vel animam interficiant."[18] The gloss to Leviticus 20:6, *anima qui declinaverit ad magos*, states:

Grande peccatum est ad magos et ariolos declinare: hoc est etiam a Deo recedere. Sunt autem magi intelligibiles, qui in nomine Domini falsa prophetant; sunt arioli deceptores et adulatores, qui veneficis verbis multorum corrumpunt et a veritate avertunt.[19]

These texts, and indeed most other Old Testament texts dealing with *magi* and other practitioners are generally treated alike by the glossators of the early twelfth century. Since several of these texts were not commented upon by Augustine, these glosses cited above would appear to derive from the ninth-century tradition or from the early scholastic glossators themselves. The glosses uniformly condemn magical practices, and sometimes they list them, as in the gloss to Deuteronomy 18:9–11. Denouncing all forms of magic, the glossators, however, do not go beyond denunciation. Only the gloss to Exodus 22:18 is explicit, and it states that while magic is to be equated to heresy, the *maleficus* is not to be killed, but excommunicated.

The most famous passage in the Old Testament, Saul's invocation of the spirit of Samuel by the witch of Endor, is treated by the glossators in a similar way. The gloss's treatment of the whole episode is quite brief, and only the gloss to the *magus* in 1 Samuel 18:9 is noteworthy:

Magi utuntur sanguine humano, et contactu mortuorum in maleficiis et divinationibus arioli solis verbis, id est incantationibus divinant. Pythius dicitur Apollo harum artium cultor, a quo Pythonissae, id est divini: hos Saul quasi zelo legis delevit, quia, ut aiunt, a daemonibus coacti David regem esse futurum praeconabantur.[20]

The injunctions of Exodus, Leviticus, and Deuteronomy and the story of Saul and the spirit of Samuel (or, as medieval theologians pointed out, following St. Augustine, the demon having the appearance of Samuel) were thus explained by the twelfth-century biblical commentators, who linked magic to heresy and whose works constitute an important chapter in the semantic history of such terms as *magia, maleficia, divinatio, veneficia, ariolus,* and *incantatio*. The commentators, explaining to their students the laws and history of Israel, preserved and transmitted the terms of the Vulgate and something of the force of patristic, especially Augustinian, disapproval of magic. They also on rare occasions added views of their own, particularly the commentator on Exodus 22:18. Their sucessors, however, such as Robert Pullen, Peter Lombard, and Peter Comestor, tended not to discuss these texts, and it is plausible that twelfth- and early thirteenth-century theologians derived their knowledge of magic and its identification with heresy from the *glossa ordinaria* alone.[21] The infrequency with which later twelfth-century theologians discuss magic indicates that the observations of the Fathers and the glossators were probably satisfactory as far as the needs of theologians went. Such texts as those cited above would suffice to explain the tone of John of Salisbury, as well as that of Peter the Chanter of Paris and other theologians of the turn of the century, who said little more about magic than to condemn it, along with, and in the same places as, prostitution, gambling, and acting. The very slight concern displayed by Peter the Chanter with anything remotely to do with magic is indicated by his restriction of any mention of it to the section of the *Verbum abbreviatum* dealing with judicial ordeals and the use of *sortes* and *sortilegia* to tempt God.[22] The discussions of the glossators and the slight use made of magic by theologians until the early thirteenth century emphasizes a point made earlier: a great deal of what is commonly called "medieval" witchcraft belief must be identified by the nature of the sources that discuss such topics, the purpose of the genres in which such discussions occur, and the kinds of writers who do (or, as here, do not) show much interest in the topic of magic. The much cited text of Exodus 22:18, for example, appears to have been interpreted by no one in the twelfth century according to its literal meaning, and the most prestigious theological source, the *glossa ordinaria* to the Bible, although it plays the important role of equating magic with heresy, explicitly states that the magician, like the heretic, should be excommunicated, not killed.

Like Hugh of St. Victor, twelfth-century biblical commentators left no room for any kind of legitimate magic at all. Heavily dependent upon St. Augustine and other patristic writers, their strictures governed the views of theologians down to the thirteenth century, when the condemnation of magic and heresy alike occupied theologians' attention far more than it had in the twelfth century. It remained for later theologians and biblical commentators to impose a literal interpretation on Exodus 22:18.[23] The figurative interpretation of twelfth-century theologians, however, coupled with Hugh of St. Victor's denunciation of magic, was more than sufficient to stigmatize all forms of magic and to lay the groundwork for its universal condemnation in succeeding centuries.

THE MAGICIAN AND CANON LAW IN THE TWELFTH AND EARLY THIRTEENTH CENTURIES

The penitentials, capitularies, papal letters, conciliar canons, and early collections of canon law in which most of the early medieval legal ideas about magic are found gave way in the mid-twelfth century to a systematic revision of law and to the beginnings of a scientific jurisprudence. In 1140 Gratian, a monk of Bologna and one of the greatest legal scholars of all time, published his *Concordia discordantium canonum,* commonly called the *Decretum,* in which he attempted to systematize the legal doctrines of the Church according to the critical and analytical methods of some of his predecessors and the new method of scholastic logic.[24] Gratian's *Decretum* constitutes a juridical watershed in European history. The earlier attempts of Burchard of Worms and Ivo of Chartres and others to produce a rational, systematized body of ecclesiastical law were overshadowed by Gratian's work and its immediate popularity. It became the standard teaching text in the schools, and it and the comments of masters upon it became the introduction to ecclesiastical law for the next eight centuries.

The second, and larger part of the *Decretum* consists of *causae,* imaginary legal cases, which are broken down into analytical questions, *quaestiones,* and solved by selected texts from Church authorities called *canones.* Linking the *canones* and *quaestiones* together and leading the reader through the complex law are comments of Gratian himself, the *dicta,* either before (*ante*) or after (*post*) a particular text. A series of texts not originally in the *Decretum,* called *paleae,* were added by later twelfth-century scholars, but the whole work and its organization are Gratian's. For an authoritative text to be found in the *Decretum,* and hence in the law, it must exist either as a *canon* or as part of the *dicta Gratiani ante* (d.g.a.) or *dicta Gratiani post* (d.g.p.) or as a *palea.* For legal purposes, the rich and extraordinarily varied earlier literature on magic was effectively reduced to what Gratian chose to include. It is impossible to consider Gratian's own opinions on the magic of his own time, and so one cannot speak of his opinions as one can, for instance, of that of John of Salisbury. It is, however, possible to examine Gratian's discussions of magic carefully in order to ascertain exactly what in magic concerned ecclesiastical lawyers. A great deal has been written about canon lawyers' development of the ideas of magic and witchcraft, but these observations are often made by scholars unfamiliar with the law itself. As we will see, the topic of magic in canon law from Gratian on was extremely limited, generated few later new texts, and in general did not exercise the lawyers' interests or imagination.

The twenty-sixth *causa* of Gratian's *Decretum* presents the case of a priest, excommunicated by his bishop as an unrepentant magician and diviner, who is reconciled to the Church at the point of death by another priest, without the bishop's knowledge. It is within the framework of this case that most of Gratian's texts concerning magic are found. The remainder are found in *causa* 33, *quaestio* 1, *canones* 1–4, which we will consider below. *Causa* 26 is divided into seven questions, all of which touch upon the process of divination. The first question asks what *sortilegium* is. It contains one canon, a text from Isidore of Seville's *Etymologies*, which defines *sortilegi* as those who "under the name of a false religion by those things which are called the *sortes sanctorum*, practice the technique of divination, or, by the careful inspection of scriptures, seek to discover the future."[25] The second question asks whether *sortilegium* is a sin. Gratian cites several historical instances of approved *sortilegium* in his *dictum ante* c. 1, and the first few canons appear to approve it. Gratian's proof texts, however, are canons 6–11, in which he draws heavily from St. Augustine, especially *De doctrina christiana*, 19–21, *De civitate Dei*, and the *Confessions*. Gratian's conclusion is that *sortilegium* is indeed a sin because it necessarily involves the invocation of demons. Questions 3 and 4 list the kinds of divination. The fifth question asks whether magicians and diviners, if they do not cease their activities, ought to be excommunicated. Gratian answers in the affirmative:

Those who participate in the cult of idols are to be separated from the communion of the faithful. Hence, as the Apostle Paul says in his epistle to the Corinthians [1 Corinthians 5:9-11] "If a certain brother is named a fornicator or a miser or a worshipper of idols, do not so much as eat with him."[26]

The first eleven canons in question 5 consist of a series of texts from early popes, churchmen, and councils forbidding various forms of magical practices and uniformly condemning their practitioners to excommunication. Canon 12 is the famous "witch-text," *Episcopi*, called the *Canon Episcopi* because individual canons in the works of Gratian and others were usually referred to by their first word or words.[27] The *Canon Episcopi* is an unusual text, partly because it says a number of different things, and partly because it is attributed to a church council of whose work it is certainly not a part. Gratian, however, who relied heavily upon the patristic writers and early church councils, understood it to be a part of the work of the Council of Ancyra of 314, probably because in his source, Ivo of Chartres' *Panormia*, it is listed under the work of that council. In fact, the *Canon Episcopi* appears for the first time in the canonical collection of Regino of Prüm early in the tenth century, and its form is clearly that of a capitulary of the ninth century, although some scholars have suggested that Regino himself either created it by combining several lost capitularies or perhaps invented it himself. It was used by Burchard of Worms and Ivo of Chartres.

The *Canon Episcopi* states:

Bishops and their officials must labor with all their strength to uproot thoroughly from their parishes the pernicious art of sorcery and malefice invented by the Devil, and if they find a man or woman follower of this wickedness to eject them foully disgraced from their parishes. For the Apostle says, "A man that is a heretic after the first and second admonition avoid." Those are held captive by the Devil who, leaving their creator, seek the aid of the Devil. And so Holy Church must be cleansed of this pest. It is also not to be omitted that some wicked women, perverted by the Devil, seduced by illusions and phantasms of demons, believe and profess themselves, in the hours of night, to ride upon certain beasts with Diana, the goddess of pagans, and an innumerable multitude of women, and in the silence of the dead of night to traverse great spaces of earth, and to obey her commands as of their mistress, and to be summoned to her service on certain nights. But I wish it were they alone who perished in their faithlessness and did not draw many with them into the destruction of infidelity. For an innumerable multitude, deceived by this false opinion, believe this to be true, and so believing, wander from the right faith and are involved in the error of the pagans when they think that there is anything of divinity or power except the one God. Wherefore the priests throughout their churches should preach with all insistence to the people that they may know this to be in every way false and that such phantasms are imposed on the minds of infidels and not by the divine but by the malignant spirit. Thus Satan himself, who transfigures himself into an angel of light, when he has captured the mind of a miserable woman and has subjugated her to himself by infidelity and incredulity, immediately transforms himself into the species and similitudes of different personages and deluding the mind which he holds captive and exhibiting things, joyful or mournful, and persons, known or unknown, leads it through devious ways, and while the spirit alone endures this, the faithless mind thinks these things happen not in the spirit but in the body. Who is there that is not led out of himself in dreams and nocturnal visions, and sees much when sleeping which he had never seen waking? Who is so stupid and foolish as to think that all these things which are only done in spirit happen in the body, when the Prophet Ezekiel saw visions of the Lord in spirit and not in the body, and the Apostle John saw and heard the mysteries of the Apocalypse in the spirit and not in the body, as he himself says "I was in the spirit"? And Paul does not dare to say that he was rapt in the body. It is therefore to be proclaimed publicly to all that whoever believes such things or similar to these loses the faith, and he who has not the right faith in God is not of God but of him in whom he believes, that is, of the Devil. For of our Lord it is written "All things were made by Him." Whoever therefore believes that anything can be made, or that any creature can be changed to better or to worse or be transformed into another species or similitude, except by the

Creator himself who made everything and through whom all things were made, is beyond doubt an infidel.[28]

The *Canon Episcopi* says a number of different things: First, it insists that bishops and other clergy must drive *sortilegium* and the magical art from their territories. Second, the canon denounces the beliefs of certain wicked women that they are transported about at night by Diana (other commentators add the names of other pagan divinities: Herodias and Holda). The canon then goes on to say that these beliefs are part of the illusory tricks of Satan. Third, the canon denounces as infidelity the belief that any creature can be transformed into another species or likeness. The extended description of demonic illusions in the second part of the canon helps to explain the general intense dislike exhibited by moralists and theologians toward illusors and the art of *praestigium*.

Canons 13 and 15 of question 5 derive from the thirteenth Council of Toledo and from St. Augustine and denounce clergy who practice the *opera maleficiae* and declare the works of magicians to be illusory. Questions 6 and 7 deal with the more general problem of giving the last rites to condemned sinners. They say nothing of magic.

Gratian's texts in this *causa* represent little in the way of innovation except in their selectivity. All of them are derived through Ivo of Chartres, and most of them go back to Burchard's *Decretum*. Many of them consist of patristic texts, particularly Augustinian texts, and it should be noted that the revival of the patristic literature permits Gratian to bring twelfth-century church law more closely into line with the writings of the most influential early churchmen. In the process, of course, a great deal of the earlier literature on magic found, for example, in Burchard, earlier penitentials, and Carolingian capitularies is omitted. Thus, Gratian's selectivity, his strong reliance on patristic texts, and his omission of many of the varieties of magical beliefs so exhaustively itemized by Burchard especially characterizes the treatment of magic in this part of the *Decretum*. Gratian intensified and lent the great authority of his work to these texts, but the texts clearly deal with the magical arts and their condemnation. Only one text, part of a canon, describes and denounces a superstition later important in witchcraft beliefs, that of night-flight with Diana. Gratian's concerns here are virtually identical with those of Ivo and John of Salisbury: learned magic, sacrificing to demons, and the belief in night-flight and shapeshifting. One distinctive feature of both Ivo and Gratian is their turning away from the exhaustive lists of superstitions in the penitentials and restoring the condemnations of the Church Fathers, early popes and councils to positions of emphasis.

Causa 33, the only other place in the *Decretum* where Gratian discusses magic, is part of a series of *causae* devoted to the topic of impediments to marriage. Among these impediments was the question of male impotence induced by magic (*maleficia*), and causa 33 deals with this topic. Only canon 3 of *quaestio* 1 directly deals with the problem of impotence caused by magic. This text is taken from Ivo, but it originated in Hincmar of Reims' ninth-century treatise *De divortio Lotharii*, which, as we have seen in Chapter 1, was an important opinion involved in the case of a ninth-century imperial divorce. The canon, *Si per sortiarias*, states that if a man is rendered impotent by magic and his impotence is not ended by penitence, exorcisms, prayers, almsgiving, and the like, the marriage may be ended. This text, far more than any other, including the *Canon Episcopi*, was of interest to canon lawyers because it touched the vital area of developing marriage law and thus represented a problem they encountered far more often than they did magicians.[29] The canon states clearly that *maleficium* may indeed cause impotence, and a number of other twelfth century sources, the most famous of which is the autobiography of Guibert of Nogent, indicate that such cases were notable and of great general concern.[30] As will be seen in the next chapter, canonists continued to concern themselves with impotence inspired by *maleficium* through the thirteenth and fourteenth centuries, as did Thomas Aquinas in a text to be considered below.[31]

Gratian's texts became the basis for the training of all ecclesiastical lawyers, and in the ecclesiastical courts of the twelfth century these were the texts used to solve the problems of working lawyers and judges. When questions of magic came into the court's purview, it was these texts to which lawyers would turn, even through other twelfth-century writers, primarily theologians and moralists, also wrote on the subject. As the description of *causa* 26 suggests, Gratian considerably narrowed the juristic purview of magical practices. *Causa* 26 was also the central place in the *Decretum* for Gratian's discussion of *superstitio*. As we have seen, Gratian's proof text is from chapters 19–21 of Augustine's *De doctrina christiana,* and from the *De civitate Dei.* The bleak injunctions of the bishop of Hippo became the lawyers' guide through the problems of superstition and magical practices. Augustine's unreleting hostility toward all forms of magic shaped strongly lawyers' attitudes and opinions in the twelfth and thirteenth centuries.

Shortly after it appeared, the *Decretum* because the primary lawbook in ecclesiastical circles, and its analytical and systematic approach to law itself helped to separate law as a discipline distinct from theology. Gratian's own view was probably that theology was a broad enough field to encompass the law. But the teaching of Gratian's text, the analogy with the study of the *Corpus iuris civilis* of the revived study of Roman law, and the intense work of the teachers and students at Bologna, Paris, and elsewhere, soon showed signs of creating a distinct discipline and profession on the basis of Gratian's work and the commentaries upon it that began to appear soon after 1140. These commentaries, the glosses, are especially important for European intellectual history because they reflect both the general response over time to the texts that became the foundations of ecclesiastical law and because they reveal what lawyers learned about the application of the texts to the actual practice of law. Although many of the early commentators restricted themselves to the meaning of particular terms and a clarification of the cases under discussion, much of their work dealt with the links between the legal texts and theology.

The *Summa* of Paucapalea, one of the earliest commentaries on the *Decretum,* says little about *causa* 26, usually explaining the terms and clarifying the references to scripture and to the writings of the Fathers, especially Augustine.[32] The *Summa* of Magister Rolandus gives short shrift to the varieties of divination: "These *questiones,* if I am not mistaken, were shown by St. Augustine to be useless in his book *De natura demonum.*"

Rolandus goes on to say that all *sortilegi* and *divini* who do not desist from their superstitions are to be excommunicated, as is shown by innumerable canons. Neither of these commentators has anything to say concerning impotence induced by *maleficia.*[33] Stephen of Tournai, whose *Summa* was composed around 1160, takes his commentary virtually entirely from Paucapalea and Rolandus, except for one or two personal observations. In considering the types of divination, Stephen remarks offhandedly: "We are neglecting the third and fourth *questiones,* and we will leave their materials to the reader of poets and philosophers." Of *quaestio* 5, Stephen simply echoes Rolandus: "This question requires no distinctions, because all *sacrilegi et similes,* if they do not desist, are to be separated from the Church." When Stephen turns to *causa* 33, *quaestio* 1, however, he offers a much longer comment than the other two *magistri.* He argues that the inability to consummate a marriage derives either from natural frigidity or from *maleficium.* If a marriage is afflicted by frigidity, and if the woman does not wish to be married, the marriage may be dissolved. If *maleficium* is involved and penitence does not allay it, the marriage may be dissolved, but if husband and wife disagree as to who is at fault, the numbers of compurgators and the processes of divorce are described. Stephen adds the touching point that if the wife does not want a divorce, she may remain, "and if not as a wife, then at least as a sister." Stephen then discusses conflicting canonist opinions concerning the nature of the matrimonial bond, a topic that consistently engaged canonists' attention through the next several centuries.[34]

A commentary roughly contemporary with that of Stephen is the *Summa Parisiensis.* Its gloss to *causa* 26 is very brief. In considering question 1, the author points out some difficulties:

It is first asked what are *sortilegia*. This question is much more to be defined than definitive. It is resolved, however, by a single chapter, from Isidore, although not thoroughly.[35]

In discussing *sortes*, the author remarks that although they were permitted in antiquity, they are forbidden today. In dealing with questions 3–4, the author simply observes that the divisions in Gratian's text are those of the Roman encyclopedist Varro, thus perhaps clarifying Stephen of Tournai's remark that he leaves such enumeration to those who read the poets and philosophers. In the case of question 5, the author is adamant: *Divini* and *sortilegi* are to be excommunicated if they do not cease. Of this there is no doubt: *super hoc nulla dubitatio*. "Here it is said that *sortes* are nothing other than *divinationes et maleficia*." In regard to *causa* 33, *quaestio* 1, the *Summa Parisiensis* raises the same question as the *Summa* Stephen of Tournai. It seems that the question of the role of *maleficia* in the general issue of the dissolvability of a marriage attracted far more canonist attention, and generated much livelier disagreements, than the material on divination, *sortilegium*, and other forms of magic.

The *Summa* of Rufinus, also dating from the late twelfth century, notes that "*sortilegium* and *auguratio* and similar superstitions . . ."[36] are kinds of heresy, at least in those who have received the faith of Christ." In discussing question 5, Rufinus echoes Gratian and the other commentators: "It is true without distinction that *sortilegi et similes*, who refuse to desist, are to be excommunicated. Clerics who make such consultations deserve to be deposed and perpetually placed in a monastery." Laymen are to be assigned a penitential period of five or seven years. In considering *causa* 33, question 1, Rufinus, like the author of the *Summa Parisiensis* and Stephen of Tournai, reflects the conflicting views and difficult legal problems that cases of frigidity and *maleficia*–caused impotence presented to Church lawyers, with the broad room for fraud and collusion they offered, and with the acute social pressures they reflected. Like the other canonists considered here, however, Rufinus has no doubt that impotence may be inflicted by *maleficia*. The problem facing the canon lawyers is not the nature of *maleficium*, upon which they tacitly agree, but upon the complexities of marital law and the problems posed by such cases.

The reticence of canon lawyers concerning the question of magic was not restricted to the twelfth century. As we will see below, the thirteenth century witnessed some further development of these strictures, but not a great deal. Thus, in spite of the variety of discussions of magic and related practices in chronicles, moral stories, and discussions of legitimate knowledge, canon law remained relatively poor in original discussions of these questions. Schulte cites a text from a thirteenth-century canonist of Brandenburg, a Magister Baldwinus, who responds to the question (in his discussion *de sortilegiis*), "But what of certain wicked women who believe and say that on nights they have ridden with Diana or Herodias upon certain beasts, crossed on them over many lands, obeyed their commands, and permitted themselves to be called to their service to perform better or worse things, or are enabled to be transformed into another species?" Baldwin states that they are to be rejected by the Church, since they are inspired by the wicked spirit, who creates these *phantasmata* for them, which are purely illusory. He would be a fool who thinks that things which have only a spiritual existence could effect material transformations. Whoever believes these things to be true does not have right faith, "and beyond doubt is an infidel and worse than a pagan." Baldwinus's comments are perfectly conventional and are obviously directed at the illusory character of the women's beliefs.[37] Thus, well into the thirteenth century, canon lawyers echoed the thought of John of Salisbury and Gratian. It appears that not until the revival of learned magic and changes in theology during the late thirteenth century did such canonist opinion appear insufficient for dealing with magic and, later, witchcraft. The category *sortilegium*, in canon law, at least, was restricted to those cases discussed by Gratian. However imaginative the language of chroniclers and moralists became, it found little echo in the law of the Christian community. It is reflected somewhat more clearly in the new penitential handbooks of the later twelfth century.

MAGIC AND WITCHCRAFT IN THE TWELFTH- AND THIRTEENTH-CENTURY PENITENTIALS

One of the most fruitful sources for the history of beliefs in magic and related practices has been the penitentials of the early Middle Ages.[38] From the middle of the twelfth century through the thirteenth century and after, another series of penitentials appeared, although these have not generally been used by historians, partly because modern editions have been lacking until recently, and partly because theologians and legal sources have dominated research.[39] Beginning with the penitential of Alain of Lille, and including the works of Bartholomew of Exeter, Robert of Flamborough, Thomas of Chobham, and St. Raymond of Peñafort, these penitentials have much to say of magic and related practices and beliefs. Their primary purpose was to assimilate the enormous amounts of dogmatic and juridical material produced by popes, Church councils, and individual theologians during the twelfth and early thirteenth centuries into a form suitable for confessors and penitents alike. These works were designed as part of the Church's new pastoral movement, and they were intended by their authors to provide an educational, as well as a penitential experience for those who used them. The confessor examined the conscience of the penitent, and the penitent in turn learned as much about his or her religion as had been learned in church or, until the thirteenth century, through sermons. These books, which reached as least as wide an audience as the works of theologians and canon lawyers, reflect a strong interest in and fear of magic in all its forms. Although the penitentials reflect the same condemnation of magic that we have seen in the work of Hugh of St. Victor, the theologians, and the canonists, their fear of it is considerably greater.

The penitentials of the late twelfth and early thirteenth century were influenced by both theology and canon law. All of them show familiarity with Gratian's *Decretum*. The greatest of the penitentials, that of Raymond of Peñafort, was, of course, written by the compiler of the *Liber Extra* of Pope Gregory IX. The penitential of Bartholomew of Exeter concerns itself with magic under the heading *De divinatione*. This heading covers a number of condemned beliefs and practices, some of which clearly include folk-customs and common superstitions. It is, however, particularly significant for the assimilation of this kind of popular (and perhaps by the late twelfth century, somewhat old-fashioned) belief to the kinds of magic traditionally condemned by the Fathers and by theologians and canonists during the twelfth century.[40]

Robert of Flamborough's *Liber Penitentialis* contains two separate sections dealing with magic:[41] Book 3, c. 3, *de sortilegio*, condemns those who offer sacrifices to demons, baptize images, and practice image magic with the eucharist. Book 5, c. 6, *de divinatoribus*, condemns other kinds of divinatory magic, at considerably greater length than Alain or Bartholomew. The *Summa Confessorum* of Thomas of Chobham, written around 1215, deals extensively with magical practices, and it treats them in the order of the seven deadly sins.[42] Thomas's *Summa* is divided into articles, *distinctiones*, and *quaestiones*. Article 7 deals with the deadly sins generally, *distinctiones* 1 through 4 dealing respectively, with penitents, *luxuria*, *gula et ebrietate*, and *ira*. Article 5, *de sortilegiis et veneficiis*, then takes up the problem of magical beliefs and practices. Divided into eleven *quaestiones*, it constitutes a thorough catalogue of most of the kinds of magic known to early thirteenth-century confessors. Thomas links *sors* with prohibited superstitions, invoking the demon, the magical properties of elements and plants, and dreams. He places great emphasis upon the vulnerability of humans to diabolic temptation, and in this aspect of his work, too, he displays what has come to be a thirteenth-century characteristic attitude: the vulnerability of humans to diabolic temptation and the role of the demon in all forms of magic, from popular superstitions to the most formal and learned kinds. Works such as these and their successors—which never fail to condemn magic uniformly and which combine all kinds of magic, from popular superstitions to learned magic, under a single rubric—turned the scattered condemnations of the eleventh century, coming from diverse sources and possessing little binding force, into the beginnings of a systematic concept of diabolic temptation and human vulnerability. The confessors, approaching the subject of magic through these systematic works, could obtain a more consistent idea of the beliefs and fears of their penitents than earlier penitentials had solicited. In addition, by taking the confessor through the mind—conscience and imagination—of the penitent, the psychology of temptation and the variety of beliefs concerning magic could be homogenized, and the emergence of sinful magic could be recognized by all who used these penitentials. Aided by the texts brought together by Gratian and Raymond of Peñafort, the confessors of the thirteenth century and the theologians who taught them at last had a manageable body of literature on which to build a theory of the prevalence and danger of magic. Simultaneously with the fear and repression of heresy, the growing awareness of and fear of magic on the part of theologians and lawyers drew the two closer together in the penitentials.[43]

Unlike the earlier penitentials (including Burchard's, the *indiculi superstitionum* of Church councils and synods, and the Carolingian capitularies), however, the new penitentials of the twelfth and thirteenth centuries dealt with popular beliefs and superstitions against the articulate background of twelfth-century theology and canon law.[44] As will be shown in later chapters, this systematizing process, perhaps as much or more so than scholastic ontology, helped to produce an extensive list of condemned popular superstitions that confessors and inquisitors could understand and measure against a complex framework of theology and law. Among the most distinctive features of the new penitential literature was its general acute awareness of the active demonic role in temptation, the variety of human weaknesses that made humans temptation–prone, the insistence that much sin (and nearly all sins touching upon *maleficia*) was the result of willing human collaboration with the devil, and the general apprehensiveness (not surprising in an age that witnessed an intensive pastoral movement in ecclesiastical life) concerning idolatry and superstition. These penitentials were aimed at a world that, although predominantly lay, was also exclusively Christian, and therefore subject to careful ecclesiastical scrutiny in all parts of its life. The monastic writers who had condemned magic in the Carolingian period and heresy in the twelfth century did so out of a generally dismal view of the possibility of lay salvation and a willingness to attribute the worst conceivable motives and acts to erring laypeople. The late twelfth- and thirteenth-century writers of penitentials, however, began with greater hope for the salvation of laypeople, but for that very reason they were more acutely aware of the dangers of much of lay life, particularly in the areas of *maleficia, idolatria,* and *super-stitio*. It is this quality of responsibility for the good lay life that gives the penitentials' treatment of magic its distinctive and novel character.

NOTES

1. On the organization of knowledge generally, see James A. Weisheipl, O. P., "Classification of the Sciences in Medieval Thought," *Mediaeval Studies* 27 (1965): 54-90. Weisheipl discusses several of the classifications mentioned below, but he does not consider magic. See also R. W. Hunt, "Introductions to the *Artes* in the Twelfth Century," in *Studia Mediaevalia in Honorem admodum Reverendi Patris Raymundi Joseph Martin* (Brussels, 1949), pp. 85-112, and R. W. Southern, *Medieval Humanism and Other Studies* (Oxford, 1970), pp. 42ff and charts I & II; M.-D. Chenu, *Nature, Man, and Society in the Twelfth Century,* trans., J. Taylor and L. K. Little (Chicago, 1968) pp. 1-48. There is a good introduction to the field in *The Didascalicon of Hugh of St. Victor,* trans. Jerome Taylor (New York, 1961), pp. 3-39. Further discussion may be found in Mary Martin McLaughlin, *Intellectual Freedom and its Limitations in the University of Paris in the Thirteenth and Fourteenth Centuries* (New York, 1977), pp. 336-37.

2. Alfons Hilka and Werner Söderhjelm, *Petri Alfonsi Disciplina Clericalis.' 1. Lateinische Text, Acta Societatis Scientiarum Fennicae,* 28, no. 4 (Helsinki, 1911). Translated, with an introduction by Joseph Ramon Jones and John Esten Keller in *The Scholar's Guide* (Toronto, 1969). See also Lynn Thorndike, History of Magic and Experimental Science (New York, 1923-58) 2:69-73.

3. Hilka and Söderhjelm, *Disciplina Clericalis.*

4. These charts are printed and discussed in R. W. Southern, *Medieval Humanism,* pp. 42ff and Charts I & II. Southern does not discuss the place of the magical arts in these schemes for the organization of knowledge.

5. Thorndike 2:78-82.

6. See Thorndike's remarks, ibid., p. 80.

7. Charles Henry Buttimer, ed., *Hugonis de Sancto Victore Didascalicon de studio legendi,* Studies in Medieval and Renaissance Latin, vol. 10 (Washington, 1939), VI. xv. The translation is from the valuable work by Jerome Taylor, *The Didascalicon of Hugh of St. Victor, A Medieval Guide to the Arts* (New York, 1961), pp. 154-55; Thorndyke 2:8-16.

8. Weisheipl, "Classification of the Sciences," pp. 72-81.

9. See below, Chapter 4.

10. See, e.g., Marie-Therèse d'Alverny, "Astrologues et théologiens au XIIIe siècle," in *Mélanges offerts à M.-D. Chenu,* Bibliothèque thomiste, 37 (Paris, 1967, 31-50, for a vigorous defense of the legitimacy of astrology as a branch of legitimate study, waged by astrologers against the complaints of some theologians. See also T. O. Wedel, *The Mediaeval Attitude toward Astrology* (New Haven, 1920).

11. Although some forms of astrology were accepted theoretically, no individual astrologer was safe from the charge of dealing with forbidden knowledge.

12. See below, Chapter 4, p. 106.

13. See below, Chapter 7, p. 163.

14. *Glossa ordinaria, PL* 113:1, col. 261, ad Exodus 22:18. No historian of witchcraft, as far as I know, has ever pointed out that this interpretation was standard in twelfth-century theology. The shift to a literal interpretation came later. On the early meanings of such terms as *exterminari*, not meaning killing or physical punishment, see Henri Maisonneuve, *Etudes sur les origines de l'Inquisition* (Paris, 1960), p. 306, and pp. 76, 154.

15. *Patrologia Latina* 113:1, cols. 202-9, ad Exodus 7-8. The magicians of Pharaoh occupied the concern of theologians far more than the canonists. See, e.g., Rupert of Deutz, *De Trinitate* (PL 167, cols. 594-608).

16. *PL* 113:1, cols. 207.

17. *PL* 34, cols. 601-2.

18. *PL* 113:1, cols. 352-53.

19. Ibid., col. 354.

20. Ibid., cols. 552-53. The case of Saul and the witch of Endor was discussed by many theologians. Their consensus was that Saul had spoken with a demon, not the spirit of Samuel himself. See Bede, *Quaestiones in libros Regum,* I, c.8 (*PL* 93, cols. 454-55); Rupert of Deutz, *De Trinitate, In Libros regum liber secundus,* c. 17 (*PL* 167, cols. 1115-16).

21. Peter Comestor, *Historia scholastica, Historia Libri Deuteronomii* c.8 (*PL* 198, col. 1253).

22. *Verbum abbreviatum,* c. 17 (*PL* 205, cols. 226-233 at p. 232). See also c. 49 (cols. 153-56). See also Baldwin, *Masters, Princes and Merchants,* 2 vols. (Princeton, 1970) vol. 1, pp. 198-204.

23. See below, Chapter 6.

24. Modern edition, Ae. Friedberg, *Corpus Iuris Canonici . . . Pars Prior, Decretum Magistri Gratiani* (Leipzig, 1879). I cite here the edition of Venice, 1595, with the ordinary gloss. All references to the *Decretum* will be internal.

25. W. M. Lindsay, ed., *Isidori Hispalensis Episcopi Etymologiarum sive originum,* 2 vols. (Oxford, 1911), Lib. 8, p. 28. See also above, Chapter 1.

26. Decretum C.26, q.5, (d.g.a.) c.1.

27. The *Canon Episcopi* has been extensively studied and commented upon. The best discussion of the text and its transmission is to be found in Jeffrey Russell, *Witchcraft in the Middle Ages* (Ithaca, 1972), pp. 291-93. See also Henry Charles Lea, *Materials Toward a History of Witchcraft,* ed. and comp. Arthur Howland (Philadelphia, 1938), 1:178-202.

28. Lea, *Materials,* 1:178-180.

29. For the canonists on marriage generally, see E. Esmein, *Le mariage en droit canonique,* 2nd ed., rev. R. Genestal, 2 vols. (Paris, 1929–36); for this problem, see vol. 1, pp. 241-250; J. Dauvillier, *Le mariage dans le droit classique de l église* (Paris, 1933). For a sampling of cases in a specific kingdom, England, see Richard Helmholz, *Marriage Litigation in Medieval England* (Cambridge, 1974), pp. 53-54, 87-90. Helmholz' work suggests that in England,

natural impotence seems to have been a far greater concern than impotence caused by *maleficium*. A full thirteenth-century development may be seen in Hostiensis, *Summa Aurea* (Venice, 1581), book 4, *De frigidis et maleficiatis et de impotentia coeundi*, pp. 240-44.

30. See John Benton, *Self and Society in Medieval France: The Memoirs of Abbot Guibert of Nogent (1064?–1125)* (New York, 1970), I, c. 12, pp. 63-68, and Benton's introduction.

31. See below, Chapter 4, p. 97.

32. *Die Summa des Paucapalea,* ed. J. F. von Schulte (Giessen, 1890), pp. 107-10.

33. *Die Summa Magistri Rolandi,* ed. F. Thaner (Innsbruck, 1874), pp. 109-12.

34. *Die Summa des Stephanus Tornacensis,* ed. J. F. von Schulte (Giessen, 1891), p. 231.

35. *The Summa Parisiensis on the Decretum Gratiani,* ed. T. P. McLaughlin (Toronto, 1952), pp. 232-34.

36. *Die Summa Decretorum des Magister Rufinus,* ed. H. Singer (Paderborn, 1902), pp. 423-28. Although they are not in themselves legal sources, the illustrations to Gratian manuscripts suggest some of the parallel attitudes to these topics on the part of these who commissioned the decoration of the mss. See A. Melnikas, *The Corpus of the Miniatures in the Manuscripts of Decretum Gratiani, Studia Gratiana* 16-18 (Rome, 1975), vol. 2, pp. 833-62 (c.26) and vol. 3, pp. 1029-58 (c.33).

37. J. von Schulte, *Die Geschichte der Quellen und Literatur des Canonischen Rechts* (reprinted, Graz, 1956), vol. 2, p. 503, n. 35. Baldwinus seems to have studied at Bologna before 1250 and is familiar with the major canonist writers before Innocent IV, Bernard of Parma, and Hostiensis. The work of these and other later thirteenth-century canonists, both edited and unedited, however, does not appear to differ significantly from that of Baldwinus.

38. See Gabriel Le Bras, DTC 12, cols. 1160-79. See F. W. H. Wasserschleben, *Die Bussordnungen der abendländischen Kirche* (Halle, 1851), and H. Schmitz, *Die Bussbücher und die Bussdisciplin der Kirche* (Dusseldorf, 1898) (both reprinted at Graz, in 1958); John T. McNeill and Helena M. Gamer, *Medieval Handbooks of Penance* (New York, 1938); John T. McNeill, "Folk-Paganism in the Penitentials," *Journal of Religion* 13 (1933): 450-66. A recent selection of some of these is Cyrille Vogel, "Pratiques superstitieuses au début du XIe siècle d'après le *Corrector sive medicus* de Burchard, évêque de Worms (965-1025)," in *Études de civilization médiévale (IXe–XIIe siècles) Mélanges offerts à Edmond-René Labande* (Poitiers, 1974), pp. 751-61.

39. See P. Michaud-Quantin, *Sommes de casuistique et manuels de confession au moyen age, du XIIe au XVIe siècle* (Louvain, 1962).

40. Adrian Morey, *Bartholomew of Exeter* (Cambridge, England, 1937), pp. 271-74.

41. *Liber Penitentialis,* ed. J. F. Firth, (Toronto, 1971), pp. 158, 258-64.

42. F. Bromfield, *Thomae de Chobham Summa Confessorum* (Louvain–Paris, 1968), pp. 466-87.

43. The *Liber Poenitentialis* of Alain de Lille is in *PL* 210. For developments

after 1215, see Michaud-Quantin, pp. 34-53. See also S. Kuttner, "Ecclesia de occultis non judicat," *Acta Congressus Iuridici Internationalis,* vol. 3 (Rome, 1936): 227-46. Russell's *Witchcraft in the Middle Ages* discusses only the *libri poenitentiales* before the twelfth century, pp. 43-100.

44. There is a summary discussion of conciliar decrees on magic in Lea, Materials, vol. 1, and in Robert-Léon Wagner, *"Sorcier" et "Magicien"* (Paris, 1939), pp. 52-67, 100-27, as well as in the general treatments of Jeffrey Russell and Joseph Hansen.

4

The Systematic Condemnation of Magic in the Thirteenth Century

MAGIC, SCHOOLS, AND SCHOOLMEN IN THE EARLY THIRTEENTH CENTURY

The magicians referred to in eleventh-century northern Italian rhetoric and in the twelfth-century courts of John of Salisbury, are to be found in greater and greater numbers in the schools of the late twelfth and thirteenth centuries. The influx of Arabic and Greek science, specifically, and the widespread interest in natural science, generally, help to explain the strong claims for the legitimacy of astrology and the attraction of astrology and similar subjects for some of the best students and teachers of the period.

Robert Grosseteste, as student and master, appears to have taught astrology at Oxford, and his *De prognosticatione seu de impressionibus aeris*, written at Oxford probably in the first decade of the thirteenth century, suggests the powerful attraction of astrology for even the ablest students and masters.[1] Like William of Auvergne, who will be discussed more fully below, Grosseteste appears to have been especially attracted by the subject of astrology, although as he grew older and probably became more familiar with the varied uses to which magic and astrology were put outside the schools, he withdrew his admiration and attacked astrology vigorously. In his *Hexaemeron*, Grosseteste applied to astrology the theological arguments that we have seen cited from Augustine to Hugh of St. Victor.[2] Grosseteste's criticism is of two different kinds. First, he argues, astrology is a necessarily uncertain science that professes to depend upon certainty of timing, observation of the heavens, and heavenly influences occurring seconds or minutes apart. He states that "there is not yet sufficient certitude concerning the motions of the heavens . . ." for astrology to be accurate.[3] Grosseteste's second attack on astrology is not scientific; it is theological. Astrology reduces the dignity of humanity to a purely corporeal nature. By subordinating the rational mind to the necessity of corporeality, the astrologers are "enemies of human nature. . . . and blaspheme against God." "Astrologers of this sort are seduced and seducers, and their teaching is impious and profane, written at the dictation of the devil, and therefore their books ought to be burned. And not only they, but those who consult them are lost."[4] The bishop of Lincoln has come a long way from his heady student and early teaching days, and the development of Grosseteste's thought concerning astrology suggests the high initial attraction that it and other studies offered in the excitement of the late twelfth-century schools.

A contemporary of Grosseteste, Michael Scot, found the same interest in the schools of the late twelfth century, but Scot never condemned astrology and magic as thoroughly as Grosseteste.[5] Scot spent his life as a courtier in the service of Frederick II. He was one of the few who managed to retain the favor of both Frederick and Pope Gregory IX, a quality that argues eloquently for the courtier's skills. Besides Michael Scot's association with the court of Frederick, his importance for our subject lies in his attempts to find a compromise between the implacable hostility toward astrology and magic on the part of such thinkers as Hugh of St. Victor and Robert Grosseteste and the popularity of astrology and other forms of magic among scholars and courtiers early in the thirteenth century.

By Michael Scot's day not only did astrology and magic attract students and young masters in the schools, but necromancers and invokers of demons plied their trade in favorite places in Verona and Naples, and probably in many other cities as well.[6] Aware of the popularity of astrology and the occult arts, Scot developed the theory that there were two kinds of astrology and other forms of magic, one acceptable and one not. Perhaps he drew upon the greater ambivalence toward these subjects in the Islamic world, with which he was familiar through his studies at Toledo and Salerno and his long stay in the world of what d'Alverny has called "Mediterranean magical traditions."[7] Whatever his reasons, whether his own proclivities and career or his proximity to the Islamic Mediterranean world in which greater latitude toward magic and astrology was permitted, Michael Scot argued for a double system of permissible and impermissible magic. He condemned superstitious astrology in much the same tone as Hugh and Robert Grosseteste; *ymaginaria astronomia*, which

Scot considered a legitimate exercise of human reason, was permitted. *Mathesis* was legitimate knowledge; *matesis*, following the earlier argument of John of Salisbury, was forbidden as a form of sinful divination; *mathematica* was a legitimate discipline, but *matematica* was a science of the devil and used only for evil purposes. Michael Scot's account of the descent of divination from the demons to Ham, derived in part from Isidore of Seville, includes the legend of Gerbert, the *optimus nigromanticus* (in the sense of "natural necromancy"). Concerning the magi who witnessed Christ's nativity, a *locus classicus* of discussions concerning magic, Scot argues, with considerable etymological accuracy, that the term *magus* had the combined meanings of trickster (*illusor*), sorcerer (*maleficus*), and sage (*sapiens*) until the coming of Christianity. Since the beginning of the Christian era, the *maleficus* and *illusor* have been forbidden and condemned, and only the *magus sapiens* is part of the legitimate order of Christian knowledge. The *maleficus* is now "he who interprets characters and phylacteries, incantations, dreams, and makes ligatures of herbs." The *illusor* is now the *praestigiosus*, condemned by theologians and canonists alike.[8]

Like Grosseteste and William of Auvergne, Michael Scot, too, was familiar with magic books and with the dark side of the *scientia Toletana*. Scot was unique, however, in listing Peter Abelard as the author of at least one of these works, along with Simon Magus and other condemned necromancers, conjurors of evil spirits, and performers of incantations.[9] And Scot himself, both in his own lifetime and particularly later in the thirteenth century, was regarded by some as a legitimate scientist, but by many others as the worst sort of magician of the type Scot himself condemns in the *Liber Introductorius*. Perhaps the best known reference to his later reputation is found in Dante's *Divine Comedy*, *Inferno*, canto 20, in which Scot is condemned to walk forever with his head twisted around facing his back with other diviners of antiquity and the Middle Ages:

> Michele Scotto fu, che veramente
> de le magiche frode seppe 'l giocco.[10]

In spite of Michael Scot's disavowal of any illegal magical practices, his reputation contributed to the picture of the dangerous and blasphemous diviner, astrologer, and wonder-worker.

Scot's distinctions between permissible and impermissible magic and astrology, whether he invented them or not, became common currency during the thirteenth century and are cited in various forms by proponents of legitimate, learned magic through the seventeenth century. In order to prove the legitimacy of at least one form of magic, whether natural or hermetic, even working astrologers and magicians had to concede that there was a forbidden side to their profession. By the early thirteenth century, theology and canon law were too formidable to be denied, and their condemnation of magic and astrology—as well as divination, all forms of incantations, and ligatures—could hardly be denied or evaded. The astrologers and "legitimate" magicians therefore echoed the condemnations of theologians and lawyers, arguing only that their practices were not among the condemned practices discussed in theologians' and canonists' texts. This bifurcation of magic, with the condemnation of magic strengthened by theologians and canon lawyers and echoed by magicians themselves, and the attempts by Scot and others to clear an area of legitimate magic, contributed greately to strengthening the pejorative sense of the terms *magus, maleficus, divinator, incantator, sortilegus,* and *matematicus.* Indeed, these terms were disavowed even by the astrologers and magicians themselves. A much more tempered condemnation of magic appeared in the work of Richard Fishacre, a Dominican follower of Grosseteste later in the thirteenth century.[11] Three sorts of people try to predict the future, says Fishacre, *magi,* astrologers, and prophets. Prophets, of course, do so by God's grace. Astrologers do so "from the natural course of stars." *Magi,* however, "predict what has been revealed to them by demons." They are to be universally condemned, and they are not to be thought divine any more than the demons who inform them. The bifurcated idea of magic, which had begun in the twelfth century and had been strengthened by the claims of the astrologers and their attractions in the late twelfth-century schools, remained in force throughout the thirteenth century and beyond. Roger Bacon (himself, of course, like Michael Scot, also accused of being a magician) denounced *magia* with greater vehemence than Scot.[12] Regardless of the fortune of their personal reputations, however, the thirteenth century astrologers and magicians heavily strengthened the case against illicit magic by condemning it just as strongly (perhaps more strongly, since they were very often under attack for it themselves) as had the theologians and lawyers of the twelfth and early thirteenth centuries.

By 1225, the figure of the evil magician had begun to take on a clearer and more dangerous shape. The figure had been outlined in the rhetorical and courtly literature of the eleventh and twelfth centuries and denounced in the theological and canon law works of the same period. Condemned with the heretic, who himself emerges as a distinctive type in the ecclesiastical literature of the twelfth century, the magician finally acquires a substantive, specific art in the world of the schools and the courts of the early thirteenth century. That art is comprised by the works of Arabic and Greek philosophy and astrology, the Hermetic books, the Pseudo-Aristotle literature, and the works concerning Solomon and the *Ars notoria.*[13] Not only these works with real or pretentious claims to the status of legitimate learning, but also the simplified and popularized versions of these, the *grimoires* that circulated throughout the thirteenth century, and after contributed to the substantive dangers of magic. The classical echoes of John of Salisbury's magicians are gone. In their place is a very real body of knowledge, some of it practiced in courts like that of Frederick II, some of it handled and sampled by no less respectable thinkers and ecclesiastics than Robert Grosseteste, Michael Scot, and William of Auvergne. The theologians and canonists who returned to the attack against magic and astrology in the thirteenth century had a much clearer and more specific idea of what they were attacking than did their twelfth-century predecessors. What they were attacking looked very much like Anselm of Besate's confected magician of the *Rhetorimachia*. But now he was a magician with real books and real knowledge, and he posed a great danger, far greater than the inept Rotiland. And his knowledge was attractive; Robert Grosseteste and William of Auvergne had themselves been attracted by it, and they bitterly remembered that attraction in their later years.

William of Auvergne was born around 1180, a contemporary of Grosseteste and Michael Scot. He spent his youth at the *studium* in Paris, became a master of theology, and was bishop of Paris from 1228 until his death in 1249.[14] As bishop of Paris, William had much to do with the university, and his own experience as a student and master, like that of Grosseteste, made him particularly concerned about the availability and attractiveness of astrology and magic to students and teachers alike. He was also concerned with the dangers of astrology and magic in the community of Christians generally, and he is one of the best-informed writers on the subject that the thirteenth century produced. Far more than Thomas Aquinas, William of Auvergne collected and expanded earlier statements of opposition to magic and denounced its evils at great length.

In cc. 24–26 of his *De legibus*, William of Auvergne tells of books of magic he himself had seen and handled as a young student in Paris. C. 24 consists of a discussion on various forms of idolatry, particularly those that William calls "the insane, vain and impious idolatry of stars and heavenly lights." He goes on, in c. 25 to discuss planetary intelligences, and remarks:

Litteras etiam, et numeros similiter eisdem partiti sunt, et ad ultimum ipsum corpus humanum per partes, et membra distribuerunt eisdem; et haec omnia in libris judiciorum astronomiae, et in libris magorum atque maleficorum tempore adolescentiae nostrae nos meminimus inspexisse.[15]

Another reference to the availability of these books in Paris in the late twelfth century is in c. 26:

Haec enim omnia adeo impia, adeoque sacrilega sunt, ut sine horrore pia corda ea nec legere valeant, nec audire; unde, et nos istorum memoriam horrificam non tam perstringimus, quam etiam fugimus, et fugamus, ne majoris insaniae occasionem demus insipientibus.[16]

Like Grosseteste, William of Auvergne had flirted with astrological and magical books, and, again like Grosseteste, he repudiated everything he had read in them. To seek out such knowledge, William argues, is the vice of *curiositas*, the *libido sciendi non necessaria*. *Curiositas*, which played an important semantic role in medieval intellectual history, had come to apply to the knowledge of astrology and magic that theologians and prelates like Grosseteste and William of Auvergne had begun to discover in the schools around them by the end of the twelfth century.[17]

The extent of William's knowledge and concern of other considerations of astrology and magic is surprising, especially in contrast to such recent theologians as Peter Lombard, Peter the Chanter, and the other moral theologians at Paris. Whereas twelfth-century theologians had done little more than repeat patristic denunciations of sorcery and divination, William of Auvergne, in the *De legibus* and the *De universo*, goes into the new magic and astrology in considerable detail. Like John of Salisbury, William begins by speaking of illusions, and he distinguishes magic based upon the natural properties of objects from other forms of magic. His knowledge is extensive and his attack formidable. William insists that without demonic help and idolatry, there is little that magic can accomplish, and to accomplish anything by demonic assistance or through idolatry is sinful. The *maleficus* is guilty of idolatry and the performance of obscene rites, as well as injury. The advent of Christianity condemned all magic except natural magic to the status of *maleficia*. In short, William of Auvergne's treatises reflect sharply the appearance of magical practices, their atttraction, their necessary dependence upon the demons, idolatry, their capacity to deceive or cause injury, and their intrinsically forbidden character. By drawing together the traditional condemnation of magic and astrology and applying it to the new magic of the late twelfth and early thirteenth centuries, William of Auvergne contributed much to the increasingly sharp picture of the criminal magician, the nature of the *crimen magiae*, and the dangers it posed to all Christians. Nor was William the last bishop of the great university city to recognize the attractions of magic to its ambitious, curious, and learned scholars.

On 7 March 1277, Etienne Tempier, Bishop of Paris, issued a formal condemnation of two hundred and nineteen propositions drawn from the writings of Averroes, Avicenna, Aristotle, and several of their Latin commentators. On 18 March of the same year, Robert Kilwardby, Archbishop of Canterbury, echoed Tempier's condemnation with his own endorsement, and on 28 April, Pope John XXI, who had suggested Tempier's investigation, issued a decretal endorsing and implementing the condemnations. Historians of philosophy have given great attention to the 1277 condemnation, and with good reason; at Etienne Gilson has pointed out, it constituted a landmark in the history of medieval thought. In addition to the condemned philosophical propositions, however, Tempier's condemnation also included such items as the literary work *De amore* of Andreas Capellanus, and, little marked by historians of philosophy but directly to the point of our discussion, a book of geomancy and

libros, rotulos seu quaterniones nigromanticos aut continentes experimenta sortilegiorum, invocationes demonum, sive conjurationes in periculum animarum, seu in quibus de talibus et similibus fidei orthodoxe et bonis moribus evidenter adversantibus tractatur, per eandem sententiam nostram condempnamus . . .[18]

Aside from the great and absorbing clash of radical Aristotelianism and orthodox resistance, this condemnation of books of magic suggests that the earlier concerns of William of Auvergne were not unique to the early thirteenth century. As we will see in a later chapter, these condemnations of 1277 were echoed in the great condemnation of magic, this time by the faculty of theology of the University of Paris, in 1398. The condemnation of 1277 is echoed in the literature of demonology, law, and poetry of the same period.

MAGIC AND DEMONOLOGY

Although many earlier writers had linked the practice of magic and even some elements of astrology with service to or cooperation with the devil, William of Auvergne's concern with idolatry and demonology in the magic books he attacks is particularly pronounced, as was that of Tempier later in the century. The principles of medieval demonology had long ago been laid down in the works of the patristic period. The inclusion of excerpts from this material in Gratian's *Decretum* and the *Book of Sentences* of Peter Lombard in the mid-twelfth century, and its subjection to systematic examination and development in the schools, together with the condemnation of Hugh of St. Victor, soon helped to shape a learned demonology readily accessible to William of Auvergne and later writers, notably Thomas Aquinas. Besides the survival of formal demonology and its revival in the second half of the twelfth century, other literary genres also contributed to demonological concerns. Hagiography, for example, had long dealt with the temptations of the saint by demons and the saint's ultimate victory over them. The hagiographical tradition made the demons familiar, first to a monastic, and later to a wider society, but it also tended to reduce the demon to manageable proportions when conquered or coerced by the holy man. The literature produced in the twelfth and thirteenth century for the instruction of novices in monasteries also placed considerable emphasis upon the nature of the devil and the manifestations of his power to tempt and lead humans to destruction. In chronicles the devil became a common element of historical causation and of human motivation. In short, different literary genres depicted the devil differently and used references to him for different purposes.

The recent studies of Kelly and J. B. Russell, along with the older works of Lea and others, have effectively traced the development of Christian demonology.[19] Several aspects of twelfth- and thirteenth-century demonology, however, deserve particular emphasis here. First, the convulsions that the eleventh- and twelfth-century reform movements created in the Christian world introduced a new and subtler image of Satan and his power over humans. The opponents on both sides of the Investiture Conflict resorted to occusing their enemies of collaboration with Satan, and the Gregorian ambition to reform the world led proponents of the reform movement to analyze the world at considerable length. In earlier hagiographical and monastic literature, the world was indeed a place of violence, temptation, and chaos, prevented from feeling the full force of God's wrath only by virtue of the purity of monastic devotions. In that world, base human nature exercised its powers for evil without any limits other than those imposed by harsh Christian rulers. The world's capacity for sin was limitless. Inside the monastery, there was temptation also, and some of the most vivid literature on demonology derives from monastic sources. Although monastic writers dealt with demonic temptation, however, they dealt with it as something which could be overcome by proper discipline, counsel, and adherence to the rules of the order. If in monastic literature the devil was a formidable and subtle opponent, he could nevertheless be contained by strict application of disciplinary measures, and triumphs over his temptations were recorded in lives of monastic saints and in the literature of instruction for monastic novices. The devil was depicted ferociously, but he was depicted within a monastic world view in which he invariably met defeat or, if on occasion he was allowed to triumph over an erring or weak monk, his triumph was exemplary. In monastic literature throughout the twelfth and thirteenth centuries, this interest in Satan continued and was orchestrated into training programs for novices by writers such as Caesarius of Heisterbach and Richalmus of Schonthal. In this pedagogical literature which was produced in order to discipline the novices psychologically for their conventual life, the psychology of demonic temptation was graphically portrayed, the horrors of the world outside the monastery glaringly depicted, and the power of obedience to the monastic rule and to superiors invariably proved supreme. Such literature had other functions as well. Professor Elizabeth Kennan is currently exploring this novice literature for its psychological impact and its role in acculturating the minds and spirits of novices to the psychological world of monastic life.[20] Lester Little and Barbara Rosenwein have studied monastic spirituality and its relation to changing cultural modes of the eleventh through the thirteenth centuries.[21] For present purposes, it is important to note two features of monastic treatmen of demons: First, demonic temptation was subtle, and monastic liturgical life, especially at Cluny, was designed to represent a continual combat with Satan.[22] Second, within the world of the monastery, this literature played a specific and clearly defined role. When its elements were transposed to the secular world—in art, sermons, and theological writings—members of the secular world had no such defenses as had the novice monks with which to overcome such ominous and implacable forces. One function of the reform movement was precisely to sanctify the world outside the monastery, and part of this process was to reveal that world as plagued by demonic forces as was the secluded, highly structured, and ultimately resourceful world of the monk. Motifs and ideas that had a controlled existence inside the monastic psyche, had a very different existence in the untrained and unsupported minds of secular clergy and laypeople. Besides the general monastic condemnation of the world as a place of violence and temptation, there was added in the eleventh and twelfth centuries a psychology of temptation that had originated in the monasteries and against which the secular world had few defenses. The invective of the reform movement, increasing manifestations of dissent, and the new emotional content of monastic and lay devotion alike all sharpened the vulnerability of the world to the temptations and violence of the devil.

In the world of novice-instructional literature, Satan's victims are usually secular clergy and laymen. Caesarius of Heisterbach, in several well-known *exempla*, tells of laymen who called up the devil or had learned secular clerics do it for them, of demons who took on familiar shapes to deceive monks and others, and of erotic and blasphemous activities performed by those outside the monastery walls or by fallen monks.[23] Caesarius several times uses the figure of the cleric skilled in invoking the devil and other forms of necromancy, and such figures, as we have seen, were generally thought to exist in the late twelfth and early thirteenth centuries. Caesarius does not directly condemn the practice, perhaps because his concern is getting the demon into the story and less with the mechanics of how the demon arrives. There are enough known cases of clerical divining and invoking demons, however, to suggest that Caesarius was using a familiar topic.

A number of modern scholars have traced the role of dissent and the growth of heretical movements in influencing twelfth-century demonology. The importance of these movements constitutes a second major aspect of twelfth-century demonology. The growing concern over the nature of evil in the twelfth century is illuminated by the most important of all the new heresies, Catharism, and its positing the existence of an evil god to explain the evils in the world. Orthodox Christianity too, faced the question of evil, and it is often in response to catharist beliefs that we see the role of the devil taking on a more important place in orthodox theology. The increasing prominence of the devil is, in a sense, an orthodox response to the Cathar explanation of evil. In addition to developing the role of the devil internally in orthodox theology, of course, the challenge of Catharism itself became an example of demonic power. The invective against heretics played an important role in sharpening the definition of the role of the devil in human life, and, as Russell and others have shown, greatly accelerated the science of demonology in the west.[24]

A third area in which ideas of demonology expanded was that of religious sentiment. A number of studies have demonstrated that devotion in the twelfth century took on a highly charged emotional content. As R. W. Southern in particular has shown, the fear and trembling before a remote and implacably just god that characterized devotion before the twelfth century was replaced, first in monastic and later in secular circles, with a new theology of redemption and a new sense of the divine love for humanity, a love that called for an equally emotional response from God's creatures.[25] The new emotional content of twelfth-century Christianity has been studied from many points of view, but one in particular is important for this study, that of the emotional revulsion against God's enemies. The intensification of hatred of the Jews, heretics, and anyone else who stood in the way of the apostolic life of one vision or another of Christian reform was the reverse of the coin of twelfth-century emotional Christian devotional feelings. In the eleventh century dissenters and heretics encountered the full force of hatred from the mobs who lynched them; in the twelfth century the literature of Jewish atrocities, so fertile in later centuries, first made its appearance in substantial volume; in the twelfth century the rhetorical depictions of heretics and other deviants introduced once more the patristic descriptions of orgies, blasphemies, and antihuman activities that become the commonplaces of theological literature in ensuing centuries. In this process, the devil, too, became more humanized, and his ubiquity and powers increased in proportion to the sentimentalization of religious attitudes toward God. This is a side of the twelfth century that has not often been discussed—a dark side of the twelfth-century renaissance of which demonology is only one aspect.

Thus, long before the development of a detailed scholastic demonology which has often been charged with responsibility for later ideas of witchcraft, there emerged a multifaceted demonology in the twelfth century derived from monastic literature, ecclesiastical invective, the challenge of dissent, and the new emotional tone of Christian belief. In the early thirteenth century theologians developed a more highly systematized demonology, of which the work of William of Auvergne constitutes a good example. The two greatest scholastic thinkers, however, were Albertus Magnus and Thomas Aquinas. It is in their work that much of the material discussed so far is drawn together. Far more than Aquinas, Albertus appears to have approached magic from the direction of natural science, and he draws a clear distinction between natural magic and demonological magic.[26] Thorndike suggests that the scientific writings of Albertus treat magic more liberally than his theological work; such a distinction is not difficult to understand. In his commentaries on scripture and on Peter Lombard's Sentences, Albertus was already working in a powerful theological tradition in which magic was uniformly condemned. Even in these works, however, he seems to be attempting to define areas in which magic is purely demonological and areas in which it is natural and harmless. In considering scholastic thought on magic and demonology, therefore, it is important to realize, in Albertus's case, that a systematic condemnation of magic was not incompatible with an interest in legitimate magic. In spite of that interest in natural magic, however, Albertus's condemnation of demonological magic is strictly in keeping with the views of William of Auvergne.

The case against scholastic theology as creating an ontological foundation for later witch-beliefs was made by a number of nineteenth-century scholars and has survived in a number of twentieth-century studies. In 1940, however, Charles E. Hopkin produced a doctoral dissertation at the University of Pennsylvania entitled *The Share of Thomas Aquinas in the Growth of the Witchcraft Delusion*.[27] In his thorough study, Hopkin assesses Aquinas's relation to traditional demonology, his theories on the magical arts, and the use of his work by later writers on demonology, magic, and witchcraft. Hopkin came to the conclusion that Aquinas tended to limit, rather than expand the power of demons; that Aquinas condemned *maleficia*, but that for him *maleficia* clearly meant sorcery and magic; and that, in general, he added little that was not to be found in scripture, in Augustine, and in the twelfth- and early thirteenth-century theologians. Hopkin's general conclusion states:

The chief difference between the scholastic demonology and that of the ancient sources is that the treatment has become systematic and theoretically rounded

out, as a part of the scholastic ordering of all theology. While this systematizing did not produce within itself a unified witchcraft concept, it may indirectly
have encouraged such a process in the courts of the Inquisition by setting up
an atmosphere of logical integration.[28]

Hopkin showed clearly that only Aquinas's insistence upon the apostasy of
the pact with demons was cited by fourteenth-century writers and that
although he was widely cited by fifteenth-century writers, he was cited
as the most "modern" of traditional Church authorities, not as a particular
innovator of witchcraft theory. In a later chapter we will deal with the
thesis of Hopkin and others that the Inquisition, and not scholastic theology, was responsible for the growth of witchcraft beliefs. It remains
here, since Aquinas was clearly concerned with sorcery and magic, to
consider his view of the relation between sorcery and demonology.
     Aquinas, as Hopkin clearly proved, knew nothing of the witch as that
figure emerged in the law and theology of the later fifteenth, sixteenth,
and seventeenth centuries. What Aquinas was concerned with, was that
kind of magic that had bcome, since the mid-twelfth century, of greater
and greater concern to theologians and other scholars—sorcery, divination,
and other practices that Aquinas listed under the general category of
superstitio. The fourth chapter of Hopkin's study is an exhaustive survey
of Aquinas's view of the magical arts, dealing with the *opuscula,* as well as
with the two great *summae* and the commentaries on scripture and Peter
Lomband's *Sentences.* In the *opusculum, Concerning the Occult Operations of Nature,* for example, Aquinas deals with the classification of hidden operations, condemning only those operations "that proceed from an
extrinsic principle, the bodies themselves being used by the higher agents
only instrumentally and selectedly," and these operations are condemned
only when they are used by necromancers, not when divine virtue or
good angels perform them.[29] Aquinas's explanation of the powers of
demons upon the natural world is also illustrated by the following passage
from the *Expositio in Job:*

One must then believe that with God's permission demons may disturb the
atmosphere, raise up strong winds, and make fire fall from Heaven. . . . All that
which may be accomplished by the simple movement of a thing from one place
to another may be done by good or evil spirits. Winds, rain, and other
atmospheric disturbances may thus occur solely because of the movements of
condensed vapors. Thus the natural power of the demon suffices to accomplish
these things.[30]

The *opuscula De sortibus* and *De occultis operationibus* both illustrate
Aquinas's distinction between natural and unnatural operations and his
emphasis upon *superstitio.*[31] It should be noted that a large part of

Aquinas's achievement is to relegate many of even the occult operations of nature to legitimate causes. Having done this in these works and in the *summae*, Aquinas is left with a clear idea of the essential role of demons in many classes of natural operation, and indeed, his logic compels him to emphasize the presence of human association with demons and thereby the presence of harmful or nugatory *superstitio*. As Aquinas concisely says, "Only that is called nugatory and superstitious which cannot have a certain cause [whether natural or human or divine], and this pertains to the society of demons."[32] The varieties of superstition that concern this study are those that Aquinas designates as idolatry, divination, and observances, one species of the latter being the magical arts. Here again, Aquinas provides a link among a number of different sins because of their common relation as parts of superstition. Thus idolatry, divination, and the magic arts are epistemologically linked together, as they had been in Aquinas's chief source, St. Augustine. Of the three divisions of *superstitio*, *observantiae* most clearly involve commerce with demons. Thus, in his initial discussions of magic, Aquinas treats it as a variety of legitimate knowledge, and he treats *superstitio* chiefly as a function of ignorance, either ignorance of natural causes or ignorance that its pursuit will inevitably lead to sacrilegious contact with demons.

In the *Summa theologiae* and the *Opuscula*, Aquinas sets forth his demonology on theological and epistemological grounds. In the *Summa contra Gentiles*, a work which attempts to prove the truth of Christian belief without extensive recourse to Christian sources, he attacks magic on rational and ethical grounds, focusing primarily on the uniformly evil ends of such practices. Although his views on magic are scattered throughout the vast body of his work, Aquinas's views are remarkably consistent and logically rigorous. Probably no writer before him systematized the condemnation of magic on so many different levels, and in this sense, as well as Hopkin's sense cited above, Aquinas provided formidable influence both toward the traditional condemnation of magic and toward the linking of magic with service to or subjection to the devil. Of the later meaning of *maleficia*, the witchcraft beliefs of the fifteenth, sixteenth, and seventeenth centuries, Aquinas, of course, knew nothing. Consistent with the theology of the late twelfth and early thirteenth centuries, he also drew heavily from other traditions, particularly scriptural and patristic. He also drew from canon law, particularly in *Quodlibet XI*, where he directly addressed the problem of magic:

Concerning sorcerers, it is known that some say that sorcery has no existence and that it comes simply from lack of belief or superstition, since they wish to prove that demons do not exist except insofar as they are the creatures of man's imagination; insofar as men imagine them to exist, these fantasies afflict the fearful. The catholic faith, on the other hand, insists that demons do indeed exist and that they may impede sexual intercourse by their works.[33]

Like demons, sorcery existed for Aquinas, as it had for all twelfth- and thirteenth-century writers considered so far. Aquinas's role in its history, although it had nothing to do with later notions of witchcraft, was to systematically describe and condemn magical practices, certainly not to invent them, nor to say anything about them that had not been said by earlier writers, particularly St. Augustine. By the end of Aquinas's work, however, the demonological content of sorcery was firmly outlined. Such defenses as had been made for astrology in the late twelfth century, and were to be made for magic in the late thirteenth and fourteenth centuries, now had to overcome the persuasive and voluminous arguments of Aquinas. In some respects, his demonology fitted the works of the magicians bettter than it did even that of the heretics, for the *mira* of the sorcerers can only derive from collaboration with demons and stand in contrast to the genuine *miracula* performed only by God.[34] Dependent upon scripture and Augustine among Christian sources, and Porphyry and Aristotle among non-Christian sources, Aquinas launched the most devastating attack yet on the magical arts. It was no less devastating because it was not a particularly important point of attack. Except in the *opuscula* and the *quodlibeta*, the attack was made wholly within the general context of his philosophical and theological system. In this light, his views of the inefficacy of magic without demonic aid are similar to those of Roger Bacon, and it is important to note that both thinkers use theological *and* rational arguments to condemn it.

THE MAGICIAN AND THE LAWYERS IN THE THIRTEENTH CENTURY

The attraction of legal study in the later twelfth century greatly influenced the canon law courts and the work of those ecclesiastics who made new law for the Christian world. In the late twelfth and early thirteenth centuries, collections of twelfth-century papal legal decisions and conciliar canons were made, usually by individuals for teaching purposes. In 1234 Pope Gregory IX published the *Liber Extra,* by Raymond of Peñaforte, the first official lawbook of the Church.[35] In the texts dealing with *maleficium* in these collections, in the work of glossators who commented upon them and considered their relation to Gratian's text, and in the lawbook of Pope Boniface VIII (the *Liber Sextus,* published in 1298), we can trace the canonist attitude toward sorcery and *maleficium* as it developed in the context of other disciplines.

Among the *Quinque compilationes antiquae,* two collections (the *Compilatio prima* and the *Compilatio quinta*) contained titles relating to *sortilegium.* The *Compilatio Prima* included three texts on the subject: part of the penitential of Theodore, a selection from book 19 of Burchard's *Decretum* (which assigned ten days' penance for performing *sortes* with the psalter or the gospels), and a letter from Pope Alexander III to the bishop of Grado, to be considered below.[36] The *Compilatio Quinta* added one text, a condemnation by Pope Honorius III of the practice of using *sortes* to elect a bishop.[37] In the *Liber Extra,* three of these texts comprised title 21 of book 5, the only discussion of *sortilegium* in the work.[38] The text from the penitential of Theodore and the letter of Honorius III both deal with *sortes* strictly considered. Alexander III's letter to the patriarch of Grado deals with the case of V., a cleric, who went with several infamous people to a private place, not with the intention of calling up the devil, but to perform divination with an astrolabe in order to find goods of the Church that had been stolen. Zeal and simplicity had driven him to do this. He has, however, committed a most grievous sin, and Alexander prescribes a penance for him. Neither the *Compilationes Antiquae* nor the *Liber Extra* added any more texts on the topic and, as can easily be seen, the more recent texts deal clearly with *divination.* In Bernard of Pavia's *Summa Decretalium* on the *Liber Extra,* the author cites both the texts in Gratian and the Roman law in Justinian's *Code.*[39] Evidently, these texts were to be read in conjunction with the law stated in the *Liber Extra.* The *glossa ordinaria* to the *Liber Extra,* by Bartholomew of Brescia, says nothing pertaining to other kinds of magic and focuses instead upon a literal explication of terms and the circumstances of each case. The Boniface VIII's *Liber Sextus* and the *Extravagantes* of John XXII and Clement V contain no title *De sortilegis.* The only text dealing with magic in the *Liber Sextus* is a letter from Pope Alexander IV in 1258 instructing the Inquisition that it may prosecute magicians only when their activities manifestly savor of heresy. As will be shown in the next chapter, Alexander's injunction posed no great difficulties in the early fourteenth century.

Rubric: The Inquisitors, deputed to investigate heresy, must not intrude into investigations of divination or sorcery without knowledge of manifest heresy involved.

It is reasonable that those charged with the affairs of the faith, which is the greatest of privileges, ought not thereby to intervene in other matters. The inquisitors of pestilential heresy, commissioned by the apostolic see, ought not intervene in cases of divination or sorcery unless these *clearly savour* of manifest heresy. Nor should they punish those who are engaged in these things, but leave them to other judges for punishment.

Ordinary Gloss: "clearly savour . . ." as in praying at the altars of idols, to offer sacrifices, to consult demons, to elicit responses from them . . . or if they associate themselves publicly with heretics in order to predict the future by means of the Body and Blood of Christ, etc.[40]

In sum, four new texts were added by the lawmakers of the thirteenth century to Gratian's body of texts, and most of these dealt with divination. As we have seen, the letter of Alexander III explicitly stated that the cleric V, did not intend to invoke demons, as if that were to be expected in the performance of divination, and the letter of Alexander IV tacitly distinguished between magic that was heretical and magic that was not. As we have seen, several commentators on Gratian's *Decretum* had identified magic with heresy (as had the ordinary gloss to the Bible), and no inquisitor would have had trouble in citing before him anyone accused of the practices condemned in Gratian, the *Liber Extra,* or the *Liber Sextus.* As Alexander IV's letter indicates, and as several commentators on Gratian had indicated, magic was not easy to define, and there appears to have been some uncertainty among canonists as to whether all magic was heretical or not. It should be remembered, of course, that the term *heresy* itself had ambiguous meanings to the end of the twelfth century, as did the term *magia.* The thirteenth-century canonists, at the same universities as the theologians who were commenting upon the various kinds of magic, were probably stricken by the same ambiguous feelings as their colleagues and heard the same kind of defense of some, at least, of the magical arts against the charge of heresy.

As the comments on the *Liber Extra* suggest, the texts in Gratian's *Decretum* probably were assumed to be satisfactory for the disposition of most of the cases of magic that ecclesiastical lawyers came across. The *Summa decretalium* of Johannes Andreae, who also wrote the ordinary gloss to the *Liber Sextus,* focuses exclusively on the technical details of divination and sorcery, as did the commentaries of his great predecessors, Innocent IV, Hostiensis, and Goffredo da Trani.[41] Unlike the canonists' treatment of other questions, of which political theory has been the most widely explored, there appears to have been general agreement among them on the question of magic, and little speculation or innovation in their comments.

Aside from comments directly linked to the arrangement of the legal texts, the twelfth and thirteenth centuries also witnessed the appearance of encyclopedic *summae* organized analytically by their authors. The *Summa* of Raymond of Peñafort, the compiler of the *Liber Extra,* is of particular importance.[42] Book 1, Title 11 of Raymond's *Summa* deals with *De sortilegis et divinis* and may serve as a kind of proof text for the opinions of one of the greatest thirteenth-century lawyers.

The first part of title 11 deals with *sortes* and the varieties of *divinatio.*

Raymond incorporates a number of Gratian's texts into his commentary, devoting most of part 1 to Augustine. Augustinian texts also dominate part 2 of title 11, dealing with what kinds of *divinatio* are permitted and what kinds are forbidden. Part 3 deals with the punishments for those who commit *sortilegium* and *divinatio*:

The punishment for such is multiplex; they are declared infamous, nor may they receive the eucharist, if their sin is notorious. . . . They may not be admitted [in court] as accusers. . . . If, after warnings and after excommunication they do not correct themselves, if they are slaves they may be scourged, and if they are freemen they ought to be imprisoned, and both kinds are to be ejected from the parish, their status shown to be reduced because of immorality, that is, they should be tonsured or scalped. The bishop may have this done by his own authority, but he should beware of dismembering them, killing them, or shedding their blood. And he may invoke the aid of the secular arm.[43]

To justify the invocation of the secular arm, that is lay judicial authority, Raymond cites from the first part of Gratian's *Decretum, Distinctio* 17, c. 4 *Nec licuit,* an important text in the history of the Church's relations with temporal powers in the judicial sphere. Part 4 of title 11 raises a number of general questions concerning *sortilegos et divinos*. First, Raymond asks, what if someone should ask a confessor if it is never permissible to divine by means of the astrolabe or similar means. "To this you must answer, according to all authorities, that if it involves the invocation of demons or other similar superstitions, it is in no way permitted." Raymond's second question touches upon the magical and improper use of sacramentals and the mass itself in order to achieve ends that these things were never intended to accomplish, especially those clerics who say masses for the dead in the name of one still living. Raymond's third question deals with the women who believe they ride at night with Diana, from *Decretum,* C.26, q.5, c.12. Raymond repeats the injunction of the *Canon Episcopi* that such superstitions and others, such as the belief in shapeshifting, are phantasms of the devil. Anyone who believes them is beyond doubt an infidel and worse than a pagan. Raymond's *Summa,* then, offers a comprehensive view of canonists' theories of magic in the early thirteenth century. His citations of Gratian's texts suggest the link between the topics discussed by Gratian, their categorical acceptance by the teachers in the law schools, and the relatively few specific texts included in the *Liber* of Gregory IX. Taken in all, as they are in Raymond's *Summa,* they constitute, with the discussions of *maleficia* and marital impotence, the sum total of canonist concern with magic in the thirteenth century. Taken in conjunction with the works of William of Auvergne, Thomas Aquinas, and other writers, they form a consistent, coherent view of magic and its sinful and criminal aspects. The sin of magic was associated with heresy as early as the *glossa ordinaria* on the Bible, and by the late twelfth century beyond question, it was regarded as being as evil as that of heresy. The magicians had become infamous by the sacrilegious and superstitious character of their practices alone. And lawyers, no less than theologians, reiterated that view from the late twelfth century on.

THE MAGICIAN IN HELL

The twentieth canto of Dante's *Inferno* suggests the theological summation of the topics treated so far in this chapter.[44] After having seen the panderers and seducers, flatterers, and simoniacs, Vergil leads Dante to the next *bolgia,* where the poet is immediately stricken with pity at the prospect before him. He sees a silent procession approaching, "at about the speed of those in our own day who say litanies," whose members all have their heads twisted around so that they see and weep backwards. Vergil remarks about the first of them, Amphiaros, what was true of all: "because he wished to see too far ahead in time, he looks behind and makes his way backwards." According to Dante's principle of *contrapasso,* those who provoke the wrath of God by trying to see into the future, are forced to look only at the past. To some extent, the punishment of the diviners in *Inferno,* canto 20, is related to that of the heretics in canto 10, who, because they denied the immortality of the soul, are deprived of the knowledge of what is happening at present and in the near future and recent past. They, unlike the diviners, are afflicted with a clear vision *only* of the distant future.

The first five diviners whom Vergil mentions are figures out of classical literature: Amphiaros, Tiresias, Aruns, Manto, and Eurypylus. Like John of Salisbury, Dante was willing to use classical references to condemn sins that were being committed by his contemporaries, probably because the references were to well-known figures whose magical practices were classic illustrations of the sin they committed. The remaining figures in canto 20 are contemporaries, or near-contemporaries of Dante: Michael Scot, Guido Bonatti, Asdente, and a nameless group of women, "wretched, who gave up the needle, the shuttle, and the distaff *e fecersi 'ndivine;/ fecer malie con erbe e con imago"*; that is, they made themselves diviners and, by parallel construction, *malie;* they cast spells with herbs and images. This short canto describes a variety of types of magician as they were known by the end of the thirteenth century, and Dante's treatment of them effectively sums up the theme of this chapter, the systematic condemnation of magic in the thirteenth century.

Simony, the subject of *Inferno,* canto 19, was named after Simon Magus, who was also a commonplace figure in patristic literature, typifying the magician. Like simoniacs, magicians perverted true devotion and became, as Dante says, idolaters, worshipping gold and silver instead of God. Following Aquinas and other theologians, Dante then takes up the theme of divination which, with idolatry and *observantiae*, were linked by Aquinas as three forms of *superstitio*. The first three classical figures, Amphiaros, Tiresias, and Aruns, are figures well known from the poems of Statius, Ovid, and Lucan, respectively; they illustrate precisely the kind of pagan divination—and in the case of Tiresias, shape shifting—that the Church Fathers so vehemently condemned. The fourth classical figure is Manto, la *vergine cruda,* who chose an uninhabited plot of land in the midst of a marsh to practice her *arti*; Benvenuto da Imola suggests that she resembles "one of those female enchanters who sometimes wander nude at night with their hair loose."

The long speech by which Vergil describes Manto serves several purposes. First, Dante the poet permits Vergil to correct something he himself had written in the *Aeneid*—his denial that Manto had founded the city. The role of Vergil in this canto is particularly appropriate, since in the Middle Ages the Roman poet himself had the reputation of being a magician; he figures in the story cited above, told by Gervais of Tilbury, also concerning a magician. But although Dante establishes Manto's role in discovering the site of the city of Mantua, he clears the city of the charge of having been founded by a sorceress. Those who actually built the city were attracted by its defensible position, not by the habits of its first inhabitant. For this reason, they decided to build the city and name it after Manto, *sanz altra sorte,* "without any other sign." Most translations of *Inferno* translate *sorte* as *augury,* and this too is legitimate, as long as the Latin meaning of *sors,* divination by lot, is kept in mind. By his terminology through the speech of Vergil, Dante is establishing a historical fact, but he exonerates the city of Mantua of any association with the practices of its first inhabitant. The final classical figure, Eurypylus, was associated in Dante's mind with Calchas, the Greek seer of the Trojan War. All of the classical figures in *Inferno,* canto 20, comprise the magic arts as these were condemned by Church Fathers and by later writers. Amphiaros saw illegitimately into the future; Tiresias shifted shape and sex; Aruns lived alone (like Manto) and also predicted the future; Manto practiced magical arts besides divination; Eurypylus consulted oracles and associated with diviners. Although Dante had begun to weep when he first saw the diviners, "because I saw our [human] image thus contorted," one of the diviners, Tiresias, transformed the human image, and another, Manto, fled human company, as did Aruns. By *contrapasso,* the diviners are punished by a distortion of the human image which symbolizes their own distortion of human nature through their magical arts.

The next figure, however, is not a figure from classical antiquity at all; it is Michael Scot, the court astrologer of Frederick II, whose reputation as a magician grew during the thirteenth century, in spite of his disavowal of illegitimate magic in the *Liber Introductorius*. Dante places Scott here because "he knew the game of magic frauds," *de le maghiche frode seppe 'l giocco*. Dante probably condemns Scot as an *illusor*, or a *praestigiosus*. Guido Bonatti, although Dante's contemporaries called him a repairer of roofs, seems to have taught at Bologna, and his *Liber astronomicus* was one of the most popular medieval works of astrology, being many times reprinted to the end of the seventeenth century.[45] In his book, Bonatti bitterly attacks those who deny the efficacy of astrology—and evidently there had been many—and goes on to assert the value and proven character of the discipline. Guido, a Ghibelline, is probably placed in Hell because astrology and magic, with heresy, were crimes particularly imputed to the Ghibellines in Italy, just as treason was imputed to the Guelfs. Among the strongest theological weapons that the papal party wielded against their Ghibelline enemies were the charges of heresy (see *Inferno*, 10), astrology, divination, and magic. The tradition of Michael Scot appears to have influenced Dante's image of Guido Bonatti as well.

The nameless women who are the last figures in the canto are perhaps a less well-known kind of diviner. The progression so far has been: classical figures, famous thirteenth-century *illusores* and *astrologi*, and unknown and perhaps humble women who discard their approved role of sewing, spinning, and weaving and pretend to be fortunetellers. This last group is important because it gives us an insight into the kind of magic practiced at lower social levels than the court, the town, and the university. They foretold the future and cast spells, engaging in herbal- and image-magic, probably finding lost objects, making love-charms, or working harmful spells upon their clients' enemies. These women are also important, because they are the social, as the other figures in the canto are the learned, precursors of the later victims of witchcraft persecution. Before the Inquisition was formally empowered to act against sorcerers, Dante the poet knew perfectly well the orthodox penalties to which diviners, astrologers, magicians, and fortunetellers of all kinds and ranks were condemned.

In *Inferno*, cantos 29 and 30, Dante once again deals with topics related to magic, this time in the context of shape-changers and illusors. Griffolino of Arezzo, who had been burned at the stake for being a magician, reveals himself as condemned for being a fraudulent alchemist. In general, alchemy presented problems somewhat different from those posed by astrology, divination, and magic; Dante treats the topic here and in canto 30 under the general heading of perverse deception, whether of alchemy, counterfeit coins, or individual identity. But Griffolino's reputation as a magician suggests the links between fradulent alchemy and other magical practices, for if he had not been an alchemist, he would have been punished in *Inferno* 20 with the diviners and illusors. Dante's commentators make it clear that Griffolino had the reputation, at least, of being a magician. Benvenuto da Imola says that the victim of Griffolino's deception, Albero of Siena, "fecit formari inquisitionem contra eum, qualiter exercebat magicam, quam tamen ille ignorabat."[46] The author of the *Ottimo Commento* states that Griffolino was burned as an invoker of demons and a heretic in faith, *ingiuratore de demonii, ed eretico in fede.* Although the commentators are not absolute authorities on Dante's intention, they provide an excellent view of the understanding of the sinfullness of magic and the invocation of demons that fourteenth- and fifteenth-century scholars might have. Their off-hand terminology, familiar from the invective of the thirteenth century, suggests that by the fourteenth century, condemnation of magicians to the stake was not thought of as unusual, although it may have been infrequent.

Others in Dante's world also incurred at least the reputations—and in one case the accusation—of being magicians, notably Peter of Abano and Cecco d'Ascoli. Although Peter of Abano condemned the varieties of the magical arts as soundly as any critic considered thus far, his discussion of them, his own extensive interest in legitimizing astrology, and his knowledge of poisons contributed to his formidable reputation in the sixteenth century as one of the most powerful of Italy's magicians.[47] Cecco d'Ascoli, who was burned by the Inquisition at Florence in 1327 for the crime of astrology, is in many ways a more important figure than Peter of Abano.[48] Cecco was, as John Mundy has pointed out, the first *magister* to be put to death for his opinions. Although Cecco's astrological works seem relatively innocuous, Villani's *Chronicle* suggests a more familiar reason: the jealousy of a fellow courtier of Cecco's at the court of Charles of Calabria, then Duke of Florence. Although Cecco appears to have been somewhat more determinist an astrologer than was altogether safe in the fourteenth century, it was probably a combination of an earlier condemnation and his resuming his forbidden art, along with the rivalry of a fellow courtier, that brought about his downfall.

In the career of Cecco d'Ascoli, it is important to note that one hitherto powerful protection of even the most criticized academic thinkers of the twelfth and thirteenth centuries, their immunity from the stake, was insufficient to save him, although it might have if he had been at Paris or elsewhere. His first condemnation came while he was teaching at Bologna, and that was only a sentence forbidding him to teach or practice astrology again. Cecco's case also emphasizes, as do the figures in Dante's *Inferno* and the later reputation of Peter of Abano, the uniform condemnation of magic and astrology in thirteenth-century sources. This condemnation was supported by formidable theological and legal structures and reiterated, as we will see in the next chapter, by a series of trials that once and for all announced the *crimen magiae* and completed the juridical framework of the condemnation of the magical arts.

Perhaps the classic figure of the scholar who was tainted with the reputation of being a magician himself because he wrote extensively about magic, was Arnald of Villanova.[49] A learned and complex man, Arnald was a physician respected by kings and popes, a "lay theologian" whose prophecies and proposals for reform brought him afoul of the Inquisition in France, Aragon, and Rome. A prolific writer, Arnald wrote several works directed against the claims of sorcerers. In these works he criticizes magic as sharply as Aquinas or William of Auvergne before him. His attack on sorcery, like those of Aquinas, are two-pronged. First, Arnald agrees with the theologians that the demons cannot be compelled by magicians, but receive them in order to assure their and others' damnation. Second, he attacks the physical basis for the magicians' claims, denying that lower substances can be compelled by the mind or by demonic power given by the demons to humans. The treatise *De improbatione maleficorum*, written by Arnald at the request of Bishop Jasbert of Valence to refute the claims of two Provençal monks that they could control the demons and use them for beneficial purposes, denounces the *curiositatem eorum, qui . . . garriunt asserendo se habere potentiam demones compellendi.*[50] Arnald begins by attacking the physical basis of beliefs that demons can be compelled by human intelligence; then he denies that any force except God can compel demons, and that God may give this force to holy men, but certainly not to magicians, *peccatores . . . exercentes nequissimi.* Arnald denies the powers of words, signs, images, blood, corpses, suffumigations, performed costumed or naked, in deserted buildings or other artificial places, *quoniam omnium talium fabricator est ipse demon,* and only deceived or simple people believe in them.

The frauds and invocations of magicians, the tricks of Griffolino, the increasing danger to court astrologers, and the denunciation of the Provençal monks by Arnald of Villanova, mark a new development in the history of the *crimen magiae*: the willingness and ability of authorities to prosecute such offenders, and the general agreement among theologians, lawyers, scientists, and legitimate astrologers that they should be prosecuted. The fourteenth century opened with the increasingly frequent prosecution of magicians.

NOTES

1. Lynn Thorndike, *History of Magic and Experimental Science* (New York, 1923-58) 2:436-57. See also Servus Gieben, "Bibliographia universa Roberti

Grosseteste ab anno 1473 ad annum 1969," *Collectanea Franciscana* 39 (1969): 362-418, and A. C. Crombie, *Robert Grosseteste and the Origins of Experimental Science, 1100–1700* (Oxford, 1952). The *De prognosticatione* is in L. Baur, ed., *Die philosophischen Werke des Robert Grosseteste, Bischoffs von Lincoln* (Münster, 1912). Relevant parts of it are translated and discussed in Richard C. Dales, *The Scientific Achievement of the Middle Ages* (Philadelphia, 1973) pp. 151-56.

2. Dales, *Scientific Achievement*, pp. 152-55.

3. Ibid., p. 153.

4. Ibid., p. 155.

5. Thorndike, *History*, 2:307-37; Lynn Thorndike, *Michael Scot* (London, 1965), esp. pp. 80-121; Ernst Kantorowicz, *Frederick the Second, 1194–1250*, trans. E. O. Lorimer (reprint ed., New York, 1957), pp. 339-68.

6. Thorndike, *Michael Scot*, pp. 80-88.

7. Marie-Thérèse d'Alverny, "La survivance de la magie antique," in *Miscellanea Medievalia, I: Antike und Orient im Mittelalter*, ed. P. Wilpert (Berlin, 1962).

8. One reason for the uniform medieval condemnation of *praestigiosi*, makers of illusions, was the analogy between their actions and those of demons, who parodied true creation and were described throughout the twelfth and thirteenth centuries and later as creating their *praestigium* in order to deceive mortals, capturing or at least endangering their souls. Hence, the punishment of counterfeiters and shapeshifters in Dante's *Inferno, canti* 29–30, and the focus upon illusion in such later works as Johann Weyer, *De Praestigiis Daemonum* (Basel, 1563), discussed below, in Chapter 6. The theme was taken up in a different sense in Thomas Mann's novella *Mario and the Magician*.

9. Thorndike, *Michael Scot*, pp. 119-20.

10. Dante *Inferno* 20, 11. 116-17.

11. Dales, *Scientific Achievement*, pp. 155-56.

12. Thorndike, *History*, 2:616-91.

13. Ibid., pp. 214-304.

14. Ibid., pp. 338-71. The text of William used here is *Gulielmi Alverni episcopi Parisiensis . . . Opera Omnia*, 2 vols. (Paris, 1674): *De legibus*, vol. 1, fol. 18-102; *De universo*, vol. 1, ff. 593-806, vol. 2, fol. 807-1072. See also d'Alverny, "La Survivance de la magie antique." The best recent study of William, however, is the article by Beryl Smalley, "William of Auvergne, John of La Rochelle, and St. Thomas Aquinas on the Old Law," in *St. Thomas Aquinas, 1274–1974, Commemorative Studies*, 2 vols. (Toronto, 1974), 2:11-72, esp. pp. 27-46 with recent bibliography.

15. *De legibus*, fol. 78.

16. Ibid.

17. I intend to produce an extensive study of the medieval history of *curiositas*. There is a good preliminary bibliography in Jean-Claude Fredouille, *Tertullien et la conversion de la culture antique*, (Paris, 1972), p. 413, n.1, to which should be added Hans Blumenberg, *Die Legitimität der Neuzeit* (Frankfurt, 1966). See, e.g., T. F. Crane, *The Exempla . . . of Jacques de Vitry* (re-

print ed., Liechtenstein, 1967), pp. 12-13. On the tradition of *curiositas* as a vice, see Gregory the Great, *Homiliarum in Evangelia,* book 2, Hom. xxxvi (PL 76, col 1268c), commenting on Luke 14:16–24. For a twelfth-century Cistercian use of the term, see Meyer Schapiro, "On the Aesthetic Attitude in Romanesque Art," in *Art and Thought: Issued in Honor of Dr. Amanda K. Coomaraswamy* (London, 1947), pp. 130-50; reprinted in Meyer Schapiro, *Romanesque Art: Selected Papers,* vol. 1 (New York, 1977), pp. 1-27. The section of Blumenberg's *Die Legitimität der Neuzeit* dealing with *curiositas* has been recently reprinted and expanded separately under the title *Der Prozess der theoretischen Neugierde* (Frankfurt, 1973). See also Horst Rüdiger, "Curiositas und Magie. Apuleius und Lucius als literarische Archetypen der Faust-Gestalt," in *Wort und Text. Festschrift für Fritz Schalk* (Frankfurt, 1963), pp. 57-82.

18. The text is in H. Denifle and A. Chatelain, ed., *Chartularium Universitatis Parisiensis,* Vol. 1 (Paris, 1889), No. 473, p. 543. See E. Gilson, *History of Christian Philosophy in the Middle Ages* (New York, 1955), pp. 402-9 and notes; F. Van Steenberghen, *La philosophie au XIIIe siècle* (Louvain-Paris, 1966), pp. 377-78, 483-93. See below, Chapter 6 for the condemnation of 1398. On Robert Kilwardby's own condemnation of magic, based on his reading of Hugh of St. Victor, see above, Chapter 3, part 1.

19. Henry Ansgar Kelly, *The Devil, Demonology and Witchcraft* (New York, 1974); Jeffrey Russell, *Witchcraft in the Middle Ages,* pp. 101-32; Norman Cohn, *Europe's Inner Demons: An Enquiry Inspired by the Great Witch-Hunt* (New York, 1975), pp. 60-75; Henry Charles Lea, *Materials Toward a History of Witchcraft,* ed. and comp. Arthur Howland (Phila., 1938), 1:34-105. Jeffrey B. Russell, *The Devil: Perceptions of Evil from Antiquity to Primitive Christianity* (Ithaca, 1975).

20. I am grateful to Professor Kennan for discussing some of the implications stated here with me.

21. Lester Little and Barbara Rosenwein, "Social Meaning in Monastic and Mendicant Spiritualities," *Past and Present* 63 (1974): 4-32.

22. Barbara Rosenwein, "Feudal War and Monastic Peace: Cluniac Liturgy as Ritual Aggression," *Viator* 2 (1971): 129-57.

23. H. von E. Scott and C. C. Swinton Bland, trans., *Dialogus Miraculorum,* 2 vols. (London, 1929), 1:313-17.

24. Russell, *Witchcraft,* pp. 101-32. The problems of late twelfth-century demonology were many. Orthodox theologians had to veer away from any indication that the devil was the "prince of this world," lest they hew too closely to Manicheism. Scholastic Aristotelians inclined to explain the powers of the devil in the natural world by emphasizing demonic physiology; there was certainly increased discussion of human commerce with the devil, linked to a sense of personal temptation.

25. R. W. Southern, *The Making of the Middle Ages* (New Haven, 1953).

26. Thorndike, *History,* 2:517-92.

27. Charles E. Hopkin, *The Share of Thomas Aquinas in the Growth of the Witchcraft Delusion* (Philadelphia, 1940).

28. Ibid., p. 177.

29. Ibid., passim; see also Thorndike, *History*, 2:593-615.

30. Aquinas *Expositio in Job*, c.1, *lect*, 3, *ad fin.*

31. Hopkin, *Witchcraft Delusion*, pp. 81-127.

32. Ibid., pp. 87-88.

33. Quodlibet XI, Quaestio 9, art. 10, *Utrum maleficia impediant matrimonium*, Thomas Aquinas, *Opera Omnia*, vol. 9 (Parma, 1859), p. 618. See the connection of the whole *quodlibet* with the discussions of Hostiensis above.

34. Aquinas *Summa theologiae*, pt. 2, q. 100, membr. 2, art. 1.

35. Cited in the edition of Venice, 1595.

36. *Quinque compilationes Antiquae*, ed. Ae. Friedberg (Leipzig, 1882), lib. 5, title 17, p. 60.

37. Ibid., lib. 5, title 9, p. 184.

38. Ibid., lib. 4, title 15, *De frigidis et maleficiatis*, deals with marital impotence. See above, Chapter 3, n.29 for references.

39. *Bernardi Papiensis . . . Summa Decretalium*, ed. E. Th. Laspeyres (Regensburg, 1860), ad 5.17, pp. 241-43. See also ad 4.16, pp. 175-80.

40. *Liber Sextus* 5.2.8.

41. *Johannes Andreae in quartum Decretalium Librum Novella Commentaria* (Venice, 1581) ad 5.21 *De sortilegiis*.

42. *Sancti Raymundi de Pennafort . . . Summa* (Verona, 1744), lib. 1, title 11 *De sortilegis*, pp. 102-9.

43. Ibid., p. 107.

44. All references are to the edition of Charles Singleton, 6 vols. (Princeton, 1970).

45. See Thorndike, *History*, 2:825-40.

46. Singleton, *Inferno*, 2: *Commentary*, pp. 535-37.

47. Thorndike, *History*, 2:874-947.

48. Ibid., 948-68.

49. Thorndike, *History*, 2, 841-61; P. Diepgen, "Arnaldus de Villanova de improbatione maleficorum," *Archiv für Kulturgeschichte* 9 (1911): 385-403.

50. Diepgen, Arnaldus de Villanova," p. 388.

5

The Sorcerer's Apprentice

THE GROWING APPEAL OF MAGIC

In 1256 a book of magic, since known as *Picatrix,* was said to have been translated into Spanish from Arabic at the order of Alfonso X of Castile.[1] Although the exact date of the translation into Latin is uncertain, the text is important because it presents a formidable defense of magic, impugning only the evil intentions of those who employ it. *Picatrix* has been termed by Thorndike a "work of astrological necromancy," since its principal aim is to explain the use of astrological images and the procedures for invoking demons. In its defense of magic, *Picatrix* also defends the magician. The purity of character, years of study, chastity, and devotion to the art required of the magician suggests that magicians, like professors, knights, and guild members, were considered members of a particular calling and made particular demands upon their initiates. Learning and purity are perhaps the most emphasized qualities, for the ignorant, unstudied, or amateur magician runs the risk of being destroyed by the very forces he pretends to command. This is one of the first appearances of the type of the sorcerer's apprentice, which becomes more familiar in the following centuries, in law and literature alike. The aims of the magic described in *Picatrix* are by now conventional: gain, affection and favor, erotic compulsion, thaumaturgy, weathermaking, and the creation of wondrous illusions.

Another thirteenth-century work that strongly defends magic was itself among those condemned by William of Auvergne, the *Liber Juratus,* or *The Sworn Book of Honorius,* so-called because its compiler, allegedly Honorius of Thebes, insisted that it be passed down only to those who swear that they will observe its secrecy.[2] The preface states that the pope and cardinals have wrongfully condemned the magicians on the grounds that magicians and necromancers "were injuring everyone, transgressing the statutes of holy mother church, making invocations and sacrifices to demons, and dragging innocent people down to damnation by their marvelous illusions." The magicians deny these charges, countering them with an idea already seen in *Picatrix,* that only the learned, disciplined, and pure of heart can be magicians. The magicians have therefore decided to condense their volumes of magic books into a single volume, and Honorius of Thebes has performed the vast labor. The product of his work is the *Liber Juratus.* The work itself makes strong claims, and it is perhaps the ultimate in what thirteenth-century moralists delighted to call *curiositas.* It pretends to reveal all secret knowledge, the prediction of future events, the control over demons, and all other occult sciences. Its claims are so comprehensive and so recondite that Thorndike cites it as an example of that magic condemned by St. Augustine:

[True miracles] . . . were achieved by simple faith and devout confidence, not by spells and charms composed according to the rules of criminal curiosity, the craft which is called magic or *goeteia,* a detestable name, or by the more honorable title of theurgy. For men try to distinguish between practitioners of illicit arts who are to be condemned, classing some as sorcerers [*malefici*], vulgarly so-called and concerned with *goeteia,* and other designated as praiseworthy, performing the practice of theurgy. In fact both types are engaged in the deceptive rites of demons, wrongly called angels.[3]

The fourth-century defenders of magical practices evoked the same condemnation from Augustine as their thirteenth-century counterparts evoked from William of Auvergne, Albertus, Aquinas, and Arnald of Villanova.

The accusations of moralists, theologians, canon lawyers, and such figures as Arnald of Villanova appear to have been based on fact as well as upon general fear. The observations of Grosseteste and William of Auvergne that they had handled magical and astrological books at Paris and Oxford late in the twelfth century is echoed by many more writers in the late thirteenth century. *Picatrix* and the *Liber Juratus* are merely two of the most eloquent defenses of magic that the thirteenth century produced. There were others, and there were those who read them and practiced what they taught—not only miscalculating court astrologers and physicians like Arnald of Villanova, Peter of Abano, and Cecco d'Ascoli, but lesser-known figures with less learned books whose presence is attested to in a large number of court records dating from the end of the thirteenth century. Often, they worked in the service of powerful ecclesiastical or temporal figures, but the power of their masters failed to save most of them once they were caught, and they often took the brunt of punishment from which their employers were sometimes spared. As *Picatrix* and the *Liber Juratus* indicate, the appeal of magic grew in the thirteenth century, and the crime of magic entered both spiritual and temporal courts.

MAGIC AND POLITICAL POWER: THE DEMIMONDE OF THE THIRTEENTH-CENTURY

In the mid-twelfth century, as noted in Chapter 2, John of Salisbury, Walter Map, and other moralists began to denounce a new set of vices, the vices peculiar to the court society that was just taking shape around them. In the *Policraticus,* John of Salisbury had warned that magicians, diviners, and soothsayers were particularly tempting to courtiers, and, much to John's dismay, courtiers were actively consulting them. By the end of the thirteenth century, the magician's skills, or at least his litera-ture, had increased immensely. Besides Caesarius of Heisterbach's clerical invokers of demons, William of Auvergne's academic magicians, and Arnald of Villanova's Provençal monks, there appeared in thirteenth-century courts another group of magicians. Those figures, whose history has often been obscured by the political interest in the events they helped to cause, found in the courts of the thirteenth century a particularly hos-pitable welcome. In order to understand the appeal of courts for magi-cians, apart from those observations made by John of Salisbury and others a century earlier, we must first consider the nature of courts themselves.

John of Salisbury was not, of course, the only writer who denounced the atmosphere of the court. Aside from many thirteenth-century moralists, one need only indicate the references to courts that run through Dante's *Divine Comedy,* particularly the moving and bitter soliloquy of Pierre de la Vigne in *Inferno,* canto 13. The climate of envy, deceit, the struggle for precarious favor, the fate that hung on a ruler's whim or impulse, and the difficulties that lay in wait for honest counsellors form a major, although generally unstudied theme of the *Comedy.*[4] In one or another similar form they constitute a literary genre that extends down at least to More's *Utopia* and into the seventeenth century.[5] Moralists and critics of the court tended to turn much of their literature of complaint and satire into conventional invective. On the other hand, the institution of the court and its life corresponded genuinely to many of the ills and

vices of which it was accused. And it was in the world of the court that
the earliest prosecutions on charges of magic took place.

By the late twelfth century, most of the royal and princely courts of
Europe were growing out of the rudimentary itinerant households of the
tenth and eleventh centuries. The legitimacy and history of the ruling
dynasty was a matter of pride and interest to the court, and the wealth
and splendor of the court testified to the power of its ruler. At the center
of the court stood the lord—whether noble, bishop, pope or king, his
servants and family; these were surrounded by others who attended
court either by right or by influence. Seen as a household, the court was
staffed with domestic servants and their supervisors, each with clearly
defined functions. Seen as a center of political authority, however, even
domestic servants might wield power far beyond their status because of
their friendship, connections, or simple proximity to the lord. Although
the thirteenth century witnessed the rise to power of great officers of
state, the lords of courts just as frequently listened to individual favorites
who often had no explicit authority. The court and its ruler were the
center of power, favor, wealth, and security, but the people who attended
court or worked there found that these gifts did not always circulate
through clearly marked channels, but were instead subject to obscure
influences, inexplicable favorites, momentary passions, the "hissings and
murmurings" not only of magicians, but of blood relatives, favorites,
mistresses, friends, clerics, and attendants. Throughout the world of the
court there existed both a system of clear and unambiguous authority
and command and a system of subtle and pervasive influences that
corresponded to no known rank, status, title, or legitimate claim to power.
These systems were delineated more and more clearly in the course of
the thirteenth century. In their midst a shrewd and intelligent ruler might
exploit these two systems to strengthen his own position and widen his
access to circles outside the court, as the ablest Byzantine emperors had
done since the sixth century. Trapped within two conflicting systems of
power, however, a weak or insecure ruler might be victimized by both.
This parallel existence of formal and informal systems of power is the
first distinctive feature of the medieval court.

In addition to the ambiguities of power and influence at the court,
thirteenth-century rulers were also in the process of transforming the
nature of the principality and kingdom itself, usually in favor of a cen-
tralized royal administration with a public, rather than a private, domestic
character. Thus, within the principality, the claims of the prince were
becoming increasingly novel and challenging the traditional reservoirs of
power and authority that traditionally lay outside the control of the king
himself, whether vested in independent ecclesiastical properties, the

landed wealth of great families, the privileges of corporations and towns, and even the *libertas ecclesiae*. Churchmen and great lay lords alike found themselves either servants of the new central authority or outside it completely. In spiritual and temporal affairs, the court and central authority created its own servants, far more pliable and loyal than mighty subjects with power bases of their own. The household clergy of the king—such as the Dominicans that surrounded the royal household in Paris—and the growing number of bureaucrats, often of humble birth and dependent upon the ruler alone for their advantage, could serve royal interests more efficiently than quasi-independent prelates and lords who could withdraw in times of danger or disfavor to their own virtually independent domains.

The affairs of thirteenth-century courts were not, however, entirely governmental. Royal pastimes included hunting, entertaining, and conspicuously maintaining the visible style of a great prince. These occupations drew more people into the world of the court: huntsmen, grooms, actors, jugglers, mimes, the *histriones* against whom moralists had complained since the eleventh century, singers, poets, musicians, and artists. Landless and penniless knights came as well, to compete in tournaments. Courts included scholars, clerics of all sorts, often astrologers, physicians, and usually young people in service as pages and esquires. At its fullest, the thirteenth-century royal court was packed with people from all social ranks and occupations, and since government was the court's primary business, it was difficult to keep the different realms of the court separated.

The social reality of the court is important because it served as a setting in which particular political tensions and problems came to the fore. Although thirteenth-century kings were slowly turning their power into public power, they did so only at the expense of other traditional forms of power. Since criticism of the king was ill-advised, if not impossible, criticism instead was aimed at those around the ruler, particularly those who appeared to have done nothing to warrant the royal favor and the consequent power it brought them. "The king's wicked advisors" became a common motif of royal criticism, one that exonerated the king from direct blame and shifted many peoples' hostility over political change onto the shoulders of the king's servants.[6] In addition to the problem of criticism and political tension, the court also served as a mirror of succession crises within the dynasty. In spite of the centralizing of both political theory and institutions, the succession to the crown still partook of domestic law. Legitimate and illegitimate claimants to the throne, as well as those in junior and cadet branches of the royal house who might have a claim to succeed, should anything unexpected happen to the normal course of heirs, all frequented the court as well. General political tensions and succession problems were but two of the larger political issues that plagued royal courts, but they are sufficient to indicate how the daily atmosphere of the court—part domestic household, part public center of government—provided a particular kind of arena in which larger public issues worked themselves out in particular ways.

One of these ways was public criticism. The literature of complaint and satire has been well researched, as has the homiletic literature of the thirteenth and fourteenth centuries and the more formal and permissible kinds of complaints, the *gravamina* submitted by convocations of bishops and the requests submitted by councils and assemblies. These forms of dissent and criticism remained well within the formal channels of public life. They say little to the question at hand. Other forms of criticism, however, were more effective. Gossip, slander, defamation, and other varieties of influencing those in power flourished in the courts as nowhere else. Favor at court could wax and wane unpredictably even in the best and most open of circumstances. Such circumstances of court life might be explained by obvious reasons, but the court's potential for deviousness and obscurity also suggested other explanations. The types of the wicked advisor, the over-influential favorite, the treacherous queen, the envious prince, and the ambitious parvenu all fill the literature of the courts, and these types, far from being exclusively literary commonplaces, actually reflect some of the political and personal circumstances that the inhabitants of royal courts faced. It is among these surroundings that the sorcerers and their apprentices found a place late in the thirteenth century, although, if we are to believe John of Salisbury, they had been drawn to the court at least a century earlier.

The courts of the thirteenth century, like the universities and the cities, generated not only a population that was designated according to the function of its particular members, but also a *demimonde*—in the broadest sense of that term, the sense used by Peter Brown when he discusses the rhetors, charioteers, holy men, and sorcerers of the fourth and fifth centuries.[7] Poets and artists, physicians and astrologers, ladies and gentlemen in waiting, meteorically rising favorites, and itinerant holy men, clerics, and various forms of entertainers may be said to constitute this *demimonde*. At home in the court, they often served figures inside and outside the world of the court as advisers, gossips, go-betweens, panders, and confidants. Their ambiguous social status served as a bridge between courtiers and the world outside the court. Their positions gave them great mobility and access to both information and influence. For those whose interest was the advancement of self and often corresponding harm to others, the *demimonde* was indispensable. In an atmosphere of factionalism, struggles for favor, ambition, intense personal likes and dislikes, the *demimonde* constituted the personnel at the disposal of those who wished to take advantage of the informal and devious means of acquiring power and favor. And the *demimonde,* wholly outside of any role its members may have played in the prevalence of sorcery at the court, was also an object of moral criticism and satire. The train of a strange queen brought even more distasteful figures into court; the friends of a prince, the current spiritual or astrological advisers of the lord, and the changing population of artists and entertainers replenished not only the *demimonde* of the court in reality, but provided ever new occasions for denunciations of court life.

The role of this *demimonde* has never been of great interest to historians, in one sense at least because it probably had little to do with the traditional and formal affairs of state. We do not notice it in war, nor in fiscal affairs, nor at the great court ceremonies and the operation of the law courts. Rather, it served the individuals of the court in their private ambitions and needs, usually behind the scenes, often secretly. Its very value was its mobility, usefullness, position, ambiguous status, and ubiquity. And in return, it was protected, patronized, and enriched by those it aided, at least as long as it did nothing especially dangerous and did not get found out. It linked the aristocracy and others to the magicians.

In a study published in 1972, Professor William R. Jones undertook an investigation into "The Political Uses of Sorcery in Medieval Europe."[8] Jones's richly documented survey is very suggestive of the role played by sorcery at the royal courts of England and France and the papal court between 1300 and 1450. Although Jones focuses upon the manipulation of charges of sorcery by political agents dealing with political crimes, his study is also important as an illustration of something more than the *realpolitik* of ambitious royal servants and conniving kings and popes. Jones' attitude toward the reality of the charges of magic that filled the courts intermittently for a century and a half is sceptical, and he regards the charges of sorcery more as a supplementary accusation than a real threat. As the foregoing chapters indicate, however, it is possible to take a different view. The development of the magical arts between the late twelfth and thirteenth centuries was considerable; already in the mid-twelfth century, John of Salisbury and others were complaining that courtiers were especially prone to employ them; the condemnations of these arts came not only from theologians and canon lawyers, but from many other sources in the course of the century, including no less formidable thinkers than Roger Bacon and Arnald of Villanova; the courts as institutions were particularly vulnerable at the end of the thirteenth century to the kinds of services magicians had to offer. As we consider some of these cases in the following pages, it is important to remember that belief in magic was not mere "superstition" around 1300, that magicians existed, that their books existed, and that there was a widespread fear of them. In many respects, Peter Brown's study of sorcery in the fourth and fifth centuries constitutes a model for the investigation of sorcery at the courts of thirteenth-, fourteenth-, and fifteenth-century Europe.

From the twelfth century, the figure of the historical magician appears in sources that have no reason to deny his existence. In *causa* 26 of the *Decretum,* as we have seen, Gratian posits the not unlikely case of a priest who has been excommunicated as an unrepentant magician and diviner by his bishop; Alexander III's letters tell of clerics accused of divining. Caesarius of Heisterbach takes it for an incidental commonplace that a knight who wanted to call up the devil would find a cleric who knew how to do such things, and Arnald of Villanova's *De improbatione maleficarum* discusses the case of two monks who actually claimed to do what Caesarius's priest did. Indeed, not only had magicians been denounced by the powers that one would expect—theologians and lawyers—but they were denounced by other kinds of scholars as well. *Picatrix* and the *Liber Juratus* made formidable claims on behalf of magic, ignoring the theological criticisms of the thirteenth century, and even purported to elevate the magician to a kind of priestly status and to claim for magic the status of *scientia.* Faced with such a thirteenth-century history, it is scarcely possible to doubt that the accusers of sorcerers in the fourteenth- and fifteenth-century political trials believed that the charges they levelled were real charges and that the accused had in fact committed the actions with which they were charged. It is entirely likely that many of the accused had done exactly what they were accused of doing.

There is, therefore, no reason to assume that the charges of magic in the trials discussed below were either cynical or fabricated, at least insofar as their plausibility is concerned. Thirteenth-century people were well aware of the existence of magic books and magicians who used them. The circumstances of the trials involving political sorcery will be shown to indicate that the particular circumstances in which the charges were made strongly suggested the presence of sorcery, and in fact the trials of the fourteenth and fifteenth centuries appear to have dealt with real magicians.

Peter Brown, following E. E. Evans-Pritchard, suggests that sorcery is best understood as a function of explaining misfortune on the part of those who consider themselves victims. Thus, it is important, for the historian as for the anthropologist, to understand the relationship between the accusers and the accused in witchcraft trials and to understand as well the reason why sorcery accusations are made in lieu of other kinds of charges. Granted, Evans-Pritchard considers only the Azande

people, and Brown only fourth- and fifth-century Rome. In a number of
ways, however, Brown's model seems particularly applicable to the society of the courts of late thirteenth- and early fourteenth-century
Europe. In the first place, Brown emphasizes that the magic practiced
in late imperial Rome was a learned magic, with its own discipline, literature, and professional practitioners. As we have seen in Chapter 1, Brown
argues that the great watershed between antique magic and medieval
witchcraft occurred with the advent of a totally Christianized society
around the end of the sixth century. Then,

In Christian popular opinion, the sorcerer could no longer be tolerated in the
community on the condition that he recanted his *art*: for he was now considered
to have abandoned his *identity*; he had denied his Christian baptism. . . . The
power of sorcery is gained, not by skill, but by a compact, a sealed document
delivered over to the Devil, renouncing Christ, His Mother, and one's baptism.[9]

As we have seen, Brown's model may help indeed to explain the relative
fearlessness of Christians between the seventh and the eleventh centuries
when faced with sorcery. In an age which geared its own legal institutions to the notion of immanent justice, it was understandable that a
powerful and outraged God would strike down a sorcerer, either directly
or through the actions of formidable living saints, bishops, and abbots.
As we have also seen, however, that certainty and security of a completely Christianized world began to slip during the late tenth and
eleventh centuries. The revival of learning brought with it a revival of
learned magic. Although theologians and canonists alike denounced most
of its forms, astrologers and magicians made strong defenses, especially
attempting to bifurcate the magical arts, condemning part of them as
evil, but eagerly defending another part as praiseworthy. By the late
thirteenth century, the learned magician had returned with his discipline,
books, and professional—almost clerical—status. Even careful writers
who distinguished between different kinds of magic, such as Roger Bacon
or Arnald of Villanova, acquired reputations for practicing evil magic;
careless magicians, like Cecco d'Ascoli, were burned. The paradox of late
thirteenth-century magic was that it necessarily ran afoul of the notion
of a completely Christianized society, but it also made strong claims to
legitimacy and learning. The pagan image of the learned magician once
more confronted a Christian society, and that society could not but regard
him ambiguously. As D. P. Walker has shown, the ambiguity between
spiritual and demonic magic persisted down to the seventeenth century.
    The learned magician having returned, some of the circumstances that
drove people to use magicians and to make accusations of magic against
others returned as well. The world of the late thirteenth-century courts,

of course, was not that of late imperial Rome. But some of the features of late Roman imperial life singled out in Brown's discussion suggest parallels with the thirteenth- and fourteenth-century courts of western Europe. First, the late thirteenth century witnessed considerable institutional and administrative centralization of royal government. In France this was achieved by a graded system of lesser public officials throughout the kingdom and a group of able and dedicated royal servants in Paris. In England, although the king had no group around him remotely comparable to the lawyers of Philip IV of France, he had a justiciar and treasurer, and the careers of Hubert de Burgh, Peter des Roches, and Peter des Rivaux in the reign of Henry III illuminate the balance among magnates, royal officers, the bishops, and the king that accompanied and characterized centralization of English government. The great officers of state in England were the objects of the envy of their rivals and the fear of the magnates. Without being exclusively archtypical low-born favorites, they excited resentment against themselves and they attracted resentment that might otherwise have been directed against the king. As Jones and others have pointed out, all of the following were charged with one act of sorcery or another between 1232 and 1307: Hubert de Burgh, Henry III's justiciar; Walter Langton, the treasurer of Edward I; and Adam Stratton, chamberlain of the exchequer under Edward I.[10] These early charges suggest one target of charges of the use of magic: the officer of state whose actions, success, and power threaten to override the balance among competing centers of power. In the case of Hubert de Burgh, his enemies seemed to favor the great magnates; in other cases, the resentment appears to have been directed against individuals whose favor with the king permitted them great power and wealth. Adam Stratton is the low-born royal favorite par excellence, and Edward I is said once to have called out to him, in a remark that reveals much about medieval humor, "Adam, Adam, where is the man I have created?"

These English cases are isolated episodes and suggest the lack of English interest in sorcery much before the fifteenth century. This general lack of concern (except in the fifteenth-century cases to be considered below) parallels England's general lack of concern for the later type of the witch as that type was supposed to flourish on the continent. The extensive descriptions of English cases of sorcery in the thirteenth and fourteenth centuries found in the work of Ewen and Kitteridge all point to a form of learned magic, which, if it is not as elevated as those defended by *Picatrix* and the *Liber Juratus,* is nevertheless a skilled art, one practiced by clerics or learned individuals. The well-known case of Dame Alice Kyteler in Ireland in 1324 suggests principally the opposition between a powerful and wealthy well-connected woman and an English

Franciscan bishop, Richard Ledrede.[11] The long conflict between the bishop of Ossory and Dame Alice clearly grew out of Alice's wealth and power in the district and the wealth of her son. The bishop, allying himself with Alice's enemies, launched the charges of homicide and sorcery which kept Kilkenny in a turmoil for several years. The importance of the Kyteler case is that in it one may observe the sharpening of accusations of sorcery and association with demons characteristic of other episodes of the fourteenth century. What is also noteworthy about the Kyteler case is that it is the only significant case of accusations of magic in fourteenth-century England—and it failed. The bishop of Ossory's charges were comprehensive and sophisticated, but they were insufficient to overcome the local support Alice Kyteler evidently maintained. In short, the Kyteler case, too, has a political air about it, although it falls outside the great cases of political sorcery that erupted in France at the end of the thirteenth century.

The French political sorcery trials fall into two groups. In one group, the king and his servants levelled charges of sorcery against several high ecclesiastics, notably Guichard, bishop of Troyes, and Pope Boniface VIII.[12] In 1308 Guichard was accused of having murdered the queen by means of image-magic and of having used magic on other occasions as well. Like Adam Stratton, Guichard was a royal favorite, and his character and activities appear to have made him bitterly hated by many at court. Accused of using a sorcerer to help him, Guichard, whether he actually used sorcery or not, was the victim of the court, of the milieu in which the use of magic was widely recognized. Philip IV's accusations against Boniface VIII are also part of a long and complex emnity that had its roots in Boniface's Italian affairs as well as in his conflict with Philip IV. Although the charges against Boniface are probably baseless, they mark an interesting step in the conflict between spiritual and temporal authority. During their political quarrel, Philip was able to defend some of his actions against Boniface by appealing to doctrines both agreed on. But Boniface ultimately parted from Philip, and the king of France was obliged to maintain his own security and his control over the French church against a formidable and articulate pope. After Boniface's death, the charge of sorcery was employed because charges of doctrinal heresy would have been canonically difficult to prove and because the other crimes with which Boniface was charged stemmed from traditional antipapal invective of the twelfth and thirteenth centuries. The charge of sorcery against Boniface was, in its way, an ingenious device for attacking a pope who was protected from other charges, such as that of heresy, and whose authority, in theory at least, was superior to that of the king. The accusations against Boniface and Guichard both may have been engineered by Guillaume de Nogaret,

Philip IV's minister, and it is possible that in Boniface's case, they were brought cynically. But in both cases, the charges were plausible. In the case of Guichard, more graphically than in that of Boniface, they helped explain his behavior, his success, his power in the court, and the deaths of members of the royal family. The charges against Boniface also explained his bitter and prolonged opposition to the *roi tres chrétien,* Philip IV.

Boniface VIII was not the last pope to be charged with sorcery, but the most effective accusations of sorcery took place within the French court itself.[13] Enguerrand de Marigny, a rival of Guichard and one of the bishop's accusers, was himself charged with sorcery in 1314. Although originally accused of treason and misappropriating royal revenues, he was soon accused of using sorcery to escape from prison and destroy the king. His wife, his sister and a sorceress were implicated with him. At the same time, Pierre de Latilly, bishop of Chalons, and Raoul de Presles, two former servants of Philip IV, also fell from grace and were charged with employing sorcery. All of these cases, as Jones points out, consisted of attacks on parvenu royal servants by members of the royal family or the high aristocracy. These powerful figures, whose actual authority seems not to have coincided with their natural rank, launched accusations against their opposites: men whose authority was great, but whose social rank was low. In terms of Brown's model, the low-born servants of the crown, whose own status was uncertain and could change at any moment, both made charges of sorcery and were the victims of these charges. Unlike the fourth-century Roman emperors, the kings of England and France could not protect their servants and favorites by placing them in a strictly graded bureaucracy beneath themselves. The power of the royal servants was less specific and therefore more vulnerable to those who hated and resented them. The great aristocrats who engineered the falls of Enguerrand de Marigny and Pierre de Latilly accused them of other crimes besides sorcery, but the accusation of sorcery covered the very real threat that these men posed of somehow managing to return to power, by the same elusive means they had succeeded in before. It should also be noted that the accused were not charged with performing acts of sorcery themselves but of having the assistance of professional sorcerers and sorceresses, people whose presence was well known and who were from the very *demimonde* of the world around the court.

The next round of sorcery accusations in France came in 1316, when Mahaut of Artois, the mother-in-law of Philip V, was accused of having sorcery practiced upon the king in order to restore his affection for her daughter.[14] Erotic magic too was part of the repertoire of the fourteenth-century sorcerer. Jones draws some general conclusions from the nature of the victims of sorcery accusations that are very suggestive. First, he notes that royal advisers, especially those with no personal rank and status of their own, were accused of using sorcery to attain their fortune and power. Second, "members of collateral branches of ruling dynasties, especially the ladies of cadet families, who were the symbols of dynastic controversy, likewise provided the focus for accusations of this kind." In both of these instances, opposition came from those whose own interests were blocked by the accused. The charge of sorcery itself, rather than (or along with) other crimes, was necessary to explain the power the accused exercised over the king without criticizing the king's judgement, and this device seems to have been a discovery of the reign of Philip IV. During his father's reign Pierre de la Broce played a role similar to those played by Guichard de Troyes and Enguerrand de Marigny; but, as far as is known, the accusation of enchanting the king was not made. A generation later, it was. It remains to inquire into the atmosphere that encouraged accusations of sorcery against such specific groups at the royal court of France.

We have already seen that these accusations usually fell into two areas: first, high-born members of the royal family or upper aristocracy made sorcery charges against low-born, but very highly placed and powerful royal servants, usually after the king's death. Sorcery was an explanation for the rise of the favorite, his domination of the king, and the grounds for an accusation of treason. Charges of sorcery also explained the failure of the aristocracy itself to achieve the position held by the parvenu counsellor. Second, ladies of cadet branches of the royal family, as Jones points out, stood to profit from interruptions of the natural pattern of succession, and amatory and erotic magic was a consistent part of the magical arts, one which especially troubled canonists. There is, however, an important third aspect of these trials and accusations: the magicians themselves. The great figures were rarely accused of performing magic themselves, but of using professionals to do it for them. These professionals were members of their own entourage or part of the *demimonde* of the court, and they were very familiar with the unseen workings of favor and danger in the world of the court. It is important to note that they were never the full-fledged sorcerers found in theologians' and scientists' denunciations, although the charges brought against them derived from denunciations of precisely the high and powerful magician. Instead, they were lesser figures—in a sense, sorcerers' apprentices—who were employed professionally because of their skills and reputations. The whole apparatus of denouncing magicians was levelled at these minor servants, hangers-on, domestic magicians, sorcerer's apprentices, thereby putting upon them the brunt of the charge, and often convicting them when their patrons were let off or punished lightly. The sorcerer's apprentices were destroyed in the conflicts of the powerful, having become involved in the affairs of the great and the powerful through their place in the *demimonde* of the court. Their destruction contributed an important element to the thirteenth- and fourteenth-century hostility to magic and to its concept of the magician. It brought the magician into the court—not the court of the Inquisition nor that of the village, but the royal court, where the traditional protected status of those accused of magic no longer helped. Powerful royal or princely patrons could not withstand the command of the royal court. In the case of Mahaut of Artois, in particular, the king himself was willing to make the charges public and stand by the final outcome, so seriously did he take them. When figures like Enguerrand de Marigny, Guichard of Troyes, and Mahaut of Artois could be brought to court, the magicians they had employed had no defense against prosecution themselves. In the first quarter of the fourteenth century a number of groups, traditionally protected against accusation of witchcraft, became vulnerable. Cecco d'Ascoli became the first *magister* to be burned for his ideas and for sorcery; the great figures of early fourteenth-century France were also called to trial on charges of sorcery. When such power and position failed to protect its members from accusation and even conviction, the sorcerer's apprentices had little chance of escaping, and few of them did. The case of Alice Kyteler is important in this context precisely because Alice did escape, if only barely, by exploiting her personal connections and because the charges of Richard Ledrede were not taken seriously. But the charges were ominous, and even Alice's wealth and power only barely saved her from one form of condemnation or another.

By the second quarter of the fourteenth century, the legal machinery of papal and royal courts, and episcopal courts as well, was beginning to accept charges of sorcery and to achieve convictions. The sorcerer brought to court was not, of course, the *magus* of the philosophers. Sorcery had become democratized, and the small magicians who fitted the competence of the courts became the predecessors of the later humble witches. A theory of magic and its dangers and errors that was designed for a learned, dangerous, and powerful sage was applied to lesser magicians in the fearful and insecure atmosphere of the court. John of Salisbury's warning to courtiers a century before was repeated, not by humanist moral critics, but by the most powerful figures of the early fourteenth century, and it was being repeated in the context of accusation, trial, and conviction. The *crimen magiae* was, in a very real sense, "on the books" after the early fourteenth century. Its practitioners were already those from the indistinct *demimonde* of courtiers and servants who sustained the machinery and intrigue of court life. They were charged in the hardest terms extant with political interference. By the early fourteenth century, political structures had become extraordinarily sensitive to inter-ference of all kinds, and the sorcerers appeared among the most dan-gerous enemies of the state. The question of whether sorcery was heretical or not did not need to be asked: it was clearly treasonous, and it attacked society at its most important level, that of the kingdom. It was therefore a legitimate concern of temporal courts, and its first victims brought its practitioners out of the world of the court into the courtroom. And al-though in the trials the magicians looked diminished and hardly like the figures depicted in *Picatrix* and the *Liber Juratus*, or even like those described by Aquinas and William of Auvergne, they were convicted because they were believed to practice the same condemned arts. It was difficult to bring a full-fledged magician into court except in the case of Cecco d'Ascoli, but the great magician in the abstract had been the focus of a unanimous condemnation that was applied to considerably lesser figures with great success. If the shadowy assistants of Guichard de Troyes, Enguerrand de Marigny, and Mahaut of Artois could be con-victed of the crime of magic, any magician could. Anyone accused of *maleficium* could be brought to trial before the secular courts, and, as the fourteenth century wore on, ecclesiastical courts entertained the charge as well. There was no need for an abstract magician; lesser professional magicians did as well, and they were easier to apprehend and convict, for they used their arts on the most vulnerable, and therefore the most apprehensive victims of all, the popes and the kings of France and England.[15]

The first quarter of the fourteenth century did not see the last of the cases of political sorcery in France, but similar cases appeared in greater numbers in England beginning at the end of the Reign of Edward III. The king, again dominated by a favorite—in this case his mistress, Alice Perrers—was said to be enchanted by her at a time when the judgement of the king was in question because of his great age and physical de-terioration. In 1419 Joan of Navarre, stepmother of Henry V, was accused of practicing magic to encompass the death of her late husband, Henry IV. The charges made against Humphrey of Gloucester's wife, Eleanor Cobham—of using magic against the young Henry VI—were similar to those made against Mahaut of Artois a century earlier.[16] By the mid-fifteenth century, England experienced a succession crisis similar to that of France around 1316, and the key figures involved were so powerful that charges of sorcery were virtually the only ones that could safely be made. Again the victims of the trials were the magicians, in this case the clerics Bolingbroke and Southwell and the professional sorceress Margery Jourdemayne. Once again the accusation of sorcery was hurled back and forth among the most powerful figures in the kingdom, but the convictions were of lesser folk, the *demimonde* of the court and the courtiers. In England as in France and Avignon, the charges aired in the highest of courts struck down a few of the mighty and many of their lesser servants. The convicted magicians were clearly from a far lesser social rank than of the powerful figures they were employed by; they came from an unprotected status—they were not *magistri*, royal relatives, or members of the great religious orders. And they did not necessarily function only at royal or papal courts, although it was in those settings that they first became vulnerable to prosecution. Long before the first village sorceresses became witches, the victims of the trials at Paris, Westminister, and Avignon already had created a public image of the magician—one who need not be remote and mysterious but who came from a social order that was supervised and scrutinized by many different law courts and magistrates. The courts concentrated upon the efficacy of the magician's acts, their intention, and the status of their victim, not particularly upon the magician's learning and skill. The magician need no longer be a *magister*, not even a *magister necromantiae*; his skills could be more easily acquired, and behind him, or her, lurked the shadow of the demon. The warning of thirteenth-century magic books had come true: the sorcerer's apprentice could indeed run into difficulty by carelessly or ignorantly employing the art. But the difficulties were far more consequential than being carried off by a demon. They consisted of being brought to trial in a real court by fearful judges.

THE CASE OF THE TEMPLARS

The case initiated in France in 1307 to destroy the order of Knights Templars may be considered as another step in the process whereby accusations of sorcery and related activities were brought into fourteenth-century law courts.[17] This case developed in the light of the general awareness of magic in the late thirteenth century, the particular atmosphere of court life that encouraged both its use and the accusation of its use against certain vulnerable figures, and the trials and accusations for sorcery themselves that began around 1301. The story of the fall of the Templars has been told many times, often badly, infrequently with sense and insight. The best modern versions are those of Mollat, Finke, and Lizerand, and recent years a good secondary literature on aspects of the subject has accumulated. Norman Cohn, in his recent study *Europe's Inner Demons*, discusses the Templar case in the context of accusations of sorcery, heresy, and idolatry as a necessary prelude to later witchcraft persecutions.[18] In this section Cohn's argument will be reviewed and supplemented with other material gathered from the context of this study.

The Templars, like other religious orders, notably the mendicants, were a privileged ecclesiastical corporation subordinate only to the pope. Unlike the mendicants and the universities, which ingratiated themselves with both spiritual and temporal power, by the early fourteenth century the Templars had become an immensely wealthy, cosmopolitan, and independent entity with its headquarters in Paris and its functions partaking far more of the worldly affairs of its banking houses and property than its spiritual or crusading purpose. In a sense, the Templars had lost their one rationale for existence and, as Cohn points out, they neither continued their work in the eastern Mediterranean, as did the Hospitallers, nor did they find a new area of military activity against non-Christians, as did the Teutonic Knights. It may be worthwhile to add that they also failed to cultivate the protection of the king, as did a number of the Spanish military orders. The economic and ecclesiastical advantages of the Templars, like the privileges and wealth of court favorites, generated widespread and sustained hostility among clerical and lay circles alike. Philip IV of France, their great antagonist and ultimate destroyer, is a figure about whom historians still fail to agree. The standard view of Philip's motivation in his destruction of the Templars is that of the king's desire to confiscate the Templar wealth, especially after the ruinous defeat suffered by France at Courtrai in 1302 and the tensions with Boniface VIII. Cohn suggests an alternative view, one that sees Philip as a mystic, possessed of a grand design (inspired by Ramon Lull and others) of combining a vast crusade and conversion mission supported by an army composed of the combined orders of the Templars and Hospitallers and led by a ruler known as "Bellator Rex," who would eventually become king of Jerusalem. Philip, according to this view, would himself become "Bellator Rex/King of Jerusalem," turning the government of France over to his son.

To be sure, Cohn's own work on millenarian movements and the work of J. N. Hillgarth on Lullism in fourteenth-century France strongly indicate that such ideas were in the fourteenth century air, and not only in Paris.[19] The problem in this case is the personality and view of Philip IV, for other schools of thought portray Philip as a shrewd, realistic, hardheaded pragmatist, who would have nothing, for example, to do with such proposals as that of Pierre du Bois, whose *De recuperatione terrae sanctae* displays just the sort of prophetic, reformist millenarian tone that Cohn sees in the grand design.

As the preceding section may suggest, it is necessary to disagree with both of these views of Philip in order to reach some understanding of the reason for his attack on the Templars and the accusations made by him and his officials against them. First, Philip was in extraordinary financial straits after 1305, and his financial demands on his own subjects were followed by the expulsion of the Jews of France in

1306 and the confiscation of their goods. It is difficult to see, as some historians have, Philip's destruction of the Templars as exclusively the cynical manouver of a financially pressed monarch. The studies of E. A. R. Brown and others show that Philip's attitude toward financial problems and the steps he took to alleviate them were shaped by an acute royal conscience and a genuine concern for the morality of his actions and, hence, his own salvation. On the other hand, there were other forces at work besides the debatable grand design that shaped Philip's attitude toward those he thought were a spiritual danger to the kingdom. The credibility, at least, of Philip's beliefs about the Templars is suggested by the trial of Bernard Saisset, bishop of Pamiers, Philip's accusations against Boniface VIII, and the elements of sorcery that we have seen on many minds in the thirteenth century. They were consistent with what is known of Philip's devout and acute conscience, made more acute by the seriousness of the charges launched against Philip himself in his duel with Boniface VIII. The Templars were the servants of the very papacy that had accused Philip of extraordinary crimes and offenses against God and the Church. Philip countered the charges of tyranny and oppression with charges of idolatry, heresy, fornication, and sorcery. The Church that had condemned Philip had to be proven to be not the true Church, but a blasphemous parody of the Christian Church, and the parody Church was that which Philip and his advisers accused the Templars of serving. Unable, and probably unwilling to accuse Rome, Philip contented himself with denouncing Boniface individually, and the Templars as a surrogate Church. The charges against the Templars read like an inversion of Christian belief: Christ was denied, idols were worshipped, sacraments were not respected. The leaders of the order were a kind of surrogate clergy. The initiation ceremonies involved lascivious acts that included homosexuality; the purpose of the order was to enrich itself. Finally, the order met in secret, at night. These charges, spread out over 127 articles, can be compared to traditional anticlerical invective and reformist criticism: antisacramentalism and idolatry directly contradicted the Church's great thirteenth-century emphasis upon sacraments, particularly that of the consecrated host. Idolatry, as we have seen, was a charge launched against the Church by heretics in the twelfth century and against heretics themselves in the twelfth and thirteenth centuries. Idolatry was also one of the most important allegations cited in the growing condemnation of magic and sorcery. This was evidenced especially by the use of book 10 of St. Augustine's *De Civitate Dei* by Aquinas and other theologians. Sexual laxity was a common item in anticlerical invective. Secret meetings were condemned in the thirteenth century as they had been in schools and heretical gatherings in the twelfth. These charges, and the extraordinarily grotesque illustrations of them contained in the full accusations, were circulated throughout the kingdom by royal servants who had had much experience in conveying the king's opinions to a larger public. The fall of Acre in 1291 sharpened Christian consciousness of the divine wrath, which was the common explanation for crusade failures: the sins of the Christians prevented God from favoring them with victory. The sins of the Templars could also be blamed for the loss of Acre. Thus far, the argument suggests that Philip could have conscientiously believed the charges against the Templars without having been either a millenarian visionary or a financial opportunist.

Were the charges true? It is impossible to avoid agreement with Finke and Cohn and to say that they were not. Were they credible, not only to the general public, but to Philip himself? The answer should be affirmative. Philip's conscience, the attack on Boniface and Bernard Saisset, the expropriation of the Jews, the atmosphere of suspicion and frustration at court which lashed out against Guichard de Troyes in 1308, again at the memory of Boniface in 1311 and left a legacy of hostility that turned against Enguerrand de Marigny and Pierre de Latilly in 1314, all suggest that Philip was prepared to believe in the truth of the accusations. Similar, if not as ambitious and elaborate, accusations were made against Beguines and Beghards, and there was an old vocabulary of invective against closed corporations whose activities were carried on in secret.

To fill out the charges, there was the testimony of witnesses and confessions made by some members of the order itself. In these, rather than in the charges themselves, there occur the elements that connect the charges against the Templars with the common beliefs of heresy and magic among clerical and lay writers of the thirteenth century: infanticide, magical potions to bind those who drink them to the secrets of the order forever, lasciviousness, and the renunciation of Christ and the worship of idols. These lesser accusations and confessions link the major charges against the Templars firmly to contemporary beliefs concerning heretics and magicians.

The case against the Templars, like the political sorcery trials that shortly followed it in France, Avignon, and England, brought two major criminal elements into accusations of sorcery: a specific and central accusation of idolatry, which, as we will see in the next chapter, became a major concern in the criminal character of sorcery, and the consciousness of a fearsome attack on a vulnerable Christianity. The vulnerability of Christendom was first declared in the twelfth century at the onset of heterodox movements. It appeared just as the outward expansion of Christian conversion of pagans came to a halt, and it was encouraged by the dream of world reform that inspired Gregorians and heterodox Christians alike. Such a declaration of vulnerability was, in fact, a way toward increased power: as the Gregorians claimed, the Church was vulnerable to the abuses of laymen and wicked clergy. In order to correct that vulnerability the Church had to possess the independence and authority to protect itself. It built those characteristics in its internal strengthening in the twelfth century and in its external dealings with temporal authorities, emperors and kings. By the late thirteenth century, temporal authorities, too, could exploit this sense of vulnerability. England and France complained of their powerlessness to prevent papal exploitation of their ecclesiastical resources; royal authority to tax was regarded as contingent upon a state of emergency, usually an invasion or threat of invasion from without the kingdom, or a revolt within it. Sorcery too threatened the king through the court, and it threatened the king's "natural" advisers by enabling upstart favorites to override their own rights. It threatened ambitious regents or heirs apparent by interfering with the natural order of succession. It threatened whole kingdoms when it was practiced by wealthy, powerful, and independent institutions within the kingdom. Just as heresy was the Church's focus of vulnerability, sorcery was the state's. The presence of magicians and idolaters threatened not only the king personally, literally putting his salvation in doubt, but it also threatened to bring the wrath of God down upon the kingdom. To be evil in early fourteenth-century France in this sense was to do what the Templars were accused of doing, to employ sorcery for personal ends as advisers and relatives of the king were accused of doing. For these were the dangers by which the kingdom measured its own vulnerability. And institutions growing stronger do so by declaring themselves vulnerable, in danger. They learn how to take the appropriate steps to offset that vulnerability, and in doing so they acquire new strengths.

MAGICIANS AND POPES IN THE EARLY FOURTEENTH CENTURY

The accusations against Boniface VIII and the Templars made by the king of France and the scurrilous invective that circulated against Boniface in Italy throughout his pontificate, helped to introduce the idea that charges of blasphemy, sorcery, and idolatry could be launched against the pope himself.[20] Indeed, Clement V was himself the subject of a number of rumors, and Augustinus Triumphus of Ancona dedicated to him a book warning of the grave dangers of consulting diviners and other kinds of magicians. Augustinus' treatise appears to repeat conventional theological and canonist denunciations of these practices. As if these circumstances were not enough to trouble the papacy, the early years of Clement's successor, John XXII, brought yet new difficulties. The move of the papacy to Avignon, not yet clearly a long sojurn, had increased the factionalism among the cardinals and their courtiers and servants; papal finances were exhausted, and the administrative machinery that later marked one of the few successes of the Avignon papacy was not yet in place. In addition, in 1314 and the following years, further trials for sorcery were troubling the royal court of France. In 1317, John XXII faced the case of Hugues Géraud, bishop of Cahors, who was accused and convicted of attempting to take the pope's life by means of sorcery and poison.[21] Other cases of sorcery at the papal court were discovered, and in 1319 Bernard Delicieux was tried and convicted of the possession of magic books, although he escaped a condemnation for the actual practice of sorcery.[22] Virtually from the very beginning of his pontificate, John XXII was involved in the problem of criminal sorcery, this time within the papal court itself.

The case of Hugues Géraud suggests parallels with several of those who were tried around the same time in France. In all cases, professional magicians were accused and confessed and appear in fact to have committed the crimes they were accused of. The magic they practiced was either harmful or amatory, but in both instances it was of a kind clearly forbidden, and explicitly forbidden during the course of the thirteenth century, when its practices and substance became better known. Its condemnation did not impede its development, and although it is difficult to gauge the statements of Roger Bacon and Arnald of Villanova and the "pope and cardinals" of the preface to the *Liber Juratus*, these diverse sources reflect a genuine concern that the practice of magic was proliferating at an alarming rate. This certainly seemed to be the case in the years immediately following 1316 at Avignon. In 1318 Robert Mauvoisin, archbishop of Aix, was charged with magical practices, although he was not convicted. Robert appears to have become attracted to astrological magic during his student days at Bologna and to have continued that interest, along with deplorable incompetence as a prelate, at Aix.[23] In the same year, John XXII condemned several clerics at Avignon for possessing and using the books and instruments of magic. The case of Bernard Delicieux in 1319 was followed in the same year by a letter to the diocese of Poitiers, in which the pope told of a case of sorcery that he had encountered earlier when he was a judge. A woman, accused of sorcery (*maleficium*) refused to confess until she was tortured, when she confessed all.[24] Hugues Geraud was not the first sorcerer that John XXII encountered.

It is not necessary to posit from these cases between 1317 and 1319 that John XXII was particularly afraid of witches. As was the case with Philip IV, he was especially in a position to be victimized by attacks of magicians, and the temper of the late thirteenth and early fourteenth centuries did not require especial fear of sorcerers or excessive "superstition" in order for rulers to make charges of magic. In this instance, Thorndike's scepticism of John's alleged credulity is probably correct, and further prosecutions of 1319 and 1320 uncovered more magicians and instituted further trials. The year 1320 witnessed the uncovering of a plot engineered by Galeazzo Visconti of Milan to kill the pope by means of aconite and image magic. As Thorndike points out, this episode also indicates that Dante Alighieri was acquiring the reputation of a magician, because Galeazzo is alleged to have said that he had tried and failed to bring Dante to Milan to perform the necessary magic.

In 1320 a letter from William, cardinal of Santa Sabina, to the inquisitors of Carcassone and Toulouse urged them with papal permission to undertake the investigation of sorcerers within their jurisdictions:

Our most holy father and lord, by divine providence Pope John XXII, fervently desires that sorcerers, the infectors of God's flock, flee from the midst of the house of God. He ordains and commits to you that, by his authority against them who make sacrifice to demons or adore them, or do homage unto them by giving them as a sign a written pact or other token; or who make certain binding pacts with them, or who make or have made for them certain images or other things which bind them to demons, or by invoking the demons plan to perpetrate whatever sorceries they wish; or who, abusing the sacrament of baptism, themselves baptize or cause to be baptized an image of wax or of some other material; and who themselves make these things or have them made in order to invoke the demons; or if unknowingly they have baptism, orders, or confirmation repeated; then, concerning sorcerers, who abuse the sacrament of the eucharist or the consecrated host and other sacraments of the Church by using them or things like them in their sorcery, you can investigate and otherwise proceed against them by whatever means available, which are canonically assigned to you concerning the proceeding against heretics. Indeed, our same lord amplifies and extends the power given to Inquisitors by the law as much as the office of the Inquisition against heretics, and, by his certain knowledge, likewise the privileges in all and singular cases mentioned above.[25]

In 1258, as noted above, Pope Alexander IV was asked by inquisitors whether or not sorcery came under their purview. Alexander's answer, which was part of a series of statements dealing with the scope of the inquisitors' inquiries, was included in the *Liber Sextus*, Boniface VIII's great lawbook, in 1298.[26] The ordinary gloss to the *Liber Sextus* was compiled by Johannes Andreae around 1300, and Johannes's comment on Alexander's text noted that:

[Sorcery and divination that *clearly savor* of heresy include] praying at the altars of idols, to offer sacrifices, to consult demons, to elicit responses from them, . . . or to associate publicly with heretics in order to predict the future by means of the body and blood of Christ, etc.

William of Santa Sabina's letter specifically charges the inquisitors of Carcassone and Toulouse with carrying out, in effect, precisely the instructions that Alexander IV's letter and Johannes Andreae's gloss issue: the sorcery they are to prosecute is precisely that kind of sorcery that manifestly savors of *heresy*.

In 1323 or 1324 Bernard Gui wrote one of the most widely circulated manuals of inquisitorial procedure.[27] As a number of historians have noted, Bernard's manual says nothing whatever about "witchcraft," but it does mention sorcerers of the kind encountered by John XXII and anticipated by Alexander IV and Johannes Andreae, and it contains a formula for abjuration by a sorcerer.[28] Bernard describes precisely the kind of sorcery condemned in William of Santa Sabina's letter of 1320. As we will see in the next chapter, this view of the inquisitor's duty to prosecute charges of sorcery was continued in the even more influential inquisitor's manual of Nicholas Eymerich, written in 1376 and widely circulated through the sixteenth and seventeenth centuries. It is in Eymerich's manual that the first text is found of a decretal issued by John XXII in 1326, *Super illius specula*:

> Grievingly we observe . . . that many who are Christians in name only . . . sacrifice to demons, adore them, make or have made images, rings, mirrors, phials, or other things for magic purposes, and bind themselves to demons. They ask and receive responses from them and to fulfill their most depraved lusts ask them for aid. Binding themselves to the most shameful slavery for the most shameful of things, they allay themselves with death and make a pact with hell. By their means a most pestilential disease, besides growing stronger and increasingly serious, grievously infests the flock of Christ throughout the world. By this edict we warn in perpetuity, guided by the sound counsel of our brothers, all and singular who have been reborn at the baptismal font. In virtue of holy obedience and under threat of anathema we warn them in advance that none of them ought dare to teach or learn anything at all concerning these perverse dogmas, or, what is even more execrable, to use any of them by whatever means for whatever purpose. . . . We hereby promulgate the sentence of excommunication upon all and singular who against our most charitable warnings and orders presume to engage in these things, and we desire that they incur this sentence *ipso facto*.[29]

Super Illius specula illustrates the vehemence with which sorcerers have come to be condemned, not only in the works of theologians, canon lawyers, and publicists, but in the working law of a jurist-pope. The letters of William of Santa Sabina and John XXII draw to a close the noose left open by Alexander IV, although they do not exceed the injunctions of the earlier pope. Although some historians have questioned the reason as to why either or both of these letters were not included in later collections of canon law, the *Extravagantes*, it would seem simply that they were not necessary. Alexander IV's decretal and Johannes Andreae's ordinary gloss were in no way exceeded by these letters. The letters simply mobilized a permission that was implicit in the earlier papal letter, and by the mid-fourteenth century, inquisitors, bishops, popes, and secular magistrates alike knew very well in what ways sorcery and magic could automatically become heretical. The importance of these texts does not lie in their relation to canon law—except insofar as they were in perfect conformity with it—but rather in the conviction that magic was flourishing and that action had to be taken to stop it. Those who were caught up in the search for magicians, it should be noted, were, with a few exceptions, the same sort of people convicted in France. They were not the high, learned magicians, but their assistants, the small practitioners of the art—clerics, monks, laymen and laywomen, all professional magicians. They were also from the *demimonde* of the court and the town, royal and papal. As the fourteenth century wore on and the charges of political sorcery became diverted into other channels, the charges of maleficent or heretical sorcery continued to be launched without interruption at the same kind of people, usually from the middling and poorer classes of court, town, and clergy. The learned sorcerer had generated the hostility which was vented on the sorcerer's apprentice.

The actions taken by John XXII have been shown to be perfectly consistent with the views of Alexander IV on the Inquisition's competence to try cases of magic. In 1270, a *Summa de officio inquisitionis* gave a formulary for the interrogation of idolaters and *maleficii*.[30] The interrogatory begins with the association of *maleficii* and demonic invocation and it goes on to enquire about love- or hate-magic, necromancy, the observation of auspicious or inauspicious days and festivals, baptizing images, and other magical offenses already clearly condemned in canon law and recognized in Johannes Andreae's gloss as manifestly savoring of heresy. When Bernard Gui wrote the *Practica inquisitionis* in 1323/4, at the height of John XXII's prosecutions of magicians, he too focused on *sortilegium* and *divinatores*. In his manual, Gui included formularies of the abjuration of magical practices and for the degradation of clerics (religious or secular clergy) convicted of practicing magic. In Avignon, at about the same time, the jurist Oldradus da Ponte wrote a *consilium* on behalf of a man accused of magical practices.[31] Oldradus began by stating that "in all crimes in which condemnation may result, there must be lucid and clear proofs." "And if this is true of any crime, it is much more so in the case of heresy, in which at the same time criminal condemnation and civil punishments result and the posterity of the convicted bears perpetual infamy." In arguing for the mitigation of accusations against Johannes de Partimachio, Oldradus argues that "simple *sortilegium*, love potions, and the consumption of an unconsecrated host do not manifestly savor of heresy." He argues that making images in order to achieve the love of a woman pertains more to superstition than to heresy, citing Augustine, *De Civitate Dei*, book 10, and Aquinas to support his claim. He argues that will and intention distinguish *maleficium*, and that although worshipping the demons is indeed giving to another creature that which should be given to God alone, invoking a demon so that the demon may tempt a woman (temptation being, as the Saviour himself said, the demon's function) may be deplorable, wretched, and a mortal sin; it nevertheless is not heresy. Finally, Oldradus, argues, Johannes de Partimachio was infatuated with the woman and driven out of his senses. Furthermore, he points out that Johannes was interrogated by two members of the Order of Preachers, that the testimony against him was often conflicting, that there is supposition of hostility towards him on the part of his judges, and that Johannes should be piously and mercifully absolved of the charge of heresy by his judges. Oldradus's *consilium* is an excellent and courageous lawyer's brief. It makes, as briefs often do, a great many arguments on behalf of his client, not all of which are as strong as others. Oldradus is perhaps on strongest ground in claiming a defense resembling insanity for his client. When he treats theological arguments in attempting to distinguish between true and false invocation of demons, or between simple and, presumably, complex *sortilegium*, he is on far weaker ground. His charge that the trial has used irregular procedures, however, is an important one. As we will see in a later chapter, it became one of the most conspicuous aspects of later trials for sorcery and witchcraft in the sixteenth and seventeenth centuries.

Around 1330, when Zanchinus Ugolini wrote his treatise *Super materia hereticorum*, he too raised the question as to whether inquisitors ought to investigate *divinatores, incantatores, sortilegi, idolatriae, magici seu mathematici*, as well as heretics. Zanchinus cites Gratian's *cap. Episcopi*, but it must be noted that he cites it only to argue against the belief in shapeshifting, and he does not mention the night-ride:

If is indeed heretical to believe that anything outside of God could be divine, or that anything might be made to become, or to change from another thing except by God, who is the creator of everything, as is shown by the said symbol, and in the first chapter of St. John's gospel, and is shown in C.26 q.5 *capitulum Episcopi*, and in the *capitulum Nec mirum*.[32]

Zanchinus goes on to distinguish between licit and illicit *sortes* and defines other types of magic. He then goes on almost literally to reiterate Alexander IV's statement on the competence of the Inquisition to try magicians. Like Johannes Andreae, John XXII, Bernard Gui, and William of Santa Sabina, he agrees that there are many magical arts that clearly savor of manifest heresy and that these are well within the province of the inquisitors. The ecclesiastical punishments for these acts include being denied the eucharist, being declared infamous, being separated from family, and excommunication. Zanchinus, however, also points out that there are secular punishments for magic, citing the *Code* of Justinian, and indicating that the ultimate secular punishment is the death penalty. It is to these texts in the *Code* and to other secular laws that Alexander IV made reference when he said that magicians whose actions do not manifestly savor of heresy should be left to their own judges.[33]

Thus, the first quarter of the fourteenth century witnessed a number of cases of magic in temporal and spiritual courts and a considerable litera- ture ranging from papal letters and conciliar canons, to canonists and moral theologians like John of Freiburg, to lay jurists and lay theologians like Arnald of Villanova. There is nothing in canto 20 of Dante's *Inferno* that would be out of place in this literature, and by the middle of the fourteenth century, the question of inquisitorial competence to deal with magic was well understood and universally approved. The moral criticism of John of Salisbury and William of Auvergne had acquired a juridical dimension and a strong theological affirmation. The magician's most formidable enemy turned out to be the pope, backed by theologians and canonists, clerics and laymen, lay theologians and poets. What is un- avoidable in this period is the unanimity with which all sectors of society condemned magic and the truly formidable strictures against magic that existed in many different kinds of literature. The developing demonology of the twelfth and thirteenth centuries, and the definition and prosecution of heresy had certainly contributed their part to this process, as Russell, Lea, and others have shown. But the *crimen magiae*, itself denounced and defined for several centuries, was sufficient in itself to form the basis of later images and charges of witchcraft. The witch of the late fifteenth, sixteenth, and seventeenth centuries derived from the magician more than from the heretic.

NOTES

1. Lynn Thorndike, History of Magic and Experimental Science (New York, 1923-58), 2:813-24. H. Ritter and M. Plessner, eds., *"Picatrix": Das Ziel des Weisen von Pseudo-Magriti*, Studies of the Warburg Institute, vol. 27 (London, 1962).

2. Thorndike, *History*, 2:283-89; Norman Cohn, *Europe's Inner Demons: An Enquiry Inspired by the Great Witch-Hunt* (New York, 1975), pp. 176-79; D. P. Walker, *Spiritual and Demonic Magic from Ficino to Campanella* (Lon- don, 1958), Index, s.v. "Picatrix."

3. Augustine *De civitate Dei* 10.9; Thorndike, *History*, 2:283. Book 10 of *The City of God* is particularly important here, not only for the reference to *theurgia*, but because it deals with the question raised by the Platonists as to whether men should sacrifice to God or to the *daimones*. Chapters 2 through 8 deal with perfect sacrifice to God as ordained by God and discuss the doctrine of the angels. Chapters 9 through 11 condemn the Plationists' doctrine of demons and place particular emphasis upon the errors of demon-worship. Chapters 12 through 25 return to the theme of the worship of the true God. Chapters 26 through 32 consist of a final refutation of demon-worshipping. The whole book is a major statement on Augustine's part, one that became the basis of later dogma, including that of Aquinas (see above, Chapter 4). On the general importance of book 10, see J. O'Meara, *Porphyry's Philosophy from Oracles in Augustine* (Paris, 1959) and Peter Brown, *Augustine of Hippo* (Berkeley and Los Angeles, 1969), p. 307.

4. The various elements of Dante's treatment of court life, which includes, of course, the life of exiles as guests at court, are scattered throughout the *Commedia*. See, e.g., *Inferno*, 4, 5, 13, 18, 26-28, 34; *Purgatorio* 7, 11, 20; *Paradiso* 6, 13, 16, 17, 19.

5. J. H. Hexter, *More's Utopia: The Biography of an Idea* (Princeton, 1952), pp. 99-157.

6. See Joel T. Rosenthal, "The King's Wicked Advisors and Medieval Baronial Rebellions," *Political Science Quarterly* 82 (1967), pp. 595-618.

7. Peter Brown, "Sorcery, Demons and the Rise of Christianity: from Late Antiquity to the Middle Ages," in Brown, *Religion and Society in the Age of St. Augustine* (New York and Evanston, 1972), pp. 119-46. See above, Chapter 1.

8. William R. Jones, "Political Uses of Sorcery in Medieval Europe," *The Historian* 34 (1972): 670-87. I am much indebted to Professor Jones for having discussed his paper with me, and for having commented on several of the points in this section when an earlier version was given at the Western Michigan Medieval Conference, at Kalamazoo, Michigan, in 1976. I have profited immensely from his work.

9. Brown, "Sorcery, Demons, and the Rise of Christianity," p. 141.

10. Jones, "Political Uses of Sorcery," and Alice Beardwood, "The Trial of Walter Langton, Bishop of Lichfield, 1307–1312," *Transactions of the American Philosophical Society*, n.s., vol. 54, pt. 3 (Philadelphia, 1964).

11. Most historians of magic and witchcraft have retold the story and included extensive bibliographies; e.g., Cohn, *Europe's Inner Demons*, pp. 198-232; Jeffrey Russell, *Witchcraft in the Middle Ages* (Ithaca, 1972), pp. 188-93.

12. A. Rigault, *Le procès de Guichard, évêque de Troyes* (Paris, 1896); T. S. R. Boase, *Boniface VIII* (London, 1933); A. Corvi, *Il processo de Bonifacio VIII* (Rome, 1948).

13. G. Lizerand, *Clement V et Philippe le Bel* (Paris, 1910); P. Dupuy, *Histoire du differend d'entre le Pape Boniface VII et Philippe le Bel Roy de France* (Paris, 1655); Jones "Political Uses of Sorcery," pp. 674-78.

14. Charles T. Wood, *The French Appanages and the Capetian Monarchy, 1224–1328* (Cambridge, Mass., 1966), with references cited.

15. These figures, who are very elusive and not always obviously associated with the great courtiers, may be important for other reasons as well; below the level of the high learned magician, and well above the level of the village and urban people accused of magic, they may form an important link between high and low beliefs concerning sorcery. They are not mentioned in Richard Kieckhefer's otherwise very illuminating study of the relations between popular and learned culture in the matter of witchcraft, *European Witch Trials* (London, 1976).

16. Jones, "Political Uses of Sorcery," pp. 682-86, with sources cited.

17. G. Lizerand, *Le dossier de l'affaire des Templiers* (Paris, 1923); H. Finke, *Papsttum und Untergang des Tempelordens*, 2 vols. (Munster, 1907); Malcolm Barber, "Propaganda in the Middle Ages: The Charges against the Templars," *Nottingham Medieval Studies* 17 (1973): 42-57, but Barber's conclusions about general magic and witchcraft are not to be trusted. See also C. R. Cheney, "The Downfall of the Templars and a Letter in their Defence," in Cheney's *Medieval Texts and Studies* (Oxford, 1973), pp. 314-27; Cohn, *Europe's Inner Demons*, pp. 75-98.

18. Cohn, *Europe's Inner Demons*, pp. 75-98.

19. J. N. Hillgarth, *Ramon Lull and Lullism in Fourteenth-Century France* (Oxford, 1971).

20. Such charges, as we have seen above, had been launched as early as the tenth century, were reiterated in the eleventh and twelfth as part of the Investiture Conflict and its literary legacy, and reappeared in the fourteenth and extended into the fifteenth. There is no study of this papal tradition of accusations of magic.

21. E. Albe, *Autour de Jean XXII, Hugues Géraud* (Cahors-Toulouse, 1904); K. Eubel, "Vom Zaubereiwesen anfangs des 14. Jahrhunderts," *Historisches Jahrbuch* 18 (1897): 608-31.

22. B. Haureau, *Bernard Délicieux et l'inquisition albigeoise* (Paris, 1877).

23. For background, see general, Thorndike, *History*, 3:18-28; Cohn, *Europe's Inner Demons*, 192-97;

24. J. M. Vidal, *Bullaire de l'inquisition française au XIVe siècle et jusqu'à la fin du grand schisme* (Paris, 1913), pp. 51-52.

25. Joseph Hansen, *Quellen und Untersuchungen zur Geschichte des Hexenwahns und der Hexenverfolgung im Mittelalter* (Bonn, 1901), pp. 4-5.

26. *Liber Sextus* 5. 2. 8.

27. See the bibliographical citations below, Appendix II.

28. Selections in Hansen, *Quellen*, pp. 47-65.

29. Hansen, *Quellen*, pp. 5-6. See also Anneliese Maier, "Eine Verfügung Johanns XXII über die Zuständigkeit der Inquisition für Zaubereiprozesse," in Anneliese Maier, *Ausgehendes Mittelalter* (Rome, 1964), pp. 59-80.

30. Ibid., pp. 42-44.

31. Ibid., *Quellen*, pp. 55-59; S. Leutenbauer, *Hexerei und Zaubereidelikt in der Literatur von 1450 bis 1550* (Berlin, 1972), pp. 53-58.

32. Hansen, *Quellen*, pp. 59-63.

33. See below, Chapter 6.

6

The Magician, the Witch, and the Law

THE THEOLOGICAL BACKGROUND OF LATE MEDIEVAL BELIEF IN MAGIC

When the "typical" figure of the witch was drawn up during the fifteenth and sixteenth centuries and began to be the object of numerous and extensive persecutions between the early sixteenth and the late seventeenth centuries, the means of defining witchcraft and maleficent magic rested upon both theological and juridical bases. This section will treat theological concepts of magic and magicians as they are expressed in several distinct, but related theological genres: biblical exegesis, the *summa* genre of encyclopedic handbooks for the instruction of preachers and confessors, the records of decisions of theological faculties, and individual works of theology from the fifteenth century. Law in its turn recognized and followed theological opinion, but it was administered in different courts by different kinds of personnel, from secular lay and ecclesiastical officials to inquisitors. The second section of this chapter will focus upon the changing legal attitude toward maleficent magic and witchcraft, from thirteenth-century Roman and canon law to the courts of the sixteenth century. The third section will deal with an important area in which law and theology meet, the problem of heresy and the relation of methods developed to deal with it to the persecutions of magicians and witches later. The fourth section will consider the parallel emergence of a new learned magic in the fifteenth and sixteenth centuries and its relation to the witchcraft persecutions. The fifth and final section will sum up the arguments of this book as they bear upon the concepts of magic and witchcraft found in the *Malleus Maleficarum* and similar treatises in the sixteenth century and expressed in the climate of the actual prosecutions of magicians and witches in the sixteenth and seventeenth centuries.

One of the most frequently cited biblical texts of the fifteenth and sixteenth centuries that dealt with magicians (and later was applied to witches) was Exodus 22:18, "*Maleficos non patieris vivere*," "Thou shalt not suffer a witch to live." Like many old Testament judicial injunctions, however, this text, as we have seen above, was not interpreted as literally binding upon Christians in the twelfth century. Although I have not found a specific commentary upon Exodus or other Old Testament texts that can be called the beginning of a new literal interpretation of *judicialia*, there is considerable evidence that the early to mid-thirteenth century witnessed the beginnings of such a process. This made possible the later medieval and early modern literalness that served as a theological foundation for the emergence of later witchcraft persecutions.

William of Auvergne, bishop of Paris from 1229 to 1249, concerned himself in the *De legibus* precisely with the question of how Old Testament injunctions were to be interpreted in the Christian era, a topic that had interested earlier biblical commentators, both Jewish and Christian, during the twelfth century.[1] The traditional Christian interpretation of the Old Testament divided such injunctions into three categories: *caerimonalia, judicialia,* and *moralia,* and the literal sense of these was treated differently by different traditions of medieval exegesis. Beryl Smalley, in her work on Ralph of Flaix and Andrew of St. Victor in the twelfth century, has suggested that already "the literal sense of the Law was evoking a new curiosity." She goes on to suggest that perhaps the Cathar denunciation of the Old Testament as being inspired by the devil may have urged a new insistence on the part of the orthodox that the *legalia* of the Old Testament were of divine origin and therefore, particularly when these coincided with contemporary Christian law or seemed to resemble its precepts, they were to be interpreted literally. The work of Moses Maimonides on the precepts of the Old Testament became generally known in western Europe in the second and third decades of the thirteenth century. Maimonides, too, presented an attempt to rationalize and justify the literal meaning of the legal precepts of the Old Testament. His work was known to William of Auvergne, whose *De legibus* makes a powerful case for the validity of the Old Testament *legalia,* claiming, among other reasons, that such precepts were instituted to combat idolatry, including magic, which still threatens God's people.

Although later thirteenth-century commentators re-emphasized the value of the spiritual levels of scriptural interpretation, other mid-thirteenth-century circumstances perhaps contributed to a tendency to interpret certain Old Testament precepts literally. The Cathar threat, as we have seen, was surely one of these. Another was the growing coercive authority of the Inquisition, supported first by the Emperor Frederick II's constitutions and by other temporal rulers, but soon permitted to exercise the ultimate "release to the secular arm" of convicted and relapsed heretics. The papal decretals of the period have been extensively studied, and by the middle of the thirteenth century Pope Innocent IV recognized that the ultimate punishment of convicted unrepentant or relapsed heretics was death.[2] As these coercive powers came to characterize the inquisitorial office and function, those Old Testament images and precepts that appeared to support such action were cited in decretals, and they may have constituted a point at which theology and contemporary canon law touched and influenced each other. By the fifteenth century, Exodus 22:18 was one of many Old Testament passages quoted in treatises on sermons and other works of theology as applying to the figure of the *maleficus* or *malefica*. Although its command may not have been considered universally binding, conditions in early and mid-thirteenth-century Europe permitted the extreme coercive powers of the Inquisition and encouraged such defenses as that of William of Auvergne of the literal authority of the Old Testament *legalia*. William of Auvergne is not widely remembered from a century that produced Thomas Aquinas, Bonaventure, Duns Scotus, and Albert the Great among many other thinkers, but he was very widely read in the fourteenth and fifteenth centuries, cited by Gerson in his own treatise against the magical arts discussed below, and generally familiar to other theologians and legists as well. Although William did not cite Exodus 22:18 specifically, his citations of other biblical texts, his insistence upon the contemporary bearing of old Testament *legalia* upon such continuing problems as idolatry, and his principle of literal interpretation generally contributed to a new life for some of the Old Testament materials discussed above and opened the door for the harshest strictures of Old Testament opinion on magicians to be employed by theologians, preachers, and confessors between the thirteenth and the sixteenth centuries.

Much of the work of the thirteenth-century theologians and canon lawyers began to be adapted for the use of confessors and preachers by the end of the thirteenth century. These *summae confessorum* or *praedicantium* were often the chief means by which later scholars, preachers, and confessors were familiar with the writings of the great thirteenth-century figures such as Aquinas or Raymond of Peñafort. Perhaps the most influential of the *summae* for confessors was the *Summa Confessorum* of John of Freiburg, written in 1297/98.[3] It was, in the words of

Leonard Boyle, its most recent and articulate student, "the most influential work of pastoral theology in the two hundred years before the
Reformation." The *Summa Confessorum* was primarily a work of theology,
and it was an expansion and modernization of the earlier *Summa de
Casibus* of Raymond of Peñafort, taking into account the theological and
canonist work of the intervening sixty years, particularly the *apparatus*
of William of Rennes of 1241, the theologians Thomas Aquinas and Peter
of Tarentaise and others, and the legal theory of the decretalists. Title 11
of book 1 of the *Summa* deals with the question *De sorteligiis et divinationibus.* John lists the various kinds of divination, including the interpretation of dreams and necromancy, and states that all of these forms and
others like them can only be accomplished by the aid of the demons. As
for their punishment,

Omnis divinatio quocunque predictorum modorum vel alio simili fiat prohibita
est et maledicta a Deo et a ecclesia tanquam ydolatria et infidelitas.

Anyone who attempts to know the future, which is only possible for God,
misapplies the law of divinity to a creature. John then cites Isaiah 41 and
Leviticus 19–20, Galatians 4, and several works of St. Augustine to justify
his conclusion. John goes on to ask whether divination accomplished by
invoking the demons is always illicit. His answer is from Aquinas, and in
the affirmative: pact with the demon is always illicit, and such activity
places the human soul in great peril. By *divinatio,* of course, John of
Freiburg refers to the generic theologians' term for all forms of condemned magic. It is worth noting that by the end of the thirteenth century the condemned forms of *divinatio* include the ordeals of water and
hot iron, as well as the judicial combat.

John notes that the *ars notoria* is also condemned, citing Aquinas as his
authority, and he condemns too the use of astronomical images and
phylacteries. He denounces the beliefs condemned in the *Canon Episcopi*
as superstitions that make the believer worse than an infidel or a pagan
and as instituted by the demons. Although John of Freiburg, like Bernard
of Pavia, notes that the penalty for these crimes in Roman law is death,
he follows Raymond in listing various spiritual punishments, from forty-
days' penance to denial of the eucharist, deposition and degradation of
clerics, excommunication, and imprisonment. In book 4, title 16, John
discusses *maleficia* in the context of impediments to marriage. *Maleficia*
may indeed make a man impotent, and John draws upon the work of
Aquinas and Hostiensis.

The *Summa Confessorum* offers little toward the classical figure of the
sixteenth-century witch, but it presents an extraordinarily impressive and
concise account of theologians' views on the varieties of magical prac-

tices and their universal condemnation. Drawing nearly equally from theologians such as Augustine and Aquinas, Scripture, and canonists such as Hostiensis, John of Freiburg produced a compendium of late-thirteenth-century theological views of *divinatio* and its various forms, cited the punishments in Roman law and contemporary ecclesiastical law, and passed these opinions down through seven generations of theologians, confessors, and inquisitors. Conciliar and synodal legislation of the fourteenth and fifteenth centuries repeated the theological consensus concerning *divinatio* and *sortilegium,* the two generic terms commonly used to designate the various magical arts.

Besides handbooks for confessors, such as the *Summa Confessorum,* the thirteenth and fourteenth centuries also produced handbooks for preachers, of which one of the most extensive was the *Summa Praedicantium* of John Bromyard, probably completed by 1348.[4] In his long article on *sortilegium,* Bromyard points out that those who profess to practice the magical arts err in three ways: they lie, since they are unable to perform that for which they are paid; they violate divine, canon, and civil law, which forbid their practices; and they err in doctrine, thereby becoming guilty of idolatry and superstition. Bromyard accuses most practitioners of these arts of having made at least a *tacita pacta* with the demons, and he cites Aquinas as his authority.

Unlike the *Summa confessorum,* the *Summa Praedicantium* provides its readers with *exempla,* and it is in his article on *sortilegium* that Bromyard repeats William of Malmesbury's story of the witch of Berkeley, as well as many other similar stories. As G. R. Owst has shown, other handbooks on vices and virtues and preaching materials also repeat this and similar stories, and it may be suggested here that one vehicle for the transmission of such *exempla* into the demonological literature of the fifteenth and sixteenth centuries was precisely the genre of handbooks for preachers. In addition to the story of the witch of Berkeley, Bromyard tells thirteen other *exempla,* from Gregory the Great's *Dialogues,* contemporary story collections, Augustine, Peter Comestor, and other sources. Like John of Freiburg, Bromyard criticizes the beliefs condemned in the *Canon Episcopi,* noting that women in this respect are found more guilty of holding them than men.[5]

When Bromyard lists the penalties for *divinatio* and *sortilegium,* like John of Freiburg, he begins by pointing out that according to civil (Roman) law, the penalty is decapitation or burning alive. Echoing Pope Innocent IV's views on the burning of heretics, Bromyard justifies the death penalty in civil law, saying "if those are worthy of death who in various lands and towns suffer death for the killing of the body, therefore those who kill the soul" are all the more worthy of death. Canon law,

Bromyard points out, again echoing John of Freiburg and others, prescribes spiritual punishments.

By the late fourteenth century, papal decretals, church councils and synods, scriptural commentary, and handbooks for confessors and preachers, all have generally agreed upon both the seriousness of *sortilegium* or *divinatio*, and its punishments. All of the definitions, descriptions of various sub-branches of the magical art, and punishments can be shown to have grown out of the thirteenth-century concerns for magic—and the prevalence of practitioners of magic—that began with William of Auvergne. There is perhaps no better summation of theologians' views on magic at the end of the fourteenth century than the *conclusio* on that subject reached by the faculty of theology at the University of Paris in September 1398 and its circulation in Jean Gerson's short treatise on the magic arts.[6]

After a brief introduction, the *conclusio* listed twenty-eight propositions, presumably those which had come before it in various ways, which it declared to be *errores*. In 1402 Jean Gerson, chancellor of the university, issued his treatise *De erroribus circa artem magicam*, apparently an expanded version of a speech he had delivered to medical students at the university. In the speech he repeated the university's conclusions in slightly altered form and listed verbatim the twenty-eight charges cited as *errores* four years before. Although the specific occasion of the 1398 *conclusio* is not known, the theology faculty may have been instrumental in condemning the magician Johannes Barrensis in 1390 (it issued other condemnations of magic in 1425 and 1426), and the *conclusio* was probably the result of the faculty's cognizance, if not specifically of this, then of other similar cases. The university had been strongly involved in the subtraction of obedience from Pope Benedict XIII just four months before it issued its *conclusio*, and in 1409 charges of employing necromancers and *divinatores* were launched against that pope by the Council of Pisa.[7] In any case, it seems clear that the theological faculty was sufficiently concerned with the frequency and danger of magical practices to issue its *conclusio* in 1398 and that Gerson agreed with it, since his own treatises against magic, although not many or long, are unremittingly hostile.[8] Therefore, the opinion of the faculty of theology of the University of Paris, and that of Chancellor Gerson, may be taken as representing the most advanced and widely respected theological thought at the turn of the fifteenth century. Given the nature of thirteenth- and fourteenth-century concerns with magic in scriptural exegesis, *summae* for preachers and confessors, and the decretals of Pope John XXII, it is worth examining the opinion of the Paris doctors on the subject.

The *conclusio* of 1398 begins with references to manuscripts covered with diverse geometrical figures and the names of demons and containing instructions for consulting demons by various means. These, the *conclusio* states, are employed not only to find hidden treasure, but to know secret and hidden things and to learn how to employ images and *maleficiis*. To Christians, to use these texts and to know the practices they describe is to be guilty of *superstitio* and *idolatria* and to become *vehementer suspecti*. The *conclusio* goes on to note that legitimate knowledge is a rightful possession, but that the pursuit of magic places the Christian on a level with Solomon, Dido, the son of Pompey, Saul, and other Old Testament figures who consulted oracles and diviners. "It is not at all our intention to derogate from licit and true traditions, sciences, and arts," but to extirpate the insane errors and sacrilegious practices of fools and beast-like humans. The *conclusio* then goes on to list twenty-eight propositions which it condemns as *errores* or as *error et blasphemia*. The first of these states "that by magical arts and *maleficia* and nefarious incantations to seek familiarity and friendship and aid from demons is not idolatry. *Error*." The second and third articles deal with the idolatrous nature of agreements with demons. The fourth states that it is idolatry to shut up demons in crystals, images, stones, rings, and mirrors. The fifth states that it is idolatry to use the magical arts, even if for a good purpose. The sixth states that it is illicit to repel *maleficia* with other *maleficia*. The eighth states that the Church does not prohibit these things irrationally. The ninth states that God did not compel the demons by magical arts. The twelfth states that the use of prayers or forms of the Christian liturgy for these purposes is idolatry. The thirteenth denies that the prophets were magicians. The twenty-third article denies that there are some good and some bad demons and that there are demons who are neither saved nor damned. The last article denies that the magical arts may lead to a vision of God or the holy spirits.

It is clear that the learned divines of the Paris theology faculty were dealing with the learned and half-learned world of magical writings and magical practices that we have seen take shape since the late twelfth century. It is also noteworthy that some of the practices they list seem to belong both to the world of learned magic and the world commonly called that of "popular superstition." By the early fifteenth century, however, the systematic theological treatment of the occult had tended to homogenize the two traditions. Thus, learned incantations, enticing demons into a crystal or a ring, knowing the names of the demons who dominate the quarters of the earth, and arguing that nonidolatrous pacts could be made with spirits, all derive from the world of learned magic and theologians' opposition to it. On the other hand, the misuse of prayers and masses, the belief in the power of phylacteries, and the use of images and incantations to change someone's affections or well-being are the charges that we have seen listed against both learned and non-learned magicians. The main elements of later witchcraft are conspicuously absent from the 1398 *conclusio*. Except for pact and the details of the practices cited above, the theological faculty of the University of Paris in 1398 knew nothing of what later became witchcraft.

Jean Gerson, who as chancellor helped to draft the *conclusio*, later repeated it in a speech to medical students, probably at Paris, and included it in his 1402 treatise *De erroribus circa artem magicam*. In the *De erroribus* Gerson sets the *conclusio* in a somewhat broader context. He writes that it is time to point out superstitious observances and that physicians are especially responsible to see that superstitions do not creep into their practice or into their patients' imaginations. It is necessary to conquer the pestiferous superstitions of the magicians "*et stultitiis vetularum sortilegarum*" who profess to effect cures by certain cursed rites. Gerson states that demons exist, that association with them in any form constitutes pact. Pact is forbidden by the Old Testament, and here Gerson cites Leviticus 19 and 22, and Exodus 22:18 *maleficos non patieris vivere*. This is the earliest citation of the Exodus text in the context of a discussion of magical practices that I have found.

It is clear that the Paris theology faculty and Gerson personally conceived magic as a form of superstition and idolatry, and they condemned it on these grounds. Gerson elsewhere notes that Romans, Arabs, Indians, and others erred on these questions, but the error of superstitious Christians who are *sortilegi et magici* are worse because they have been illumined by true faith and forbidden explicitly to use such practices. He notes that ecclesiastical judges condemn those guilty of magical practices to perpetual imprisonment, but that secular judges sentence them to the fire. God, Gerson says, sentences them to Gehenna. Both the Old and the New Testaments agree on the matter of pact with demons, and here it may be seen that the *legalia* of the Old Testament, particularly when they coincide with contemporary Christian theology, can be brought directly to bear in their literal sense upon practicing Christians. In the case of the statements of Gerson and the Paris faculty, it is possible to see a theologian's reaction to scepticism about the reality of demons (a concern that Aquinas noted), a growing apprehension of the superstitious nature of many contemporary Christian practices, and a willingness to invoke the authority of both the Old and the New Testaments to condemn magical practices. "Distinguishing the foolishnesses of certain old women who practice *sortilegium*" from the *magici* in Gerson's treatise was an important step in the shaping of the witch-figure, because it identified those women who practiced amatory magic, divination, fortune-telling, superstitious cures, and other semiprofessional occult services (as did Dante's nameless women in *Inferno*, canto 20) with the formidable learned magicians who had been the object of meticulous theological and legal invective since the late twelfth century. Not superstitious practices alone, then, but the identification of these practices with the articulately defined and decribed and condemned magical arts, brought Dante's hapless women and their successors to the attention of theologians and judges, spiritual and temporal, in the course of the fourteenth century.

A few years after Gerson, in 1437, a decretal of Pope Eugenius IV suggests the degree to which a number of different superstitious practices had become identified with the condemnations of learned magic:

The news has reached us, not without great bitterness of spirit, that the prince of darkness makes many who have been bought by the blood of Christ partakers in his own fall and damnation, bewitching them by his cunning arts in such a way that these detestable persuasions and illusions make them members of his sect. They sacrifice to demons, adore them, seek out and accept responses from them, do homage to them, and make with them a written agreement or another kind of pact through which, by a single word, touch, or sign, they may perform whatever evil deeds or sorcery they wish and be transported to or away from wherever they wish. They cure diseases, provoke bad weather, and make pacts concerning other evil deeds. Or, so that they may achieve these purposes, the reckless creatures make images or have images made in order to constrain the demons, or by invoking them perpetrate more sorcery. In their sorcery they are not afraid to use the materials of Baptism, the Eucharist, and other sacraments. They make images of wax or other materials which by their invocations they baptize or cause to be baptized. Sometimes they make a reversal of the Holy Cross, upon which our Savior hanged for us. Not honoring the mysteries, they sometimes inflict upon the representations and other signs of the cross various shameful things by execrable means.[9]

The impact of this movement in theology may be seen in many places, none described more strikingly than Johann Huizinga's treatment of fifteenth-century religious sensibility and imagination. Huizinga contrasts the devotional flowering of piety represented by Gerson and the Brethren of the Common Life, on the one hand, with the violence of these same theologians' perception of superstition, illusions and temptations by demons, and ignorant devotion. Indeed, if there is a single hallmark common to most fifteenth-century theological writings it is the marked sense of human vulnerability to demonic temptation and the description of this sense in lively, colorful, and horrendous detail. Huizinga's treatment of Alain de la Roche (1428–1475) constitutes an eloquent portrait of a theologian who touched both sides of the fifteenth-century devotional movement. Alain, a teacher of Jacob Sprenger, the author of the *Malleus Maleficarum*, accurately reflects the fear of fifteenth-century theologians:

Now, whereas the celestial symbolism of Alain de la Roche seems artificial, his infernal visions are characterized by a hideous actuality. He sees the animals which represent the various sins equipped with horrible genitals, and emitting torrents of fire which obscure the earth with their smoke. He sees the prostitute of apostasy giving birth to apostates, now devouring them and vomiting them forth, now kissing them and petting them like a mother. This is the reverse side of the suave fancies of spiritual love.[10]

We may note that the prostitute of apostasy strongly resembles the "witch goddess of the night" that John of Salisbury mentioned in the *Policraticus*. For John, she had been a delusion of simpleminded folk; for Alain, she is literally real, and she stands at the beginning of that process of articulating the witches' world that produced the *Malleus Maleficarum* in 1486 and the demonological literature and witchcraft trials of the sixteenth and seventeenth centuries.

The spiritual imagery of Alain de la Roche is far from the rational analysis and condemnation of magic in the work of Gerson, but both writers share a sense of the immediacy of the danger which magic poses to Christian society. This sense of immediacy was fueled by such demonological speculations as Johann of Frankfurt's 1412 *quaestio, Whether the power of coercing demons may be acquired by characters, figures, and by the utterance of words.*[11] This long and very detailed treatise is exhaustive on its subject, full of citations of thirteenth- and fourteenth-century theologians and canonists, and its focus is, as that of Gerson, upon the sin of idolatry and magic as a manifestation of idolatry. Demonological literature also reviewed older topics of theological discussion, particularly that concerning the power of demons to move things and human beings from one place to another. It is among fifteenth-century theologians' works, such as the scriptural commentary of Alphonso Tostado of about 1440, that the reality of the night-ride of females is first proposed and proved in detailed discourse.[12] Tostado wrote that the pagan goddesses Herodias and Diana are really demons, as are the animals which some of these women claim to ride upon. Demons cannot perform such actions with humans normally, but they can if the humans wish it and make a pact with the demons. Jordanes de Bergamo wrote a *Quaestio de strigis* around 1470, in which he, as a theologian, undertook to describe the theology of witchcraft.[13] Although Jordanes adheres to the *Canon Episcopi*, he attributes to the demons a threefold power of deluding magicians and witches: through illusion, dreams, and the demonic power of moving people from place to place. Thus, by the late fifteenth century, a new concern with demonology had begun to increase theologians' apprehension of several areas in which the demons' power and presence was thought to be most marked. Among these were magic in general, and certain kinds of magic specifically. The theologians' concern was far more directed at the general categories of idolatry and superstition and with magic as a sub-category of these than at magic alone. In this new concern, literal biblical interpretation, particularly of those Old Testament texts that appeared to address the problem of magic, gave a strong scriptural foundation to modern apprehension. As texts were cited—not only in original works of theology, but in handbooks for confessors and preachers, in *quaestiones* and *conclusiones,* and in various specialized *tractati*—such texts as Exodus 7–9 and 22:18, Leviticus 18–20, and others became literary commonplaces that were always cited in the context of theologians' discussions of various forms of magic.

Not all theologians were equally influenced by these currents. Such writers as Johann of Frankfurt and Jordanes de Bergamo, as well as Jean Vincent in his 1475 treatise *Liber adversus magicas artes,* accept fully the reality of magic, but the magic of which they speak is a form of learned magic, involving the use of baptized images, philters, rings, and other devices condemned from the twelfth century on.[14] Others, such as Petrus Mamoris, whose *Flagellum Maleficorum* was written around 1462, appear to contribute more to such notions as the assemblies of magicians.[15] In general, the theologians' concern was primarily with the nature of magic as a theological offense, and less with the particularities of magical practices. Thus, the reality of magical practices is affirmed, the pact with the demon proved, and the resulting idolatry and superstition condemned. To say, as a number of historians have, that "scholastic theology" created the foundations of later beliefs in witchcraft is, as Hopkin and others have shown, highly misleading. It is in the theology of the late fourteenth and fifteenth centuries that the preliminary steps are taken toward the later definition of the witch; in both its interpreting and teaching methods, in its literary morphology, and in its theodicy, this theology is quite distinct from, although related to, the theology of the thirteenth century. To witness the further transformation of idolatrous magic into witchcraft we must turn first to the law, and then to the problem of heresy and the Inquisition.

THE *CRIMEN MAGIAE* IN LATE MEDIEVAL LAW

The treatment of magic and related practices during the classical period of canon law, 1140–1350, was extremely limited. Not only did Gratian's *Decretum* contain few texts dealing with the topic, but the *compilationes antiquae* and the *Liber Extra* of Gregory IX contributed few additional texts. The teachers and commentators on these texts tended to repeat each other and their authorities. Their chief concern with magic was its role among the impediments to marriage, and marital cases appear to have been among the most common in which lawyers and judges confronted the problem of magic at all. The *Summa de casibus* of Raymond of Peñafort played an important role in familiarizing theologians with the sense of canon law on the subject, and in this respect, John of Freiburg's *Summa confessorum* continued that role for theologians during the fourteenth and fifteenth centuries. As we have also seen, Church councils and synods and papal decretals also mentioned magic, but, except for the text of Pope Alexander IV in 1258 distinguishing between heretical and non-heretical magic, none of the papal materials entered canonical collections. Even the many decretals of John XXII and such later letters as that of Eugenius IV, cited in the preceding section, remained outside the tradition of canonist commentary and teaching. From the early fourteenth century on, however, a number of canonists produced commentaries on Gratian's *Decretum* in the light of subsequent canonist and theological work. Among these were Guido de Baysio, Panormitanus, and Johannes a Turrecremata. Turrecremata's *Commentarius in Decretum Gratiani*, completed around 1445, suggests something of the fifteenth-century canon lawyer's approach to the texts from the classical period discussed in Chapters 3 and 4.[16]

The most striking feature of Turrecremata's commentary on C.26, q.5, *Canon Episcopi* is its extraordinary length, much greater than earlier canonists' commentaries. Second, he deals with such topics as the demons' power to create illusions, the transformation of shapes, and the question of whether "the folly of magicians abounds to a greater extent in the female or the male sex." That is, Turrecremata deals seriously with several topics that Stephen of Tournai, for example, had offhandedly remarked should be left to the poets and philosophers. His discussions are not by any means brief, and he proceeds to each topic by means of the methods of scholastic logic; that is, he states the arguments for one side of the question, then those for his own side and refutes the first set. His discussion of illusions is a professional theologian's discussion, quite foreign to traditional canonists' terseness on such subjects. Turrecremata's conclusions, however, are quite traditional. The devil can create illusions; the illusory character of the superstitions described in the *Canon Episcopi* is reiterated. The superstitious character of belief in night-flights is redefined. Demonic power cannot change the shapes of humans. Finally he argues that such superstitions are to be found more frequently in women than in men, claiming to base his conclusion upon the order of relationship to Christ and the order of temptation invented by the devil, according to the schema of Alexander of Hales. Turrecremata goes on to say, however, that he has never heard a wise man or woman testify to such beliefs, but rather "old, foolish women, sick men such as are melancholics, phrenetics, maniacs, those who are excessively fearful, boys and that kind, who are easily deluded by demons and by men." It is very difficult to see, in the canonical legal scholarship of the fourteenth and fifteenth centuries, any particularly marked notice, in the professional literature (that is, commentaries on texts or materials to aid judges), of the growing concern in theology over the general question of idolatry and superstition. The canonists, possessing only a few particularized texts, restricted themselves to commentary on those texts, and their commentary appears to have been quite conventional between the late twelfth and the late fifteenth centuries. Those writers who attempted to impugn the authoritativeness of the *Canon Episcopi* in the late fifteenth and sixteenth centuries were usually inquisitors and theologians, and they did not do so in the genre of canonist literature. Far from contributing to the growing belief in witches and the increased fear of magic in all its forms, canonists as a profession appear to have kept to the letter of the law. The *editio romana* of the *Corpus Iuris Canonici,* although it did not authenticate any text, did not repudiate *Episcopi,* either. And seventeenth-century canonists, for example Balthasar van Espen, adopted the conventional interpretations available since the late twelfth century. It appears not to have been from any change in the opinion of canon lawyers that the fifteenth-century attacks upon magic and witchcraft were launched. Therefore, to understand the legal forces that did contribute to the definition of these crimes, we must turn first to Roman law and then to the legal world of late fifteenth-century temporal and inquisitorial courts.

As we have seen in Chapter 1, the codification of Roman law in the fifth and sixth centuries preserved formidable penalties for the practice of magic. From the second century on, imperial edicts proclaimed stronger and stronger penalties, not only for injuries caused by magic, but for the practice of it and for the employment of magicians. Magic, at first forbidden when directed against the emperor (and punishable by death), was by the end of the third century punishable in all of its manifestations. By the fourth century the charge of magic made the defendant subject to judicial torture. By the time of the codifications of the fifth and sixth centuries, Roman law preserved a substantial body of legal literature concerning magic. The revival of Roman law in the twelfth century brought medieval law slowly into line with earlier Roman imperial law, although the Romanists' interest in magic does not seem to have made any significant impact upon European legal thought until the end of the twelfth and the beginning of the thirteenth centuries. From that period on, the Roman law on magic influenced the teaching of civil law and the administration of Roman law where it was still considered binding. It also influenced the temporal laws of the Italian city-states, and it strengthened the approaches to such offenses as magic and heresy taken by inquisitors and temporal authorities from the end of the twelfth century on. The revived study of Roman law contributed the formidable strictures of fourth- and fifth-century imperial edicts to the character of persecutions of heresy. These strictures inflicted the severest civil penalties on heretical belief. The papal consideration of heresy as a crime of *lèse-majesté* derived from the revived study of Roman law and had its fullest development in Innocent III's decretal of 1199 *Vergentis in senium.*[17] Innocent III and Huguccio of Pisa both drew heavily upon Roman law in defining the crime of heresy and establishing its punishments. This new juridical approach to heresy in turn influenced the laws of temporal societies, beginning with the ordinance of Louis VIII of France in 1226, which translated into royal law the strictures of canonist and papal decisions, and continuing with the ordinance *Cupientes,* issued by Louis IX in 1229. Between 1220 and 1231, imperial constitutions issued by Frederick II and promulgated by Pope Honorius III and Pope Gregory IX increased the severity of the punishments of heretics and altered the traditional accusatorial procedure in favor of the introduction of the inquisitorial procedure, another important juridical element taken over from Roman law. By the middle of the thirteenth century, Roman law had substantially altered the Church's approach to heresy and had shaped the policy of temporal authorities as well. As will be seen in the next section, the formation of the Inquisition created a new avenue for the development of new punitive forms and procedural changes that shaped not only the thirteenth-century Christian ecclesiastical policy toward heretics, but, as Jeffrey Russell has shown, contributed considerably toward the Church's attitudes toward magic and later witchcraft.

The circumstances surrounding the revival of Roman law are as important as the character of the law itself. Although many features of earlier legal systems survived into the thirteenth and fourteenth centuries—the localism of much law, the power of privilege and exemption, and the strength of custom—the character of thirteenth-century urban life in itself produced new approaches to crime and punishment. When Roman lawyers wrote tracts *De criminis,* many cities and principalities applied their principles to social phenomena of crime and to the organization of criminal law and procedure. The thirteenth century witnessed what Calisse has called "the recovery of the power of punishment" as well as a systematic approach to criminal law that was greatly strengthened by the structure of Roman law.[18] Thus, certain innovations of the period, such as the spread of torture, the introduction of the inquisitorial process, and new rules of evidence, were common to a number of societies. They were not, as is sometimes asserted, solely the invention of ecclesiastical inquisitors. Although heretics were more severely handled by the law after 1225, the same is true of all classes of criminal offenders, and one could be tortured for other offenses besides heresy and executed by public authorities acting as other than the "secular arm" of an ecclesiastical tribunal. When the legal aspects of heresy, magic, and witchcraft are considered, it should be remembered that the law in general had grown more severe, more remorseless, and more systematic, for the hardened criminal as well as for the heretic. With the abolition of the system of ordeals—and with it of the idea of immanent justice, as well as the fundamental role of community consensus in determining guilt and punishment—a new burden was placed upon the human agencies of the law. If God was not to indicate guilt, man must. As we have seen above, the system of ordeals itself was linked with traditional ideas of *divinatio* by the fifteenth century. In its place there emerged a compromise system: human agents indeed investigated, instituted prosecutions on the basis of the inquisitorial process, and instituted torture. In part, at least, the dramatic appearance of the new criminal procedure after 1225 was the result of a residual attitude toward determining guilt absolutely that required a confession when other evidence was not immediately and conclusively convincing. Thus, the residual requirement for confession increased the need to resort to torture, and the decretals of Innocent IV in 1252, *Ad extirpanda,* and of Alexander IV in 1258 and 1260 extended the domain of torture into the Inquisition itself. Torture, however, had been part of the judicial system in some Italian city-republics since as early as 1228, and its roots were neither exclusively the revival of Roman law nor the fear of heretics, but lay rather in the social structure and juridical competence of the new towns and the circumstances of crime in them. R. C. van Caenegem and others have suggested and emphasized the social circumstances that made torture attractive to the magistrates of the thirteenth-century cities. The increased power of judges and prosecutors, the idea that crime was an offense against the community rather than exclusively against a private person, and the momentary forces that swayed judges toward extraordinary mercy or extraordinary severity in assigning punishments drastically transformed criminal procedure in general and constitute the essential background against which the particular conception and treatment of heretics, magicians, and witches must be understood.[19]

It is important to note that the ambiguities and abuses of the new system remained a characteristic of European law for centuries. First, the vulnerability of the civil community to injury by criminals of all kinds, suggested above in the "political" magic trials of the early fourteenth century, increased the ferocity of criminal procedure and punishment, condoned the extraordinary power of the civil authority to institute summary procedures and extraordinary punishments, permitted secrecy, instituted new and less restricted categories of evidence, and created the idea of the *crimen exceptum,* the crime so dangerous to the civil community that the very accusation acted to suspend traditional procedural protection to the defendant and opened the way for the most ruthless and thorough kind of prosecution, undertaken to protect the state from its most dangerous enemies.[20] Not only treason, but magic, witchcraft, and other offenses became "exceptional crimes" by the sixteenth century. These offenses constituted the procedural equivalent to other ways by which the state, or the civil community, was asserting its supremacy over traditionally diversified ways of life and legal procedures and areas of power and authority outside that of the prince or the communal authorities. Seen in this light, the prosecution for magic, treason, and witchcraft by the temporal courts was of a piece with other late medieval and early modern political and constitutional developments.

Second, what had been the province of God had become the province of man, and judicial activity acquired a moral dignity and theological justification that it had not possessed much before the thirteenth century. Not only were teachers of the law called "priests" of the law, but the magistrate, on whatever level, increasingly came to be considered responsible for the spiritual, as well as the judicial proprieties of his office. Thus, especially in dealing with "crimes of mixed jurisdiction," the temporal magistrate assumed spiritual responsibilities as well as increased dignity. When, at the end of the fifteenth century, the authors of the *Malleus Maleficarum* urged the temporal courts to aid ecclesiastical officials in rooting out the crimes of magic and witchcraft, they were instituting no novelty, but invoking the moral responsibility of temporal courts that had been heightened steadily since the thirteenth century. In this light, the blessings of the instruments of torture in civil courts, the judges' solicitude for the moral condition of defendants, their exhortations to repent, the whole apparatus of civil liturgy that had been adopted from an earlier period and a more exclusively clerical milieu, all supported the discretion and responsibility of the judge and the magistrate. It also helps to explain the often noted sixteenth-century theory that God's ministers, temporal and spiritual, were invulnerable to the powers of witches and magicians once the defendants had been introduced into the judicial system.

The temporal judicial authorities of the period between the fourteenth and the seventeenth centuries, charged with protecting a vulnerable civil community and elevated to a quasi-priestly rank in order better to do so, worked with at least the rudiments of a sophisticated legal system directly or indirectly shaped on the model of Roman law. These authorities dealt with a considerably expanded sphere of public crimes and a system of the classification of crimes that, while it moved toward a degree of professional rationality, for a long period also included offenses that were primarily spiritual and which were punished, often more strongly and arbitrarily, as if they were identical to such temporal offenses as treason. The long history of the temporal authority as the secular arm of ecclesiastical courts did not end when temporal courts assumed greater independence. It was transformed into a rationale for extending judicial authority into fields hitherto exclusively the judicial province of ecclesiastical courts. In those fields it retained its powers, procedures, and apparatus of punishments that, as all commentators noted after the fourteenth century, were far more severe than those of the ecclesiastical courts. The purpose of the activities of the temporal courts was admonitory; the often spectacular and gruesome punishments they meted out were expected to act as a deterrent and disciplinary education to the public. Not only the defendant, of course, but those who aided him or her, had to be corrected. Over and against the good civil society, protected, ministered to, and educated by its princes and magistrates, the wicked society emerged in its midst, concealed by secrecy and requiring extraordinary measures to be discovered and tried. These measures, not bound by the normal rules of procedure, might contain such archaic elements as the ordeal and the traditional invective against enemies of God. But their formidable character was established through their use of the most novel and versatile legal techniques at their disposal. Indeed, the idea of the *crimen exceptum*, the extraordinary crime against the state, was one of the enduring legacies of the prosecutions of witches in the sixteenth and seventeenth centuries. Its place in constitutional law did not end when the prosecutions ended, but turned instead to other kinds of criminals and was supported by a constantly increasing apparatus of state power that, in certain parts of the eighteenth, nineteenth, and twentieth centuries, often reached terrifying proportions.

The development of such judicial attitudes as those mentioned above may be traced in the histories of criminal law of Italy, Germany, and France. Many historians of witchcraft prosecutions tend to distort the nature of punishments for witches by focusing upon them exclusively, instead of approaching them in the context of general legal history, especially that of criminal law. The very term that designated magic and witchcraft in all later sources, *maleficium*, had long had several meanings. In Roman law it meant almost any crime or delict, and Roman legal scholarship through the fourteenth century retained this general sense of the term. Although Roman law and its medieval commentators did use *maleficium* and *maleficus* to denote magicians, they also used it in the general sense of injurious wrongdoing of a criminal character. Thus, to the judges who tried magicians and witches, the *crimen maleficii* was similar semantically to other kinds of criminal injury. Other Roman legal thought concerning magic, however, and the powerful theological condemnations of magic from the thirteenth century on, slowly added more ominous overtones to the general idea of delict, so that the *crimen magiae* was a particular kind of *maleficium*, one made distinct because of its association with idolatry, demon-worship, and heresy.[21]

The broader Roman law concept of *maleficium* was preserved in several treatises on criminal law down through the seventeenth century. It is one example of the new rationale of defining crime and punishment systematically, in a specialized vocabulary, that greatly influenced temporal courts, whether they specifically employed Roman law or not. Such professional influences, the judge's role as a quasi-sacerdotal official, and the phenomenon of urban crime itself, all increased the harshness of criminal procedure and punishment and brought some crimes of mixed jurisdiction, such as magic, before the temporal magistrate. In place of the restricted system of pre-thirteenth-century law, the fourteenth- and fifteenth-century magistrate would work with wider judicial discretion, broader rules of admissable evidence, torture, and the support of ecclesiastical authorities. These elements made all criminal procedure more severe on the defendant and the convicted felon, and also upon the witnesses and accomplices. It is in the general context of criminal law after the thirteenth century that the prosecution of magicians and witches ought to be understood. Little wonder that theologians and canonists remarked that the temporal law penalized such crimes more severely than Church law. With the exception of the Inquisition, this was true.

HERESY, THE INQUISITION, AND THE CRIME OF MAGIC

"Indeed, it is proable," Maitland once remarked, "that but for the persecution of heretics there would have been no persecution of sorcerers." Many historians of witchcraft, most recently Jeffrey Russell, have confirmed Maitland's dictum in detailed studies, and there is no modern scholar who would be prepared to deny the powerful influence that not only the prosecution of heretics, but the concept of heresy in general, exerted upon the judicial life of late medieval and early modern Europe. As has been shown above, the rhetorical description of heretics derived in part from and influenced later descriptions of magicians. Russell's exhaustive catalogue of heretical traits described in the twelfth and thirteenth centuries and their reappearance, attributed to the witch, in the fourteenth and fifteenth centuries, suggests one of the most important sources, both for the changing picture of the magician and the witch and for the legal grounds upon which magic and witchcraft were pursued.

Magic had been identified with heresy as early as the fourth century, however, and the great weight of patristic, particularly Augustinian, authority influenced its identification with heresy in the work of Hugh of St. Victor and Gratian, among many other twelfth-century writers. As has been shown above, magicians were especially accused of invoking demons and using demonic aid in their arts, thereby becoming guilty of idolatry. The theme of the idolatrous magician is perhaps the most distinctive aspect of inquisitorial manuals' treatment of magic as heresy in the thirteenth and fourteenth centuries.[22] Alongside the theme of idolatry, however, there grew up the similar theme of detailing the practices of the devil's children. Thus, the literature depicting the behavioral excesses of heretics that had appeared by the middle of the thirteenth century considerably helped to fill out the detailed picture of just what demon-invocation and devil-worship included.[23] Many sources from the late twelfth and thirteenth centuries contributed to these descriptions. Chroniclers and moralists, theologians and preachers, monks and mendicants contributed to the construction of the image of the bestial heretic, degraded by demon-worship to performing the most obscene and repulsive rites, and unalterably dedicated to a hatred of the human race. Cathars, Waldensians, Luciferians, and other heretical sects became merged in the image of the absolute heretic, which in turn became the image of every enemy of Christian society. Although the inquisitors' manuals of the fourteenth and fifteenth centuries generally reflect an accurate knowledge of various heretical beliefs, the inquisitorial literature of the thirteenth century left a popular legacy in its portrait of the heretics and their activities. This legacy influenced moralists and preachers in the fourteenth and fifteenth centuries and tainted the magician as well as other kinds of heretics. The charges against the Templars, such lay groups as the Beguines and Beghards, the Brethren of the Free Spirit, the Fraticelli, and even against the friars themselves in the fourteenth and fifteenth centuries all find their roots in the invective of the thirteenth century.[24] The fevered, picturesque, and grotesque descriptions of heretical activities depicted in late twelfth-century and early thirteenth-century sources must be set against the relatively sober descriptions of heretical beliefs and activities in twelfth-century sources, and against the relatively reliable accounts of heretical beliefs in fourteenth- and fifteenth-century inquisitors' manuals. A particular example of such literary invective is contained in the decretal *Vox in Rama*, issued by Pope Gregory IX in 1233 in response to a request for aid against heretics in the Rhineland made by the friar Konrad von Marburg:

When a novice is to be initiated and is brought before the assembly of the wicked for the first time, a sort of frog appears to him; a toad according to some. Some bestow a foul kiss on his hind parts, others on his mouth, sucking the animal's tongue and slaver. Sometimes the toad is of a normal size, but at others it is as large as a goose or a duck. Usually it is the size of an oven's mouth. The novice comes forward and stands before a man of fearful pallor. His eyes are black and his body so thin and emaciated that he seems to have no flesh and be only skin and bone. The novice kisses him and he is as cold as ice. After kissing him every remnant of faith in the Catholic Church that lingers in the novice's heart leaves him.

Then all sit down to a banquet and when they rise after it is finished, a black cat emerges from a kind of statue which normally stands in the place where these meetings are held. It is as large as a fair-sized dog, and enters backwards with its tail erect. First the novice kisses its hind parts, then the Master of Ceremonies proceeds to do the same and finally all the others in turn; or rather all those who deserve the honour. The rest, that is those who are not thought worthy of this favour, kiss the Master of Ceremonies. When they have returned to their places they stand in silence for a few minutes with heads turned towards the cat. Then the Master says: "Forgive us." The person standing behind him repeats this and a third adds, "Lord we know it." A fourth person ends the formula by saying, "We shall obey."

When this ceremony is over the lights are put out and those present indulge in the most loathsome sensuality, having no regard to sex. If there are more men than women, men satisfy one another's depraved appetites. Women do the same for one another. When these horrors have taken place the lamps are lit again and everyone regains their places. Then, from a dark corner, the figure of a man emerges. The upper part of his body from the hips upward shines as brightly as the sun but below that his skin is coarse and covered with fur like a cat. The Master of Ceremonies cuts a piece from the novice's vestments and says to the shining figure: "Master, I have been given this, and I, in my turn, give it to you." To which the other replies: "You have served me well and will serve me yet more in the future. I give into your safekeeping what you have given me." And he disappears as soon as he has spoken these words. Each year at Easter when they receive the body of Christ from the priest, they keep it in their mouths and throw it in the dirt as an outrage against their Saviour. Furthermore, these most miserable of men blaspheme against the Lord of Heaven and in their madness say that the Lord has done evil in casting out Lucifer into the bottomless pit. These most unfortunate people believe in Lucifer and claim that he was the creator of the celestial bodies and will ultimately return to glory when the Lord has fallen from power. Through him and with him they hope to achieve eternal happiness. They confess that they do not believe that one should do God's will but rather what displeases Him. . . .[25]

This passage was probably inspired by Konrad von Marburg's own letter of appeal to the pope, and it suggests the influence of some of the anti-heretical invective noted above in Chapters 2 and 3. The *osculum infame*, the pallid master, the magical loss of the faith, the ritual, lasciviousness, the appearance of the demon, desecration of the host, and blasphemy all constitute the prototype of charges against later heretics and witches. The only part missing is the description of what the heretics have done to earn the praise of the demon for having served him well. Fifteenth-century theologians and moralists compiled a grim catalogue of precisely what those actions were. When their work was finished, the portrait of the heretic in Gregory IX's letter became the portrait of the witch. Heretical assemblies became witches' sabbats; the ritual deference to the master and the demon became the pact, the basis of idolatry. It is possible that the *covenança*, or oath taken among heretics in southern France, became the etymological root of the later coven of witches.

It was not merely the literary invective against heretics, itself originally borrowed in part from earlier invective against magicians, that helped to shape the later picture of the witch, but the structure and procedure of the Inquisition itself and the personnel, especially the early personnel, who staffed it. The inquisitorial process gave great authority to the inquiring magistrate, offered new rules of evidence, and permitted a number of other procedures—not all of which were irregular—in its course. It offered in some respects a rational and efficient process, one which appealed to certain levels of thirteenth-century society (for different reasons, to ecclesiastical courts, city magistrates, royal officials, and mendicant inquisitors) for other reasons than the hunting of heretics. What made the ecclesiastical inquisitorial process distinct was its utilization of untraditional juridical forms, often under the direction of mendicants with no legal experience, in a forum which had hitherto been purely penitential. The forum of conscience now opened out, in the matter of heresy, into a judicial forum in which the concealed crime of heresy was to be discovered by the new legal procedures and their practitioners. Years before Gregory IX committed the Inquisition against heretics specifically to the mendicant orders, ecclesiastical officials and temporal magistrates had co-operated in catching, trying, and punishing heretics. Episcopal courts and monastic inquisitors, notably Cistercians, had also worked together, particularly in southern France. In Italy lay individuals and lay spiritual associations vigorously inquired into the faith of their fellow citizens. Such enthusiastic hunters of heretics in the Rhineland as Conrad Dorso and John the One-Eyed, who probably acted as synodal witnesses (accusers) on behalf of the episcopal court at Worms, were joined by Konrad von Marburg, who had received three papal commissions between 1227 and 1231 to hunt out heretics in Germany. These three men, none of them specifically designated an inquisitor, accused heretics before the episcopal court, and it was in this function that Konrad von Marburg wrote to Gregory IX the description which Gregory echoed in *Vox in Rama*. The introduction of three such inexpert figures into the episcopal inquisitorial process marks one of the most important early stages of the history of the Inquisition. For Konrad von Marburg was far from being a lawyer, far from understanding the dangers of ruthlessly and pitilessly manipulating the court into condemning heretics wholesale. A mendicant ascetic, Konrad preached crusades from 1214 to 1220, and served as the spiritual director of St. Elizabeth of Thuringia between 1221 and the saint's death in 1231. As spiritual director of that much put-upon saint, Konrad inflicted his spiritual visions upon his protégé and exercised his fascination for demonology. Out of this nonlegal background, Konrad acquired considerable power over the judicial machinery of the Upper Rhineland. He translated his own interior demonology into the society of heretics in the Rhine valley, and he invoked the law to purify the society he imagined.[26] Both Konrad and Robert le Bougre, who worked at the same time in France, helped to set the tone—one of spiritual zeal coupled with a total disregard for the most elementary features of legal process—that characterized much of the Inquisition's history and was not removed even by the systematizing and regularizing of the inquisitorial process in the fourteenth century. For the procedure that later learned inquisitors used was developed in the more flexible and more dangerous days of the early thirteenth century by men like Konrad and Robert and their assistants. The great authority of the Inquisition stemmed from its direct papal authority and its exemption from the common canon law of the Church. This authority was lent to a system of investigation, accusation, trial, and punishment that shared many of its most formidable parts with the criminal procedures of other thirteenth-century societies, from the kingdom of France to the Italian city-republics. But the most ominous and destructive features of the Inquisition derived from the application of those parts in a novel way by zealous men who were trained in no law and could thereby use the law to attack spiritual dissent, no matter how deeply concealed. *Ecclesia de occultis non judicat*—"the Church does not judge hidden offenses," so said a canonist maxim in the late twelfth and early thirteenth centuries; the concealed sin was left to the forum of penitence, the confessional.[27] In inquisitorial procedure, however, it was precisely the transference of concealed offenses to the judicial forum of the Inquisition that marked the difference between the Inquisition and conventional canon law courts. The spiritual troubles of Gregory IX, Konrad von Marburg, Robert le Bougre and others took up the rhetorical descriptions of heretical activities developed late in the twelfth century and pronounced them crimes of the gravest kind; they instituted a juridical procedure that cut away traditional protections, initially operated with unprofessional personnel, and possessed virtually unlimited power. As Henri Maisonneuve points out:

[In the case of Konrad of Marburg and his role as a *testis synodalis*] it is not necessary to speak of an episcopal inquisition here, nor of a monastic inquisition, in spite of the specific affiliation of many "inquisitors," and even less of a "secular inquisition, but rather of an itinerant and formidable papal commission of inquiry *sui generis*. If it did not suppress ordinary jurisdictions, ecclesiastical and secular, it stimulated them, it goaded them, and it tended naturally to supplant them, and by that means, without doubt, to depart from the essence of legality.[28]

Maisonneuve demonstrates the process by which the papal Inquisition spread throughout Germany, northern and southern France, Aragon, and Italy. He traces the changing definition of severe corporal punishment and death, the *animadversio debita*, incapacitation, exheredation, and the death penalty, seeing in Innocent IV's decretal *Ad extirpanda* of 15 May, 1252—the most important instrument after the constitutions of Frederick II and the decretals of Gregory IX—the institutional creation of a papal Inquisition. In this decretal, not only is torture permitted and the penalty of death by fire recognized, but inquisitors are permitted to assemble staffs, archives, and other institutional structures. In Alexander IV's letter *Quod super nonullis*, discussed above, heretical magic is specified as within the Inquisition's competence, although nonheretical magic is left to the ordinary system of spiritual and temporal criminal justice. The articulation of heresy in the manuals of the inquisitors of the fourteenth century, however, logically and implacably drew sorcery too into the power of the Inquisition.

Bernard Gui's handbook for inquisitors, the *Practica officii inquisitoris heretice pravitatis*, written around 1323/24, contains a formula for interrogating those suspected of being *sortilegi, divini*, or *invocatores daemonum*, evidently considered well within the limits of heretical magic by the early fourteenth century. The accused are to be asked what they know of these subjects and from whom they learned it. The inquisitor is then to descend into particulars, and these detailed questions range over most of the topics of learned and unlearned magic familiar to most theologians of the period. Gui emphasizes the importance of inquiring about any desecration of the sacrament or profanation of ecclesiastical rites. Gui also gives the formula for abjuring magical practices as well as several formulas for the degradation of clerics convicted of such acts as well as for those convicted of using the consecrated host for *sortilegium* and *maleficium*. In 1376 Nicholas Eymeric's *Directorium inquisitorum* discussed the problems of magic and sorcery at considerable length, but his handbook, which was the best-known inquisitor's handbook through the early seventeenth century, focuses upon the idolatry of magicians, and reveals little of the detail that later described the type of the witch (see the translation below, Appendix II).

In inquisitorial literature the terminology of traditional magic was broadened to include heresy. The constitutions of Frederick II had identified heresy and *maleficium* in 1231, and the terms used to designate *sortilegium* and *divinatio* were attached to *maleficium* in the German *Richterlichen Klagspiel* around 1450: *die das volk maleficos (zaubrer) nennt . . . die schwartzen kunst oder sunst andere verbotene kunst, im latein artem divinandi . . .* At about the same time, Alfonso de Spina spoke of the *artes magicae vel divinationes.*[29]

From the Roman vagueness of *maleficium*, inquisitors and theologians appear to have directed the term to the specific meaning of magician, and to have done this between the late thirteenth and the late fifteenth centuries, although in technical studies of Roman law the older meaning of the term appears to have survived, as we have seen, into the sixteenth century. Besides drawing some of the key terms in the history of magic together (*sortilegium, divinatio, maleficium, ars magica*) inquisitorial literature went much further into the nature of the magician's acts and the character of his sin, especially idolatry, than canon lawyers appear to have done. In the work of two fifteenth-century inquisitors, Heinrich Krämer and Jacob Sprenger, and in the *Malleus Maleficarum*, the most exhaustive (and, for a century, the most conclusive) arguments are made: *divinatores* and *malefici* are regarded as being the same kind of offender, since they are punished in the forum of conscience by the same punishment. Both anticipate injury to God's creatures inflicted by demons, and both ask from the demons what should only be asked of God. In the inquisitorial literature of the late fourteenth and fifteenth centuries, the separate semantic development of such terms as *maleficus, divinator, sortilegus* gives way to a process of identifying all these terms with each other and with the magical arts. These arts, in turn, although some of them may in theory be acceptable, are continuously condemned, and that condemnation becomes stronger in the fifteenth and sixteenth centuries. In the fifteenth century the invective against heresy is applied to magicians and later to witches, by bringing them before the inquisitorial tribunals, not only of the Inquisition itself, but before secular judges as well; the ancient condemnation of magic is strengthened by its identification with idolatry, superstition, and apostasy. As Norman Cohn has pointed out, and as Richard Kieckhefer's calendar of "witchcraft" trials indicates, most convictions before the late fifteenth century were for the practice of magic seen in these terms.[30]

THE ORDEAL OF LEARNED MAGIC

At exactly the time when hitherto separate terms designating magic were drawing closer together in meaning and the inquisitorial process had begun to include magicians as heretics and apostates, there occurred a revival of learned magic that went far beyond the thirteenth- and fourteenth-century revivals and dealt with much broader ideas than the manipulation of the created world. In general, the new magic of the fifteenth and sixteenth centuries was, or claimed to be, natural or hermetic, specifically opposed to superstitious magic and deriving from Neoplatonic philosophy. Its earliest defenders, Marsilio Ficino and Giovanni Pico della Mirandola, although they claimed for their magic the highest benefits to mankind and insisted upon their freedom from illicit communication with demons, often found themselves facing the same kinds of condemnations as thirteenth-century magicians had, made more serious by the interest of the Inquisition and the attacks on magic in the fourteenth and fifteenth centuries. Ficino himself is careful to indicate that his own talismans are not those made through illicit arts, and that his songs are not to be identified with forbidden incantations to demons, of whose dangers he appears to have been very much aware. The dilemma of Ficino and other learned magicians who play so important and mysterious a role in early modern intellectual history was sharpened by the attitudes toward all forms of magic in the world in which they lived.[31]

The appeal of learned magic in the fifteenth and sixteenth centuries has been recognized by many scholars, notably Eugenio Garin:

For people sensed that here was a new way which might allow man to gain a full mastery over nature. The attempt to seize precisely those methods which medieval theology had rejected shows once again how fundamental the break with the middle ages had been.[32]

The vision enunciated by Ficino, and echoed in the following century by Trithemius, Agrippa von Nettesheim, Bruno, and Campanella, was that of increased human power over nature achieved by control of the spirits and forces that fill the universe. Ficino based his magical ideas on the hermetical treatises, but his reading was wide, and he published in translation Michael Psellos' eleventh-century treatise on magic and demonology besides much else. The anthropocentrism of literary and philosophical humanism dictated that man alone could free himself from the static, ordered world of forms and become either a divine being or a beast. As Garin states,

[T]he ambiguous reality of man consisted of the fact that he was a possibility, an opening through which one could rejoice in the inexhaustible richness of Being. He was not a being defined once and for all, immobile and secure, but was always precariously balanced upon the margin of an absolute risk . . . [in] an infinite universe which is open to all possibilities.[33]

As Garin, Thorndike, and others have pointed out, such a view was diametrically opposed to the earlier views of human nature and magic. What several historians have called "the muse of terror" lay behind medieval attitudes toward magic, and throughout the last and most learned revival of magic there raged against it and its vision of human nature the strictures first enunciated by Plato and later by the theologians and inquisitors of the fourteenth and fifteenth centuries. At the beginning of the seventeenth century, attacks came from a new quarter, from the new vision of science possessed by Francis Bacon and the logical method of Descartes. Of the two enemies of natural and hermetic magic, the theologians and inquisitors were the more dangerous; not only did they apply to the new magic the old strictures and the new punishments, but they associated the learned magicians with the unlearned witches, who had come much more sharply into focus by the late fifteenth century.[34]

The chief theological problem faced by the hermetic magicians was the Church's firm statement that there were only two kinds of spirits, angels and demons. Independent commerce with what appeared to be benevolent spirits could only be commerce with demons, and no Christian in the fifteenth century, Neoplatonic philosopher or not, could easily disagree. It is not surprising, therefore, that Ficino and Pico and their successors emphasized far more emphatically than even Roger Bacon and Arnald of Villanova that there existed two kinds of magic, which D. P. Walker terms spiritual and demonic, and that their magic was purely spiritual. Walker shows that, for all their protests, the hermetic magicians of the sixteenth century were themselves well aware of the dangers of demonic magic, even if some of them, such as Agrippa and Paracelsus, veered even closer to demonic magic than Ficino.[35]

It was no accident that the new learned magic began in Italy and that several of the most impassioned attacks on magic and witchcraft, and the earliest, also originated in Italy. As Peter Burke has recently shown, there were a number of trials for forbidden magic in fifteenth- and early sixteenth-century Italy, and the judges did not always distinguish between what historians too easily call "magic" and "witchcraft." Gianfrancesco Pico's dialogue on magic and witchcraft *Strix* (published in 1523) sums up, in its arguments for and against the belief in witchcraft, a wide range of learning and a denunciation of both learned and humble magic. In *Strix* and in his other writings against magic, Gianfrancesco Pico attacks the revival of the cult of antiquity, striking out at the targets that had exercised the Church Fathers centuries before: Orpheus, Apollonius of Tyana, and Circe. Indeed, one striking feature, especially of the *Strix*, is the author's citation of classical models, such as Medea and Circe, in his condemnation of all forms of magic.[36]

With the stirrings of the Reformation, certain implicit contradictions in late medieval theological approaches to the subject of magic became explicit, and reformers could and did attack Catholic ceremonial practices and beliefs as manifestations of demonic magic. Indeed, one of the themes that sustained much of the literature concerning magic and witchcraft throughout the sixteenth century was the diabolical magic of which the Catholic church was accused. On the other hand, H. C. Erik Midelfort has suggested that the very hardening of confessional camps in the sixteenth century led to denominational postures that necessarily excluded all of one's enemies' ideas, including those, such as scepticism toward magic and witchcraft, that might otherwise have circulated across confessional divisions.[37] The work of Johann Weyer, for example, has been regarded in different ways by different historians, precisely because it is usually read in parts, selectively. Weyer, physician to Duke William of Cleves, wrote in 1563 a long work entitled *De Praestigiis Daemonum*, which is generally remembered for its scepticism concerning the reality of the crimes of which witches were accused. What is not as often noted, however, is Weyer's unremitting hostility toward the Roman church and his accusations that many Catholic practices are manifestations of the worst kind of demonic magic.[38]

In addition, Weyer fully believes in the reality and diabolical character of learned magic, and he attacks Ficino and other learned proponents of natural magic vigorously. It was just this sort of attack that the traditional denunciations of magic had prepared, but Weyer does not cite the conventional patristic sources, relying heavily upon the Bible and his own vision of a nonmagical Christian religion. Although they appear different, the learned philosopher-magicians and the Roman churchmen are both victims of demonic illusion, both sunken in diabolic magic. In spite of Pico's humanist learning and Weyer's scepticism as to the reality of witches' actions, D. P. Walker legitimately groups these two thinkers with Thomas Erastus under the heading of evangelical hardheads:

Those who believe all magic to be demonic or diabolical and illusory; who tend to be sceptical about the reality of supernatural phenomena; who distrust all pagan philosophy, particularly Neo-platonism; who take the Bible as their supreme authority whenever possible; who in general have a sensible, no-nonsense outlook on things, usually based upon a moderate Christianized Aristotelianism.[39]

It is worth suggesting that such a view applied to the case of magicians as well as to that of witches, and many tracts against witchcraft are also directed against magicians. Indeed, Weyer directs his hostility toward magicians and Roman Catholic clergy exclusively. Jean Bodin, whose *De la démonomanie des sorcières*, published in 1580, was in large part a refutation of Weyer's "tolerance" toward the witches, is even more hostile to magicians than Weyer, and as Christopher Baxter has recently stated, "The word sorcerer here covers the lofty Neoplatonic magus of the Renaissance hermetic tradition; the lowly medieval necromancer; and the old crone of the European witchcraze."[40] In Martin Del Rio's *Disquisitiones magicae*, of 1559, sorcerers (magicians) are condemned with witches as the most pestiferous blight upon the human race.[41]

Without going further into the topic of sixteenth-century learned magic than this study requires, it seems to me appropriate to point out some conclusions suggested by the history of the figure of the magician in medieval and early modern Europe. First, although both anthropologists and historians persist in separating the crimes of magic and witchcraft, medieval theologians and lawyers did not, and many of the elements of sixteenth-century witchcraft were first brought to light in charges against magicians. A somewhat oversimplified schema of this process would state the relationship thus: from the patristic period through the twelfth century, Christian concepts of magic and denunciations of its practitioners were continuous and unremittingly hostile. In the twelfth century some of the invective traditionally directed against magicians and heretics was revived and extended, applying to both the new heretics and the increasingly evident class of magicians. Thirteenth-century theologians and philosophers attacked magic more severely, as did certain temporal and spiritual courts. As the inquisitorial process took shape, magic began to come within the purview of the Inquisition, and many of the distinct terms once used to designate learned magic—*sortilegium, divinatio, maleficium, ars magica*—were applied not only to learned magicians, but to other practitioners of "superstitious" and "idolatrous" acts, including fortune-telling, judicial astrology, medical practice, love-magic, and weather-magic. The original condemnation of the learned magicians became the general charge under which others were prosecuted as well. What Baxter has noted in Bodin's *Démonomanie*, that the term *sorcerer* included all kinds of magicians indiscriminately, is the logical conclusion of this process. Thus, the figure of the learned magician and the type of the sixteenth-century witch are not as far apart as some excessively schematized histories of witchcraft usually suggest. Although learned magic at its most intellectually respectable—whether in the *Poimander, Asclepius, Picatrix*, or the work of Ficino or Campanella—may seem at first glance far removed from the humble and lethal activities of the witches, it seems that way only to sixteenth-century apologists and twentieth-century historians. It did not seem that way to fourteenth-century theologians and inquisitors, nor to alleged sceptics like Weyer nor resolute monotheists like Bodin. The other side of the development of the figure of the witch—and it is a side just as important as the side of the magician—has been traced by Russell and others and requires a shorter presentation.

The rhetorical invective against heretics that twelfth-century monastic writers inherited from the patristic period and which, with their thirteenth- and fourteenth-century successors they turned into a minor form of literary art, was broadened to include several practices attributed to magicians and defined in ways that could be dealt with by special inquisitorial courts. Heresy, idolatry, and superstition indiscriminately merged in the person of the heretic, and the heretic merged into the witch—a figure made more formidable because of its ancestry in the invective against magic, on the one hand, and in the mentality of the Inquisition and the society it served, on the other. The final section of this book will deal with this question at greater length; here it is only necessary to emphasize again the role of learned magic in shaping, not only the witch figure, but the circumstances that led to the resolute opposition to all forms of magic in the sixteenth century. This opposition, although directed from different presuppositions, hampered the development of learned magic throughout the sixteenth century until the new assault from sceptics and rationalists killed it off in the early part of the seventeenth century. It is not common to link such figures as Bacon and Descartes with Gianfrancesco Pico, Bodin, and the sixteenth-century magistrates and inquisitors, but a link there is, one of many obscure connections between what often seem to be wholly separate worlds, the theology of the fifteenth century and the rational philosophy of the seventeenth.

THE WITCH AND THE LAW

Historians of witchcraft have faced other dilemmas besides that of whether to adopt the rationalist or romantic approach to their subject. On the one hand, the influence of anthropology on the study of history since the 1930s has suggested that techniques of anthropological investigation help to explain certain aspects of the phenomenon of the witch persecutions. A number of critics, most eloquent among them Rossell Hope Robbins, have argued against too great a dependence upon anthropology, chiefly because anthropology tends to homogenize the societies it studies. In the case of early modern European witchcraft, Robbins argues, anthropology tends to leave out specifically European features of witchcraft, most obviously the concept of the devil and the relation of the witch to the devil. Having rescued the witch from the anthropologists, Robbins and those who agree with him have been willing to leave the magician as a kind of hostage to comparative religion and anthropology in the witch's place.[42] One of the central themes in this book is that the magician, between the second and the eighteenth centuries, is just as much a particularized historical figure as the witch; in fact, the magician is older. The magician too, from St. Augustine on, made pacts with the devil, and indeed was the first to do so. The magician, whether learned or unlearned, was the type against whom those laws were first promulgated that were later applied to the witch. Many of the tracts *De strigibus* deal as much, if not more, with the evil magician than they do with the witch. Critics and promoters of the witchcraft persecutions alike—Weyer, Bodin, Del Rio, de l'Ancre—join in attacking evil magic. So strong was the opposition created in the period between the twelfth and the sixteenth centuries that it haunted Ficino and Pico, blackened the memory of Roger Bacon, Arnald of Villanova, Pietro d'Abano, Trithemius, and Agrippa, and set the stage for the appearance and legend of Faust. Pomponazzi and Campanella became suspect magicians too, and all of this occurred long before the rationalist assault led by Bacon, Bayle, and Descartes. Even that final assault was tempered by the residual theories of spiritual causation exhibited by the Cambridge Platonists and others down to the end of the seventeenth century. What Keith Thomas calls "the magic of the medieval Church" may have been the cause of dissension between sixteenth-century thinkers who defended a nonmagical Christianity and those who fought against it, but from the second to the sixteenth centuries the magic of the medieval Church remained exclusively an ecclesiastical form of magic. As Aquinas once said, it was a magic hallowed by *miracula* and divine providence; all else were *mira*, simply wonders and illusions, created by sporting and deceptive demons. No matter how learned the magician, the same process of demonic illusion that deceived the simple witch, deceived him as well. And the magician was the greater fool and the greater sinner.

Once the full variety of medieval magic has been described, it seems to me impossible not to appreciate the important place that medieval attitudes toward magic and magicians—and the nature and practice of magic on many levels itself—exerted in the thirteenth, fourteenth, and fifteenth centuries. Once even learned magic began to be actively examined and denounced, especially in the work of William of Auvergne and others in the early thirteenth century, a framework of magical activity was shaped that came to include many kinds of behavior; some of it was regarded as popular superstition and residual paganism, and more of it as one form or another of learned magic. The process did not occur at a steady rate, nor did all kinds of thinkers contribute equally to it. Canon lawyers and scholastic theologians seem to have contributed less than was once thought. Even inquisitors, once the nature and extent of the inquisitor's powers are understood, appear to have been less original and more closely tied to contemporary theological opinion than they are customarily thought to have been. Since Kieckhefer and Cohn have demolished some of the fourteenth-century cases that had long anchored the image of the sixteenth-century witch in the fourteenth century, such documents as Kieckhefer's own exhaustive list of witch trials may be read as trials for *sortilegium, divinatio,* and the illicit practice of the *ars magica.* And behind these trials and opinions, there lies an accessible body of ecclesiastical opinion on magic. The magic described by thirteenth-, fourteenth-, and fifteenth-century writers is not the eternal sort of magic, studied by historians of comparative civilizations and distinguished by anthropologists and some historians from witchcraft, either general or specific. It is a particular kind of magic, practiced through demonic power by a variety of social types from the learned magus to the sorcerer's apprentice, from the local maker of crude images and love potions to the poisoner, the midwife, and the wisewoman.

As magic came to be considered specifically the result of illicit commerce with demons, so too did heresy, and although heresy inspired the spread of inquisitorial procedure, both in special courts and generally throughout ecclesiastical and secular society, it is not surprising that those courts took cognizance of magic as well as heresy. It would be surprising if they had not. Magicians and heretics are both antecedents of the witch. Once magic is dissociated somewhat from the idea of eternal magic on the one hand, and learning on the other, it is easy to regard it as a time-bound phenomenon, the result of historical circumstances acting upon a traditional literary and theological hostility which dates from the patristic period. And this has been the argument of this book so far.

Once we have admitted that the theory and practice of magic was a historical event from late antiquity through the sixteenth century and that magic elicited a specific Christian response not fundamentally different from orthodox responses to heresy and later to witchcraft, we are forced to reassess the terminology customarily used to label magic and witchcraft. Medieval Latin and all the European vernacular languages possessed terms that were applied to magicians from late antiquity on. Although I have not been able to provide a full semantic history of such key terms as *maleficium,* I have suggested that in Latin, terms that had remained relatively discrete before the fourteenth century began to be used interchangeably after that period. When one reads *"divinatio vel ars magica,"* for example, in a fifteenth-century text, it is clear that the hitherto limited definition of *divinatio* has been expanded and become interchangeable with the term *ars magica.* The history of *maleficium* also shows narrow and broad meanings. When *maleficium* and *sortilegium* became consistently forms of *idolatria* and *superstitio,* theologians and inquisitors acquired greater freedom in dealing with them in relation to other crimes that had long been considered manifestations of *idolatria* and *superstitio.*

The interchangeability of terminology in the fourteenth and fifteenth centuries created a new context in which not only Latin terms, but vernacular terms as well could be considered as manifestations of the same sin. Thus, such terms as *Hexe, strega, wicca,* and many others, which we first find in early penitentials and sermons, came to mean a particular type of sinner and criminal which we commonly designate as *witch.* Yet they did not always mean what *witch* means, and has meant from the late fifteenth century on. In the early eleventh-century *Sermo Lupi ad Anglos,* England is chastized by the preacher because, among many other vices, *"7 her syndan wiccan 7 waelcyrian."*[43] A literal translation would read, "here there are [male] witches and valkyries." But such a translation would be erroneous in two respects: first, the preacher is speaking of magicians, not male witches, and, second, the valkyries are not the Scandinavian goddesses, but living women who practice magic. Yet the modern word "witch" comes from *wicca*, but in an etymological sense only. Lupus (or Wulfstan) certainly had no conception of the future meaning of the feminine form of *wicca*. About four centuries later, Chaucer's Friar describes the duties of an archdeacon:

> a man of heigh degree,
>
> That boldely dide execucioun
> In punysshynge of fornicacioun,
> Of wiccecraft, and eke of bawderye,
> Of diffamacioun, and avowtrye,
> Of chirche reves, and of testamentz,
> Of contractes, and of lakke of sacramentz,
> Of usure, and of symonye also.[44]

Sorcery was one of many kinds of sin whose absolution was reserved to the bishop, and the archdeacon was the bishop's legal official. Thus, the Friar's archdeacon punishes for *sorteligium* and *divinatio* and the poet, writing in English, naturally uses the term *wiccecraft*. Chaucer knew no more of fifteenth- and sixteenth-century meanings of witchcraft than had Lupus-Wulfstan four centuries earlier. The point of this short semantic excursus is that the history of usage and meaning can illuminate relationships between Latin and vernacular words and can suggest that certain terms whose meaning dramatically changes, such as *witch* and *witchcraft*, ought to be recognized as such and perhaps differentiated as to early and late meanings. As I observed at the beginning of this study, the words *sorcerer* and *witch* exist in English because after 1066 English was strongly influenced by the Romance languages. If modern English had to deal only with a term such as *wiccacraft*, many of the fine distinctions drawn between magic and witchcraft would no longer exist.

This argument runs close to a caveat of Jeffrey Russell—that to define witchcraft only as that institution described in sixteenth-century and some fifteenth-century sources, with the full panoply of pact with the demon, night-flight, the sabbat, the use of demonic power to perform supernatural acts injurious to the human race, and so forth, is virtually to deny that such a thing as witchcraft existed before 1400 or so. For the sake of semantic precision, as the preceding chapters have indicated, I am strongly inclined to take precisely that position. But any reader of Russell's rich and massively documented study would recognize that such a stand would exclude a strong tradition and an accumulation of legend; polemic, and legal and psychological attitudes would also be excluded.

Without a knowledge of these elements, it would be impossible to understand the full meaning of what was essentially a sixteenth-century phenomenon. I have argued that the figure of the magician in medieval thought and law must be reconsidered; I recognize that the type of the sixteenth-century witch was a distinct type, so distinct that it is running the risk of blurring her distinctiveness to use the word *witchcraft* without qualifying it for different historical periods. Yet the works of Hansen, Lea, Robbins, and Russell offer extremely illuminating materials and judgments about a dark and often neglected side of medieval life, and scholarship would be considerably poorer without it. Keith Thomas's phrase, "the magic of the medieval Church" has yet to be fully explored, and all of the work cited above contributes much to that exploration.

As an example of the process by which some traditional notions about magic and some formidable new notions about the practitioners of magic joined in the late fifteenth century, let us consider two of the most famous documents in the history of witchcraft, or *wiccacraft*: the bull *Summis desiderantes affectibus* of Pope Innocent VIII in 1484, and the *Malleus Maleficarum* of 1486, the great treatise on witchcraft to which the bull was always attached.

Innocent issued *Summis desiderantes* at the request of two Dominican inquisitors, Heinrich Krämer (or Institoris) and Jacob Sprenger, who had worked in southern Germany and encountered some resistance in their search for heretics. The bull formally removes all impediments to the completion of Krämer and Sprenger's mission. Its text follows:

Desiring with supreme ardor, as pastoral solicitude requires, that the catholic faith in our days everywhere grow and flourish as much as possible, and that all heretical pravity be put far from the territories of the faithful, we freely declare and anew decree this by which our pious desire may be fulfilled, and, all errors being rooted out by our toil as with the hoe of a wise laborer, zeal and devotion to this faith may take deeper hold in the hearts of the faithful themselves.

It has recently come to our ears, not without great pain to us, that in some parts of upper Germany, as well as in the provinces, cities, territories, regions, and dioceses of Mainz, Köln, Trier, Salzburg, and Bremen, many persons of both sexes, heedless of their own salvation and forsaking the catholic faith, give themselves over to devils male and female, and by their incantations, charms, and conjurings, and by other abominable superstitions and sortileges, offences, crimes, and misdeeds, ruin and cause to perish the offspring of women, the foal of animals, the products of the earth, the grapes of vines, and the fruits of trees, as well as men and women, cattle and flocks and herds and animals of every kind, vineyards also and orchards, meadows, pastures, harvests, grains and other fruits of the earth; that they afflict and torture with dire pains and anguish, both internal and external, these men, women, cattle, flocks, herds, and animals, and hinder men from begetting and women from conceiving, and prevent all consummation of marriage; that, moreover, they deny with sacrilegious lips the faith they received in holy baptism; and that, at the instigation of the enemy of mankind, they do not fear to commit and perpetrate many other abominable offences and crimes, at the risk of their own souls, to the insult of the divine majesty and to the pernicious example and scandal of multitudes. And, although our beloved sons Henricus Institoris and Jacobus Sprenger, of the order of Friars Preachers, professors of theology, have been and still are deputed by our apostolic letters as inquisitors of heretical pravity, the former in the aforesaid parts of upper Germany, including the provinces, cities, territories, dioceses, and other places as above, and the latter throughout certain parts of the course of the Rhine; nevertheless certain of the clergy and of the laity of those parts, seeking to be wise above what is fitting, because in the said letter of deputation the aforesaid provinces, cities, dioceses, territories, and other places, and the persons and offences in question were not individually and specifically named, do not blush obstinately to assert that these are not at all included in the said parts and that therefore it is illicit for the aforesaid inquisitors to exercise their office of inquisition in the provinces, cities, dioceses, territories, and other places aforesaid, and that they ought not to be permitted to proceed to the punishment, imprisonment, and correction of the aforesaid persons for the offences and crimes above named. Wherefore in the provinces, cities, dioceses, territories, and places aforesaid such offences and crimes, not without evident damage to their souls and risk of eternal salvation, go unpunished.

We therefore, desiring, as is our duty, to remove all impediments by which in any way the said inquisitors are hindered in the exercise of their office, and to prevent the taint of heretical pravity and of other like evils from spreading their infection to the ruin of others who are innocent, the zeal of religion especially impelling us, in order that the provinces, cities, dioceses, territories, and places aforesaid in the said parts of upper Germany may not be deprived of the office of inquisition which is their due, do hereby decree, by virtue of our apostolic authority, that it shall be permitted to the said inquisitors in these regions to exercise their office of inquisition and to proceed to the correction, imprisonment, and punishment of the aforesaid persons for their said offences and crimes, in all respects and altogether precisely as if the provinces, cities, territories, places, persons, and offences aforesaid were expressly named in the said letter. And, for the greater sureness, extending the said letter and deputation to the provinces, cities, dioceses, territories, places, persons, and crimes aforesaid, we grant to the said inquisitors that they or either of them, joining with them our beloved son Johannes Gremper, cleric of the diocese of Constance, master of arts, their present notary, or any other notary public who by them or by either of them shall have been temporarily delegated in the provinces, cities, dioceses, territories, and places aforesaid, may exercise against all persons, of whatsoever condition and rank, the said office of inquisition, correcting, imprisoning, punishing, and chastising, according to their deserts, those persons whom they shall find guilty as aforesaid.

And they shall also have full and entire liberty to propound and preach to the faithful the word of God, as often as it shall seem to them fitting and proper, in each and all the parish churches in the said provinces, and to do all things necessary and suitable under the aforesaid circumstances, and likewise freely and fully to carry them out.

And moreover we enjoin by apostolic writ on our venerable brother, the Bishop of Strasburg, that, either in his own person or through some other or others solemnly publishing the foregoing wherever, whenever, and how often soever he may deem expedient or by these inquisitors or either of them may be legitimately required, he permit them not to be molested or hindered in any manner whatsoever by any authority whatsoever in the matter of the aforesaid and of this present letter, threatening all opposers, hinderers, contradictors, and rebels, of whatever rank, state, decree, eminence, nobility, excellence, or condition they may be, and whatever privilege of exemption they may enjoy, with excommunication, suspension, interdict, and other still more terrible sentences, censures, and penalties, as may be expedient, and this without appeal and with power after due process of law of aggravating and reaggravating these penalties, by our authority, as often as may be necessary, to this end calling in the aid, if need be, of the secular arm.

And this, all other apostolic decrees and earlier decisions to the contrary notwithstanding; or if to any, jointly or severally, there has been granted by this apostolic see exemption from interdict, suspension, or excommunication, by apostolic letters not making entire, express, and literal mention of the said grant of exemption; or if there exist any other indulgence whatsoever, general or special, of whatsoever tenor, by failure to name which or to insert it bodily in the present letter the carrying out of this privilege could be hindered or in any way put off,—or any of whose whole tenor special mention must be made in our letters. Let no man, therefore, dare to infringe this page of our declaration, extension, grant, and mandate, or with rash hardihood to contradict it. If any presume to attempt this, let him know that he incurs the wrath of almighty God and of the blessed apostles Peter and Paul.

Given in Rome, at St. Peter's, in the year of Our Lord's incarnation 1484, on the nones of December, in the first year of our pontificate.[45]

When *Summis desiderantes* is read in the light of earlier papal letters, such as those of Eugenius IV and John XXII cited above, and still others printed by Hansen, it is clear that Innocent VIII has propounded nothing new in his letter. More than half the text is devoted to the vexing problem of local opposition to papal inquisitors; the first part speaks only of persons forsaking the Catholic faith, making pacts with devils, and thereby gaining the power to injure human beings. Despite Trevor-Roper's energetic but misguided attempt to demonstrate that in this document "a general mandate was given, or implied [for persecuting and burning witches]," there is no such mandate given or implied in the text, and Innocent VIII's idea of the sinners he was describing was virtually identical with those of his predecessors. By itself, *Summis desiderantes* would have constituted an interesting but routine papal letter in the series printed by Hansen. What has allowed historians (and demonologists) to read the letter as something more are the circumstances of its circulation. Not only was the letter routinely circulated to its addressees, but it was printed two years later as a preface to Institoris's and Sprenger's treatise, the *Malleus Maleficarum,* "The Hammer of Witches," the first printed encyclopedia of magic and witchcraft. Institoris and Sprenger elicited the decretal in the first place. What they received was a conventional papal letter concerning evil magic, most of which was directed against ecclesiastical officials who had impeded the two inquisitors' attempts to perform their papal commission. There is not a shred of evidence that Innocent VIII ever saw the *Malleus Maleficarum* or had the faintest notion of the ideas it contained. The printing of papal bulls with ecclesiological works was a particular phenomenon of the age of print itself; but the association of the bull, which was traditional and wholly unexceptional (compare it with Gregory IX's *Vox in Rama*) with the *Malleus Maleficarum,* which was neither traditional nor unexceptional, was the work of sixteenth-century writers and, of course, Institoris and Sprenger themselves. The juxtaposition of the two texts in printed editions could legitimately be understood to have misled sixteenth-century demonologists, but it is surprising that it should have misled so many historians since the sixteenth century.

The *Malleus Maleficarum,* however, is something quite unique and original. From Hansen and Lea to Robbins and Russell, scholars have analyzed and probed it for antecedents and influences. Sydney Anglo is the most recent writer to have studied the work in English. All scholars agree that the form of the work, that of a series of scholastic *quaestiones,* derives from handbooks for inquisitors, of which Eymeric's is the best example. Within the framework of *quaestiones* arranged into three major parts, however, the work is intellectually inferior to Eymeric's and hardly to be considered "scholastic" in the original sense of that term at all. What is striking about the *Malleus* is its economic use of the *quaestio* form to bring together elements from all of the diverse sources that had provided elements of the new fifteenth-century beliefs in magic in the first place. The juxtaposition of these elements in a single, concentrated, tightly argued treatise of considerably greater length than any earlier work really constituted the basis of the popularity of the *Malleus* during the next two centuries. Hansen has worked out the complicated method whereby the *Malleus* acquired the approbation of part of the faculty of theology at Cologne, and Russell has pointed out how many of the elements of the classical witch type of the sixteenth century are missing from the *Malleus.*[46] Moreover, there is no evidence that the appearance of the *Malleus,* nor its reprinting down through the middle of the sixteenth century several times, generated any greater persecutions for witchcraft and magic than had already occurred by the end of the fifteenth century. In fact, the prosecution of magicians and witches in Italy, which had begun earlier there than elsewhere, appears to have declined shortly after the publication of the *Malleus*. The *Malleus*, however, did succeed in welding together a number of hitherto distinct traditions concerning magic and, even more important, surrounded its second part, which deals with the activities of the *maleficae/malefici*, with a first part dealing with the theology of magic and a third part describing in immense detail the judicial procedures to be used against it. In no other work are theology and law so tightly linked. Even if, as I have suggested above, the *Malleus* made no discernible impact on the prosecution of magicians and witches for nearly half a century, no comparable work approached its comprehensiveness until those of Bodin and Remy, Del Rio and Boguet, at the end of the sixteenth century.

The *Malleus* drew heavily on, and consolidated, the work of fifteenth-century theologians and inquisitors such as Nider, Jaquier, and Spina. If indeed it became the standard reference text for later demonologists and magistrates, its popularity raises the question of the fundamental, as opposed to the relative, importance of such topics as Institoris and Sprenger do not consider. Russell remarks:

It is curious that they made no mention of familiar spirits, the obscene kiss, or even of the feasting and orgies of the sabbat. Nor is there any reference to the witches' or the Devil's mark, both of which became so common in the trials of the next two centuries.[47]

In the light of these and other marked characteristics of their theory of witchcraft, one is forced to reiterate the suggestion made above, that the pact, the arcane skills, and the injury to humans are the fundamental elements of learned ideas of witchcraft. Other aspects of the witches' activities, including night-flight, and the elements cited by Russell, were drawn in to the figure of the witch later and do not constitute an essential part of her activities, at least as far as the theology and law of the fifteenth century is concerned. And the fundamental crimes of the witch, seen in this light, are virtually identical with those of the earlier magician.

The social mechanisms that led accusers, inquisitors, and secular magistrates to institute the great persecutions after the middle of the sixteenth century are phenomena of the sixteenth century and have no bearing upon those mechanisms that led accusers to charge magicians in the thirteenth, fourteenth, and fifteenth centuries. The later social structure of the persecutions has begun to be studied in the important works of MacFarlane, Midelfort, and Monter, and it is beyond the scope of this book. Those new social pressures, however, were encountered by a formidable body of hostility to supernatural powers. However characteristic of sixteenth-century thought the work of Bodin, Del Rio, Remy, Boguet, and De l'Ancre is, the roots of sixteenth-century demonological thought lie in the Middle Ages, and one of the purposes of this book has been to explore those roots and to examine their influence long before the sixteenth century. There were many writers in the sixteenth century who tried to separate the categories of *magia* and *goeteia,* but from St. Augustine onward, such attempts were doomed to failure. Even though some of those who prosecuted witches were willing to make such distinctions in theory, no individual magician or witch could ever be less than apprehensive about his or her safety from a formal charge of *maleficium.* And few judges in the fifteenth century were likely to be faced with a clearcut, genuine, Neoplatonic magus; rather, they encountered more often magicians of the rank described above in Chapter 5—the sorcerer's apprentices, who had access to *grimoires* and some high learning, but used their arts to effect forbidden results, thereby veering close to the popular magic of the local witch.

The range of a broad definition of evil magic made it easy for judges to include local superstitious practices in different corners of Europe. But the framework was in place first, and the old notion that later witchcraft persecutions originated in the encounter between learned inquisitors and popular practices from the most isolated, usually mountainous regions of Europe, must be discounted. The learned judges had plenty of time and opportunity to develop a theory of magic in the cities of the plain—in Italy, Flanders, Burgundy, and France—and there they found the middle-level practitioners who were their first victims.

Nor were these judges always inquisitors. The association of the Inquisition with trials for magic and witchcraft dates from the end of the thirteenth century to the end of the sixteenth. Both Lea and Burr have commented upon Italy and Spain, the strongholds of the institutional Inquisition, as being the first places to discontinue witchcraft prosecutions. Such prosecutions had begun in temporal courts in the thirteenth century, moved into the Inquisition's sphere between the thirteenth and the seventeenth centuries, and lasted in ordinary ecclesiastical and secular jurisdictions long after the Inquisition ceased to concern itself with witchcraft, although it continued to prosecute magicians after it had ceased prosecuting the witches. A public may shape its image of the magician—or of the deviant or the gangster—in a form very different from the actual magicians—or deviants or gangsters—who appear before its courts; but it prosecutes the image, not the particular criminal before it, and public opinion often fails to be swayed in the direction of the latter, regardless of how much evidence is accumulated to indicate that it is wrong. Many legal institutions, therefore, have been regarded by criminologists as generally an improvement over traditional methods: the inquisitorial process; efficient, professional personnel; the denial of imminent justice; the regularizing of categories of crime and the standardizing of punishments. All of these worked in the fifteenth and sixteenth centuries *against* those accused of magic and witchcraft.

In general, the changing historical meaning of the *crimen magiae* must be studied in the whole context of late medieval and early modern criminal law, spirituality, and moral criticism. Magic and witchcraft, like other forms of social deviance, change their content—and their practitioners—over time. In the courts, schools, and confessionals of the period between the twelfth and the sixteenth centuries, the sin and the crime of magic acquired particular definitions and particular forms of condemnation, many of them based upon earlier forms of depicting heretics and earlier patristic depictions of the *crimen magiae*. "The crime of magic is as the crime of rebellion," said the Book of Samuel, and priests, magistrates, and kings alike treated both in their civil liturgies and spiritual disciplines. The late sixteenth and early seventeenth centuries witnessed a new exertion of spiritual and temporal power precisely against these forms of deviance, armed with effective and virtually irresistible legal forms and an evangelical conviction of righteousness. In these circumstances the great witch prosecutions of the period began.

The literature that guided the later prosecutions, however, condemned the magician as well as the witch. This study has attempted to show how the condemnation of magic in various circumstances between the time of the Church Fathers and the sixteenth century took form and when and where the appearance of demonstrably real practitioners of magic gave a new immediacy to older forms of condemnation. Far more than the well-known figure of Merlin, medieval magicians generated the condemnations of spiritual and temporal authorities. Those condemnations were later applied to witches, as were others. The law, whether archaic or early modern, was remorseless in its condemnation and treatment of both. By the early seventeenth century, the Neoplatonic magus might, like Prospero, drown his books and finally repent. The sorcerer's apprentice and the witch had no such recourse; where they could not hide, they must be burnt.

NOTES

1. See above, Chapter 4. The best recent study, one that has greatly informed the following pages, is Beryl Smalley, "William of Auvergne, John of La Rochelle and St. Thomas Aquinas on the Old Law," in *St. Thomas Aquinas, 1274–1974, Commemorative Studies*, 2 vols. (Toronto, 1974), 2:11-72.

2. There is a large literature on this subject, from H. C. Lea, *A History of the Inquisition in the Middle Ages,* 3 vols. (Philadelphia, 1887) to Henri Maisonneuve, *Études sur les origines de l'inquisition,* 2nd ed. (Paris, 1960), esp. pp. 243-366.

3. See P. Michaud-Quantin, "A propos des premiers *Summae confessorum,*" *Recherches de théologie ancienne et médiévale* 26 (1959): 264-306, and most recently and magisterially, Leonard E. Boyle, O. P., "The *Summa Confessorum* of John of Freiburg and the Popularization of the Moral Teaching of St. Thomas and of Some of His Contemporaries," in *St. Thomas Aquinas, 1274– 1974, Commemorative Studies,* 2 vols. (Toronto, 1974), 2:245-68; see also P. Michaud-Quantin, *Sommes de casuistique et manuels de confession au moyen age, du XIIe au XVIe siècle* (Louvain, 1962). I have used the edition of Augsburg, 1476, for the text of John of Freiburg's *Summa Confessorum* discussed here. See also the discussion by Thomas Tentler, Leonard Boyle, and others in C. Trinkhaus and H. Oberman, eds., *The Pursuit of Holiness in Late Medieval and Renaissance Religion* (Leiden, 1974), pp. 103-40.

4. For this discussion I have used the Venice, 1586 edition of Bromyard's *Summa Praedicantium.* For the date, see Leonard E. Boyle, O. P., "The Date of the *Summa Praedicantium* of John Bromyard," *Speculum* 48 (1973): 533- 37. Besides Th.-M. Charland, *Artes Praedicandi* (Paris-Ottawa, 1936), see the works of G. R. Owst, *Preaching in Medieval England* (Cambridge, 1926) and *Literature and Pulpit in Medieval England* (Cambridge, 1933). The most recent contribution to the discussion of the influence of sermons on literature is Siegfried Wenzel, "Chaucer and the Language of Contemporary Preaching," *Studies in Philology* 73 (1976): 138-61.

5. It is important to point out that Bromyard here is not simply echoing the earlier humanist antifeminism of John of Salisbury and other twelfth-century moralists, but rather reflects the new and much more virulent antifeminism of the later Middle Ages, an element of immense importance in the later development of the witch-figure. Bromyard was, of course, not alone. In Nicholas of Lyra's vast *Postillae,* the most popular biblical commentary of the later Middle Ages, written in the first half of the fourteenth century, the author in his comment on Exodus 22:18 emphatically corrects the vulgate Latin term *maleficos,* noting that the Hebrew term is feminine and that the term should be understood *sortilegam.* I have used the Basel, 1501 edition of the *Postillae,* printed with the *glossa ordinaria* and the interlinear gloss, vol. I, fol. 170v. See *The Cambridge History of the Bible,* ed. G. W. H. Lampe, vol. 2 (Cambridge, 1969), pp. 155-308, esp. 197-220.

6. The text of the *conclusio* may be found in the *Chartularium universitatis Parisiensis,* ed. H. Denifle and A. Chatelain, Vol. 4 (Paris, 1897), no. 1749, pp. 32-36. For Gerson, see Jean Gerson, *Oeuvres complètes,* vol. 10 (Paris, 1973), pp. 77-90; Lynn Thorndike, *History of Magic and Experimental Science* (New York, 1923-58), 4:114-31.

7. See Margaret Harvey, "Papal Witchcraft: The Charges against Benedict XIII," in *Sanctity and Secularity: The Church and the World, Studies in Church History,* ed. Derek Baker, vol. 10 (Oxford, 1973), pp. 109-16.

8. See Thorndike, *History,* 4:114-31, for a discussion of all of Gerson's works

on magic and astrology. Vol. 10 of the *Oeuvres complètes* prints the relevant texts on pp. 73-143. In addition, see D. G. Wayman, "The Chancellor and Jeanne d'Arc. February - July, A. D. 1429," *Franciscan Studies* 17 (1957): 273-303.

9. Joseph Hansen, *Quellen und Untersuchungen zur Geschichte des Hexenwahns und der Hexenverfolgung im Mittelalter* (Bonn, 1901), pp. 17-18. In general, Hansen's collection of excerpts from papal bulls, pp. 1-37, should be consulted.

10. Johann Huizinga, *The Waning of the Middle Ages* (reprint ed., New York, n.d.), p. 199. See the similar remarks concerning Jacopo Passavanti in Millard Meiss, *Painting in Florence and Siena after the Black Death* (New York, 1964), pp. 74-104.

11. Hansen, *Quellen*, pp. 71-82.

12. Ibid., pp. 105-9.

13. Ibid., pp. 195-200.

14. Ibid., pp. 227-31.

15. Ibid., pp. 208-12.

16. Hansen, *Quellen*, 112-18. Turrecremata was a theologian writing on canon law, but he appears to have been generally well-informed on recent canonist thought.

17. See Henri Maisonneuve, *Études sur les origines de l'inquisition* (Paris, 1960) and the Introduction, by Walter Ullmann, to Henry Charles Lea, *The Inquisition of the Middle Ages: Its Organization and Operation* (New York, 1969).

18. "Il *Tractatus Criminum*" in Hermann Kantorowicz, *Rechtshistorische Schriften* (Karlsruhe, 1970), pp. 273-86; Carlo Calisse, *A History of Italian Law* (Boston, 1928), pp. 400-32; A. Pertile, *Storia del Diritto Italiano*, vol. 5, *Storia del Diritto Penale*, 2nd ed. (Bologna, 1966), esp. pp. 434-62; G. Dahm, *Das Strafrecht Italiens im ausgehenden Mittelalter* (Berlin, 1931); R. His, *Das Strafrecht der deutschen Mittelalter* (Weimar, 1935) vol. 2, 5, 27 on secular magistrates' authority to punish blasphemy and sorcery.

19. See the references below, Appendix II, and W. Engelmann, *Die Wiedergeburt der Rechtskultur in Italien* (Leipzig, 1939); Hans von Hentig, *Die Strafe*, vol. 1 (Berlin, 1954).

20. Ullmann, Introduction to Lea, *Inquisition*, p. 42, citing the *Liber Sextus* 5, 2. 8.; H. C. Lea, *Materials Toward a History of Witchcraft*, ed. and comp. Arthur Howland (Philadelphia, 1938), 1:244-45; 2:648. The *crimen exceptum* is an important category of legal thought in itself and important, also, in its role as part of the early European legal legacy to modern states. The notion of a crime, or category of crimes, that is at once so horrendous and so threatening to the state that the mere accusation suspends normal legal procedure and institutes special procedures, has never been studied. Its relation to the *crimen magiae* is only one part of its long and complex history. See Norman Cohn, *Europe's Inner Demons* (New York, 1975), pp. 229, 253.

21. Only two of the many scholars who have studied the problem of witchcraft have attempted to consider the semantic history of the term *maleficium*:

Cohn, *Europe's Inner Demons*; Robert-Leon Wagner, *"Sorcier" et "magicien" Contribution à l'histoire du vocabulaire de la magie* (Paris, 1939). Although both works are important, neither is conclusive on this point.

22. See below, Appendix II.

23. Many texts are cited, not always systematically or completely, in Lea, *Materials*, and Hansen, *Quellen*. See also Lea's *History of the Inquisition*.

24. For two unrelated examples, see Robert E. Lerner, *The Heresy of the Free Spirit in the Later Middle Ages* (Berkeley and Los Angeles, 1972), and Penn R. Szittya, "The Antifraternal Tradition in Middle English Literature," *Speculum* 52 (1977): 287-313.

25. *Monumenta Germaniae Historica, Epistolae saeculi XIII e regestis Pontificum Romanorum*, vol. 1, p. 435.

26. Cohn, *Europe's Inner Demons*, pp. 266-67, cites the standard bibliography on Konrad von Marburg. It has not been emphasized enough, however, that Konrad's own spiritual career generated a view of demonology that greatly influenced Gregory IX and other thirteenth-century writers.

27. S. Kuttner, "Ecclesia de occultis non judicat," *Acta Congressus Iuridici Internationalis VII Saeculo a Decretalibus Gregorii IX*, vol. 3 (Rome, 1936), 225-46. Kuttner does not go beyond the early thirteenth century, but his study shows the considerable change that traditional canonist thought would have to undergo.

28. Maisonneuve, *Études*, p. 259.

29. Hansen, *Quellen*, pp. 122-23; 145-49.

30. Richard Kieckhefer, *European Witch Trials: Their Foundation in Popular and Learned Culture, 1300–1500* (London, 1976), pp. 106-47. This very valuable compilation of known trials touching on magic and witchcraft between 1300 and 1500 permits the historian to easily locate a vast number of cases and to check the data supporting each. In my investigation of Kieckhefer's table, it seems to me that all of the trials deal with what can justly be called sorcery and was probably understood in traditional contexts by the judges. On the growth of lawyers, magistrates and judges as an influential group in early modern culture, see William J. Bouwsma, "Lawyers and Early Modern Culture," *American Historical Review* 78 (1973):303-27.

31. The field of learned magic has been considerably illuminated in recent years with the appearance of a number of works of high quality and great intelligence: Frances Yates, *Giordano Bruno and the Hermetic Tradition* (London, 1964); E. Garin, "Considerazioni sulla magia," and "Magia ed astrologia nella cultura del Rinascimento," both in Garin, *Medioevo e Rinascimento* (Bari, 1961), the second having been translated into English as "Magic and Astrology in the Civilization of the Renaissance," in E. Garin, *Science and Civic Life in the Italian Renaissance*, trans. Peter Munz (New York, 1969), pp. 145-65; D. P. Walker, *Spiritual and Demonic Magic From Ficino to Campanella* (London, 1958; reprint ed., Notre Dame, Ind., 1975). A very learned and neglected text is C. S. Lewis, *English Literature in the Sixteenth Century, Excluding Drama*, Oxford History of English Literature (Oxford, 1954), Introduction, "New Learning and New Ignorance," pp. 1-65. Thorndike, *History*,

vols. 4 and 5, are still indispensable. Wayne Schumacher, *The Occult Sciences in the Renaissance* (Berkeley and Los Angeles, 1972) is less reliable than the foregoing works. On Ficino, see Paola Zambelli, "Platone, Ficino e la Magia," in *Studia Humanitatis. Ernesto Grassi zum 70. Geburtstag*, eds. E. Hora and E. Kessler (Munich, 1973), pp. 121-42.

32. "Magic and Astrology," trans. Munz, p. 149. As I suggest below, others' perceptions of Ficino's new magic did not represent a break with medieval views. See also Will-Erich Peuckert, *Pansophie* (Berlin, 1956).

33. Ibid., p. 153.

34. See P. M. Rattansi, "Alchemy and Natural Magic in Raleigh's *History of the World*," *Ambix* 13 (1965): 122-38. Rattansi's highly suggestive theory that magic was condemned by Aristotelians and promoted by Platonists has been taken rather uncritically by recent historians; Platonic condemnations of magic, through Augustine and Hugh of St. Victor, formed the basis of later medieval and renaissance attitudes, as has been shown above.

35. Walker, *Ficino Campanella*, pp. 85-126.

36. *Ibid.*, pp. 146-52; Peter Burke, "Witchcraft and Magic in Renaissance Italy: Gianfrancesco Pico and His *Strix*," in *The Damned Art: Essays in the Literature of Witchcraft*, ed. S. Anglo (London, 1977), pp. 32-52; Gene Brucker, "Sorcery in Early Renaissance Florence," *Studies in the Renaissance* 10 (1963): 7-24. The history of prosecutions for magic and, later, witchcraft, in Italy in the fifteenth and early sixteenth centuries has, on the whole, been neglected by historians of witchcraft. The works cited here constitute an exception. The urbanized life of Italy, the considerable development of criminal law in the secular courts, and the general learning of Italian theologians and inquisitors such as Bernard of Como and the layman Paulus Grillandus, strongly suggest that the conceptual framework of magic included later witchcraft. The contribution of humanism has yet to be assessed.

37. "Witchcraft and Religion in Sixteenth-Century Germany: the Formation and Consequences of an Orthodoxy," *Archiv für Reformationsgeschichte* 62 (1971): 266-78; see also Midelfort's splendid study *Witch-hunting in Southwestern Germany, 1562–1684: The Social and Intellectual Foundations* (Stanford, 1972).

38. Most recently, see Christopher Baxter, "Johann Weyer's *De Praestigiis Daemonum*: Unsystematic Psychopathology," in Anglo, ed., *The Damned Art*, pp. 53-75.

39. Walker, *Ficino to Campanella*, p. 144 (cf., 144-88). The search for a "nonmagical" Christianity has not been extensively considered by historians of the sixteenth century.

40. Ibid., pp. 171-78; Ursula Lange, *Untersuchungen zur Bodins Démonomanie* (Frankfurt, 1970); Christopher Baxter, "Jean Bodin's *De la Démonomanie des Sorciers*: The Logic of Persecution," in Anglo, ed., *The Damned Art*, pp. 76-105.

41. Walker, *Ficino to Campanella*, pp. 178-89; Henri Busson, *Littérature et théologie* (Paris, 1962), pp. 9-32. Del Rio is an interesting thinker whose life and work have been insufficiently studied.

42. Most recently, in his Introduction to *Witchcraft: Catalogue of the Witchcraft Collection in Cornell University Library* (Millwood, N.Y., 1977), pp. xvii-xviii. See also Jeffrey Russell, *Witchcraft in the Middle Ages* (Ithaca, 1972).

43. Dorothy Bethurum, *The Homilies of Wulfstan* (Oxford, 1957), p. 273; see also Dorothy Whitelock, *Sermo Lupi ad Anglos* (London, 1952). I am grateful to Malcolm Parkes for this reference.

44. F. N. Robinson, ed., *The Works of Geoffrey Chaucer* (Boston, 1957), p. 89.

45. Trans. G. L. Burr, reprinted in Kors and Peters, *Witchcraft in Europe*, pp. 107-12.

46. Russell, *Witchcraft*, p. 232; Hansen, *Quellen*, pp. 360-407.

47. Russell, *Witchcraft*, p. 232.

Appendix I

Res fragilis:
Torture in Early European Law

I.

Rationalist historians of the nineteenth century wrote with a sense of freedom from the institutions of the past and a sense of hope for the future that have since generally disappeared from modern historiography. Having identified the enemies of reason and humanity, having described and denounced them, they—and the society for which they wrote—were at last free of them. Barbarism, superstition, despotism, theology; these terms, in the work of Lecky, White, Lea, and others, stand like gravestones over institutions and beliefs that meticulous scholarship and philosophical hostility had condemned, once and for all, to the buried wreckage of a hopelessly irrational past. When Henry Charles Lea began the final section of his first major historical work, *Superstition and Force,* he looked back at his earlier chapters on compurgation, the judicial duel, and the ordeal and summarily described all of these as "the resources devised by human ingenuity and credulity when called upon to decide questions too intricate for the impatient intellect of a rude and semi-barbarous age." He then linked these with the subject of his last chapters, judicial torture:

There was another mode, however, of attaining the same object which has received the sanction of the wisest lawgivers during the greater part of the world's history, and our survey of man's devious wanderings in the search of truth would be incomplete without glancing at the subject of the judicial use of torture.

Compurgation, the judicial duel, and the ordeal all belonged, as Lea well knew, to a universe of legal and social ideas that had come under heavy attack and was largely destroyed, at least in the judicial sphere, during the late twelfth and early thirteenth centuries.[1] Judicial torture, however, belonged to a new order of jurisprudence, one whose disappearance from the lawbooks of European and American societies was not complete itself until the nineteenth century, and many of whose traces still constitute the bases of substantive and procedural law in modern societies. Lea wrote with the confident assurance that torture, like the duel and the ordeal, had finally vanished from the world, although he also noted, as have other scholars, the ambiguous place of judicial torture in the rational legal universe of early modern Europe. In the history of western law, torture plays a role that seems to echo at once both a remote and archaic legal universe and, in the decades since Lea's death in 1909, an appallingly contemporary one. The earliest protests against judicial torture in the modern world came from the Italian jurists of the thirteenth century. Two of the most eloquent, immediate, and recent protests come from the French jurist Alec Mellor and the philosopher Jean-Paul Sartre.[2]

A succinct explanation of the appearance of torture in the courts of thirteenth-century Europe was provided in 1892 in an address given by James C. Welling to the Anthropological Society of Washington:

From this formal species of proof [*duel, ordeal, and compurgation*] men pass to a matter-of-fact species of proof, according as their reasoning powers grow stronger and their appliances for the rational discovery of truth become more and more available in the domain of justice. In this passage of the human race from a ceremonial and formal species of negative proof to a rationalistic and substantive species of positive proof, the method of proof by the intervention of torture occupies a place which may be described as a sort of "half-way house" situate between these two typical and distinctive forms of judicial procedure.[3]

Welling belonged to Lea's generation and shared Lea's belief that his world had seen the end of judicial torture—one of the best intentioned and least securely founded beliefs of that optimistic generation. According to Lea and Welling, judicial torture constitutes a kind of bridge between irrational and rational legal universes, a significant, if repugnant, step in that process by means of which rules of evidence, the authority of judicial enquiry, and the extention of legal reasoning came to constitute a great humanizing force in the conflict between the underlying principles of social organization and the momentary, but terrible, exigencies of social fear. Lea and Welling both knew also that judicial torture had been used long before the Middle Ages in far more sophisticated systems of jurisprudence, and our own time has witnessed its vigorous resurgence. If judicial torture is a bridge between different legal universes, it is a bridge that has been crossed several times in both directions.

Torture is one of those signs of increased social rationalism that praisers of rationalism often neglect. The capacity to inflict pain willfully and consciously and, on a civil scale, to institute systems of terror, is a characteristic feature of most human societies during most periods of their history, but judicial torture is always a product of an increased reliance upon reason. Historians of those highly reasonable centuries, the twelfth and the nineteenth, often fail to see many of the consequences of discarding several of the old irrational bonds to which society had become accustomed in favor of a greater reliance upon human energies and the capacity of human analysis. The rejection of compurgation, the duel, and the ordeal around 1200 meant, to be sure, a new reluctance to depend upon the intervention of the supernatural in affairs that men felt able to deal with by their own agency. In the twentieth century torture has reappeared under a similar guise, that of state necessity, when it is used to deal with crimes or the threat of crimes whose enormity and deviousness appear to render due process ineffective. The temptation to exceed the traditional limits of the law, or to institute judicial novelties hitherto repugnant to the law, in order better to protect those institutions and principles that the law itself was designed to protect usually implies both an acute sense of social danger and a failure of confidence in the efficacy of traditional legal institutions. Those who approved the use of torture in the thirteenth century were thus, in their own way, humanists; that is, they chose a means of judicial enquiry that relied solely upon human agency to determine complex instances of disputed truth. They were inspired by a new concept of legal personality and responsibility, they developed new judicial procedures to accommodate it, and they grew particularly cautious in designing safeguards for their new procedures.

Henry Charles Lea's study of judicial torture between the sixth and the eighteenth centuries is more than a chapter in remote and archaic legal history. Lea realized that the history of legal procedure is far more than the excessively specialized and recondite subdivision of *Rechtsgeschichte* that scholars often make it appear to be. Like Maitland, he knew that procedure, like all public ritual in traditional societies, is an integral part of social experience that cannot be understood outside of the cultural matrices of the period under consideration. "The history of jurisprudence is the history of civilization," Lea remarked in the later editions of *Superstition and Force,* and Lea's own meticulous scholarship and astute sensitivity to the multiple interactions of life and law between the eighth and the eighteenth centuries made his works not only landmarks in American historical scholarship, but pathfinding contributions to social and cultural history as well.

II.

In Greek and Roman law, torture was contingent upon two conditions: unfree personal status and particularly heinous crimes. Slaves could legally be tortured because they did not possess legal personality and the responsibility of free men. In cases of particularly significant crimes, especially treason, even free men appear to have been generally immune from torture until the end of the first century of the Roman Empire. In spite of the revolting detail in which Suetonius describes the penchant for torture on the part of several first-century emperors, particularly Tiberius, Caligula, and Domitian, judicial torture did not make inroads into criminal procedure, except for cases of treason, until the second and third centuries A.D.[4] The increased and more precisely focussed authority of the state, the wider role of imperial officials in the conduct of civil and criminal cases, and the absorption of Roman jurisprudence and legal education into the administrative bureaucracy of the Empire, all contributed to the new role of judicial torture. A new usage of procedural terms, in which, for example, the old term for the interrogation of witnesses, *quaestio*, became synonymous with torture (hence, the Medieval Latin *quaestio* and Old French *question*, both of which mean torture) as torture became a normal part of the interrogation of both the accused and witnesses, reflects these profound changes in procedural law. By the fourth century, torture had become a standard element in criminal procedure, and the circle of heinous crimes for which even the upper level of free men, the *honestiores*, might be tortured widened perceptibly to include sorcery and other crimes. With the publication of the *Theodosian Code* in 438 and the *Corpus Iuris Civilis* of Justinian in 534, *tormentum*, originally an aggravated sentence of death, was used interchangibly with *tortura* and *quaestio*. The torturers, the *tortor* and *quaesitor*, were legal officials, and the standard definition of *quaestio* became that of the jurist Ulpian as embodied in the *Digest* of Justinian: "*Quaestio* should be understood to mean the torment and suffering of the body in order to elicit the truth."[5]

The new legal universe of the Roman Latin West after the sixth century generally reduced the place torture had attained in Roman law. Although many of the law codes of the Germanic kingdoms of Europe retained some traces of the Roman law of torture, particularly in the cases of slaves, but occasionally, as in Visigothic Spain, in the cases of free men as well, the concept of legal personality in these Germanic laws generally prevented free warriors from being subjected to torture, or, indeed, to any judicial process remotely resembling a modern trial. The ubiquity of the accusatorial procedure, according to which the outcome of a case depended more upon an outright denial of charges or a resort to the judicial duel, compurgation, or the ordeal, considerably restricted the freedom of the judge to ascertain fact, the compulsory power of the public order, and the diminution of personal public status. From the seventh through the twelfth centuries, men might challenge the truth of each other's accusations in a duly constituted court by offering the oath of innocence, sometimes supported by the oaths of others (compurgation), or they might reject an accusation by submitting, or having someone else submit on their behalf, to one form or another of the ordeal, or they might offer to fight a judicial duel. But no court could countenance the possibility of torturing a free man. Slaves, serfs, and strangers might still be tortured, but this was precisely because they lacked what free men had: a specific legal status, a kindred, and an immunity from all but the first accusatorial step in the judicial process.

The history of European law from the seventh through the twelfth centuries is in large part the history of the transformation of this particularized and limited role of judicial procedure. In the lapidary phrase of Sir Henry Maine, it witnesses the transformation in law from "status to contract," and it includes not only a legal revolution, but a new theology and new concepts of the social bond as well. As Lea points out, the legal universe of the period 600–1200 was largely irrational; that is, disabled from inquiring except by the most limited and rigid procedures into the full dimensions of a legal offense, courts at the last resort relied upon divine intervention to determine issues that the personal status of the accuser and the accused made impossible to settle by any other form. Judicial procedure is, of course, a form of social control, and the legal procedures of this period were consonant with the social conceptions of early medieval society. The status of individuals and the limitations upon judicial procedure, as much as the concept of immanent justice, shored up the courts of early medieval Europe.

In the course of the eleventh and twelfth centuries, the forces that had sustained this legal universe were themselves transformed. The intellectual and political attacks upon the ordeal and the judicial duel grew stronger as new ideas of legal bonds drove out older ideas.[6] The revival of Roman law studies in the eleventh and twelfth centuries led to new conceptions of the role of law in society at the same time as a new interest in Roman antiquity gave rise to new influences in historiography, literature, and the visual arts. The social dimension of the "Renaissance of the Twelfth Century"—in terms of both social theory and social institutions—has often been slighted in favor of the traditional approach of the history of ideas. Yet it is hardly too much to say that the period between 1050 and 1250 witnessed not as the least influential of its many transformations a legal revolution, the detailed history of which constituted an indispensible commentary upon other profound changes in European society. The appearance of new judicial procedures, the growth and activity of new ecclesiastical and secular courts, the changed character and the distribution of legal education and the concurrent growth of a new legal literature, and the broadened spectrum of careers open to those trained in the law all constituted part of this revolution, and both the social and intellectual changes of this period constitute the backdrop of the reappearance of torture in the courts of the thirteenth century.

III.

The first documentary evidence of the reappearance of torture in Western Europe is found in the *Liber Juris Civilis* of the city of Verona of 1228, and torture appears in the criminal sections of the laws of a number of other Italian city-republics during the ensuing few decades, in the *Constitutiones Regni Siciliani* of Frederick II in 1231, and, in Castile, with its tradition of continuing torture, in the *Fuero Juzgo* of Ferdinand III in 1241 and the *Siete Partidas* of Alfonso X in 1265. The victim of torture in most of these instances was the notorious criminal; as the laws of Vercelli of 1241 observe, "No man ought to be tortured or executed unless [he is known to be] a common rogue, a thief, or a man of ill repute." The appearance of torture under these circumstances was not, it should be said at the outset, solely the result of the renewed study of Roman law. Rather, as R. C. van Caenegem has suggested,

in the last analysis it was the needs of criminal practice and new principles for the pursuit of criminals that were responsible for the reappearance of torture in Europe, and not the revival of Roman legal studies. It seems that the renewal of Roman law and the reception of torture in ecclesiastical practice were the result of the diffusion of the inquisitorial procedure in Europe.[7]

Indeed, so much casual historiography has indiscriminately linked torture both to the revival of Roman legal studies and the ecclesiastical Inquisition, that it is necessary to clarify the origins of torture in early thirteenth-century criminal procedure.

Besides the accusatorial process, there were other specialized judicial procedures in pre-twelfth-century Europe, although these were often not widely used or were suitable only for particular sets of circumstances. In certain circumstances, as early as the ninth century, a category of *mala fama*, ill-repute, existed in the Carolingian courts, and anyone in this category might be condemned by a judge if he refused to exculpate himself by oath or by ordeal. Also in the ninth century, a notorious offense could be prosecuted by the judge without an accuser, and by the twelfth century the necessity of an accuser could be dispensed with in cases involving *infamia*. As a later lawyer remarked, "In the inquisitorial process, the judge himself does not take the part of the accuser, but *infamia* stands in the place of the accuser or denouncer." Such phenomena as the episcopal visitation to the ecclesiastical institutions of a diocese in canon law and the visitation of royal judicial representatives to a district in secular law both established the requirement that the inhabitants of such places were obliged to inform the proper authorities of crimes committed since the last visitation. In ecclesiastical and secular terms, this practice was known as the *denunciatio*, and some writers linked it to several scriptural and patristic references to social correction in early Christian communities.[8] Because of the enduring idea that only a charge brought by an accuser was a complete charge, convictions under these forerunners of the inquisitorial process tended to result in lighter penalties, and in some cases authorities required a full confession from the accused in addition to conviction by *inquisitio* in order that a full penalty might be imposed. Out of these specialized and tentative beginnings, there emerged by the twelfth century a consensus that in certain kinds of cases another procedure than the accusatorial might be used, one which eventually placed considerably greater latitude and power in the hands of the judge than the older procedure, one which dispensed with the traditional accuser and substituted either a denouncer (who might have to furnish proof), or, eventually, a court official, the *promotor*, who formally made charges. Even during these changes, however, some traditional rights of the accused remained relatively undisturbed: he might be informed of the names and the evidence of witnesses and examine them and refute their testimony himslf; he was not yet subject to torture; he might have the aid of counsel, and although all his testimony had to be given under oath, another novelty, courts generally conducted such hearings warily.

The most significant aspect of the inquisitorial procedure was the elimination of the necessity of the liable accuser and the increased latitude and power of the courts and of the authorities they represented. Human agency, rather than supernatural, was responsible for investigating the truth or falsehood of an accusation, and the increased judicial liability that had been traditional in ecclesiastical communities now became a presupposition of secular communities as well. The overriding need to protect the public order and to punish crime constituted the background for the adaption of the earlier inquisitorial procedures to new social uses. From the experiences of the notorious heretic, the offending member of a religious community, and the ill-famed villager, a new judicial procedure had been shaped that gave great power to the judicial authorities and imposed a new kind of liability upon the accused.

That liability and that power did not develop everywhere in the twelfth century in quite the same way. As Maitland has pointed out, what is peculiar to England is not the dissatisfaction with waged "laws" and supernatural probations, nor the adoption of an "inquisition" or "inquest" as the core of the new procedure, but in the form that the inquest takes, or rather retains. By instituting the Grand Assize and the four Petty Assizes Henry II had placed at the disposal of litigants in certain actions that "inquest of the country" which ever since the Norman Conquest had formed part of the governmental machinery of England. His reforms were effected just in time. But for them, we should indeed have known the inquest, but it would in all likelihood have been the inquest of the canon law, the *enquête* of the new French jurisprudence.[9]

Nor, it must be said, were all of the later repugnant features of the inquisitorial process immediately clear, either to churchmen or to French jurists, in the course of the twelfth century. The inquisitorial procedure offered what to a modern litigant would seem very familiar and acceptable: avoidance of rigid and excessively formalized charges; an airing of testimony and a weighing of evidence, with opportunity for rebuttal, that was unavailable under the accusatorial process in its eleventh- and twelfth-century forms; the possibility of a trained judge who might act equitably in establishing procedure and weighing intangibles. At its outset in the twelfth century, at least, inquisitorial procedure seemed to reflect precisely that increased reliance upon reason, conscience, and a broadened concept of the social order that historians have otherwise praised in other aspects of the life of the period.

What caused the inquisitorial process which, in spite of Maitland's disclaimer for England, might have remained simply a new procedure giving the court greater investigatory powers, first, to admit torture, and second, to produce the well-documented procedural abuses of the thirteenth and fourteenth centuries? The sharpened concept of treason in the twelfth century and the thirteenth-century concept of heresy as a kind of treason to God certainly constituted opportunities for the laws of treason in Roman jurisprudence to be invoked once again, although in England those suspected of treason were probably not tortured—and even then rather by orders of the monarch or of Council—until the sixteenth century.[10] Van Caenegem's suggestion that the reappearance of torture is attributable to new concepts of criminal law has much to offer. For it was not the heretic who was the first to be tortured in the Italian laws of the early thirteenth century, but the notorious criminal. Torture was first used in the treatment of criminals, particularly, it may be supposed, those accused of concealed crimes in which the identity of the guilty party was not immediately discernible, although strong suspicion of the accused, based upon ill-repute, may well exist. It is but a short step from instituting torture for those strongly suspected of committing a crime to trying those suspected of heresy, an offense much more heinous and more difficult to prove. As Pope Innocent IV observed in 1252 when for the first time he sanctioned the use of torture by the Inquisition, if torture is appropriate for those who break the laws of men, then it is more than fitting for those who break the laws of God.

The twelfth century saw new outbreaks of heresy, and the newly reorganized Church attacked it in areas of society with which ecclesiastical courts were generally unfamiliar.[11] The apparent magnitude of heretical society, the new authority of the Church, and the problems of discovering intellectual crime generated considerable ecclesiastical and lay concern, and the new legal procedure of the inquisitorial process (particularly in cases in which accusers were often hard to find, or unwilling to testify) offered a judicial approach to the problem. The Inquisition, or, technically, the Holy Office, took shape in the third quarter of the twelfth century and the first half of the thirteenth. Its agents were members of the new Orders, at first aiding, then growing independent of, the normal diocesan jurisdiction. In their hands, which were not, at first, necessarily the hands of trained lawyers, the inquisitorial procedure developed its earliest oppressive features, the concealment of the identity of witnesses and the content of evidence, the refusal of counsel, the demands to identify accomplices, the admission of evidence from hitherto unsuitable witnesses, and, in 1252 in the decretal *Ad extirpanda,* the introduction of torture. Henceforth, the inquisitorial process became burdened with perversions of rational procedure that exceeded the accusatorial system and the ordeals at their worst. By the end of the thirteenth century articulate Inquisitors such as Bernard Gui wrote learned and rational handbooks describing and justifying Inquisitorial procedure, and Gui was followed by Nicholas Eymeric and others, whose arguments were echoed in the ecclesiastical literature of the fifteenth and sixteenth centuries and in the literature of those secular courts which adopted both the inquisitorial procedure and its excesses and produced its own learned analyses in the sixteenth and seventeenth centuries.

Yet, in spite of perversion and excess and judicial incompetence, not all manifestations of the inquisitorial procedure, even those which retained torture, developed along lines identical to the ecclesiastical institution. As Walter Ullman has shown, there quickly grew up a cautionary literature concerning the excessive and improper use of torture almost as soon as the institution of torture itself reappeared.[12] Indeed, the lawyers themselves appear to have been among the first and the severest critics of the institution, and, by the sixteenth century, even the trained lawyers of the Inquisition in Rome and Spain became suspicious of the efficacy of torture, long before such suspicions acquired enough weight in the world of secular jurisprudence to begin the process of eliminating torture in the eighteenth and nineteenth centuries. By then, judicial torture and the inquisitorial process had long been used to perform the same grisly service for the monarchies of the sixteenth and seventeenth centuries that they had performed for the Church in the thirteenth and fourteenth—the enforcement of orthodox belief and conduct by a drastic curtailment of traditional judicial liberties and the development of an infallible instrument for detecting concealed and forbidden intellectual forms of dissent, from treason to witchcraft.[13]

The history of judicial torture and of the legal procedures that afforded opportunities for its appearance in thirteenth-century Europe is thus part of a larger chapter in social and intellectual history, as well as a topic of concern to social scientists and jurists who may be more interested in its twentieth-century manifestations than in its Roman and medieval origins. For the thirteenth-century lawyers who first cautioned against its random use, torture was a *res fragilis*, a delicate matter, which, although admissible in certain instances, could easily abort the judicial processes it was originally intended to serve. Those lawyers' warnings should not be taken lightly, nor should their limited approval of its use so obscure the humanitarian vision of twentieth-century investigators that they reject both approval and criticism together. For torture was not, as the decades since the publication of Lea's book have clearly shown, an historical aberration whose death knell was sounded, once and for all, by the irresistible onset of the Age of Reason and the legislative enlightenment of the states of Europe in the late eighteenth and early nineteenth centuries. The means of precise analysis offered by legal history and social science ought not to be expended in describing the history of such institutions as torture solely for the purpose of patronizing what Lea called "the impatient intellect of a rude and semibarbarous age," but for studying those configurations of social forces that permit, and then encourage, such instruments of public power. Lynn White once remarked that "to know the subliminal mind of a society, one must study the sources of its liturgies of inflicting death."[14] There are many other social liturgies whose sources require the same study, sources that produced both the medieval lawyers' reservations of the *res fragilis* and the enormities of the totalitarian state.[15]

NOTES

1. The best recent study of these circumstances is John W. Baldwin, "The Intellectual Preparation of the Canon of 1215 against Ordeals," *Speculum* 36 (1961), pp. 613-36; the fullest study is that of Hermann Nottarp, *Gottesurteilstudien*, Bamberger Abhandlungen und Forschungen, Bd. II (Munich, 1956).

See also the works cited in the introduction to Henry C. Lea, *The Ordeal* (Philadelphia, 1973).

2. Alec Mellor, *La Torture* (Paris, 1949), the most learned and humane of modern scholarly studies; Jean-Paul Sartre, Introduction to Henri Alleg, *The Question,* trans. John Calder (New York, 1958). Cf. Sartre, p. 17: "If patriotism has to precipitate us into dishonour; if there is no precipice of inhumanity over which nations and men will not throw themselves, then why, in fact, do we go to so much trouble to become, or to remain, men?"

3. *The Law of Torture: A Study in the Evolution of Law* (Washington, 1892), p. 2.

4. See Theodor Mommsen, *Römische Strafrecht* (rep. Graz, 1955), pp. 401-11. A recent summary is included in Peter Garnsey, *Social Status and Legal Privilege in the Roman Empire* (Oxford, 1970), pp. 141-47; 231-16.

5. *Digest* 47.10.15.41; cited by Garnsey, p. 141.

6. The most recent general study is that of Christopher Brooke, *The Twelfth Century Renaissance* (New York, 1969), with a good bibliography. There are particularly important discussions in R. W. Southern, *The Making of the Middle Ages* (New Haven, 1953) and G. Le Bras, ed., *L'Histoire du droit et des institutions de l'église,* Vol. VII, *L'Age classique, 1140–1378,* by J. Rambaud-Buhaut and Charles Lefebvre (Paris, 1965). See also the sources cited in Lea, *The Ordeal.*

7. "La Preuve dans le droit du moyen âge occidental. Rapport de synthèse," in *La Preuve,* Recueils de la Société Jean Bodin, Vol. XVII (Brussels, 1965), pp. 691-755 at 740. See also the older but valuable work of A. Esmein, *A History of Continental Criminal Procedure,* trans. J. Simpson (Boston, 1913) and Walter Ullmann, "Reflections on Medieval Torture," *Juridical Review* 56 (1944), pp. 123-37.

8. For the development of notoriety, see Jean Philippe Lévy, *La Hiérarchie des preuves dans le droit savant du moyen-âge,* Université de Lyons, Annales, Troisième série, Droit (Paris, 1939), pp. 32-66; see also the studies in the volume *La Preuve* cited in the preceding note.

9. F. Pollock and F. W. Maitland, *The History of English Law,* 2nd. ed., Vol. II (Cambridge, 1968), p. 604.

10. For the history of torture in England, see David Jardine, *A Reading on the Use of Torture in the Criminal Law of England Previously to the Commonwealth* (London, 1837); L. O. Pike, *A History of Crime in England* (London, 1873); Leonard A. Parry, *The History of Torture in England* (London, 1934); R. B. Pugh, *Imprisonment in Medieval England* (Cambridge, 1968); Pollock and Maitland, Vol. II, *passim.*

11. The standard work is Henry C. Lea, *A History of the Inquisition in the Middle Ages* (Philadelphia, 1887), 3 vols. There exist a number of abridged versions, and of these particularly useful for the aspects of legal procedure is Henry Charles Lea, *The Inquisition of the Middle Ages: Its Organization and Operation,* with an Historical Introduction by Walter Ullmann (New York, 1969). On the Church's search for heretics and its attitude toward legal procedure, see Austin P. Evans, "Hunting Subversion in the Middle Ages,"

Speculum 33 (1958), pp. 1-22; Henri Maisonneuve, *Etudes sur l'origine de l'inquisition,* (Paris, 1960).

12. "Reflections on Medieval Torture," above, n. 7. See also Walter Ullmann, *The Medieval Idea of Law as Represented by Lucas de Penna* (London, 1946), pp. 159-61.

13. Much of this literature is briefly surveyed in Henry Charles Lea, *Materials Toward a History of Witchcraft,* ed. Arthur Howland (Philadelphia, 1939), Vol. II.

14. "The Legacy of the Middle Ages in the American Wild West," *Speculum* 40 (1965), pp. 191-202 at 199. That such social liturgies exert a continuing and dangerous fascination is obvious to any citizen of a twentieth-century state. See the informative study by Hans von Hentig, "The Pillory: A Medieval Punishment," in his *Studien zur Kriminalgeschichte* (Bern, 1962), pp. 112-28: "There is a metempsychosis of human concepts. Certain punishments which have been abolished as utterly ineffectual, and even damaging, emerge again and get hold of the mind. Being fit dischargers of emotional tensions, they are restored by the return of men of similar emotional instability."

15. The comparative character of legal procedure, particularly as it may apply to the policies of the twentieth-century state in its treatment of criminal and political offenses has not received the attention of many scholars. A particularly original comparative study on these lines, whose footnotes are often as stimulating as the main argument itself, is Mirjan Damaska, "Evidentiary Barriers to Conviction and Two Models of Criminal Procedure: A Comparative Study," *University of Pennsylvania Law Review* 121 (1973), pp. 506-89. Professor Damaska offers considerably less simplified observations on the relation of the inquisitorial procedure to torture than my remarks above.

The greatest work on the history of judicial torture is that of Piero Fiorelli, *La tortura giudiziaria nel diritto comune,* 2 vols. (Milan, 1953–54), an exhaustive and massively documented study that is not likely to be replaced. Among shorter works, that of Alec Mellor, *La Torture* (Paris, 1949) is certainly the most learned and humane and makes an eloquent plea against the revival of judicial torture in the twentieth century. In German, the work of Franz Helbing and Max Bauer, *Die Tortur. Geschichte der Folter im Kriminalverfahren aller Zeiten und Völker* (Berlin, 1926) has extensive documentation. There is a large bibliography of works on recent instances of judicial torture, although many alleged surveys either fail to take historical questions into account or attempt to indict the institution of torture by the use of misplaced psychological investigation or generally uncritical indignation. The work of George Ryley Scott, *The History of Torture Throughout the Ages* (London, 1949) is of this last type and should be used with caution.

The most scholarly general history of criminal procedure is the old work of A. Esmein, *A History of Continental Criminal Procedure,* trans. J. Simpson (Boston, 1913). Two early articles by Walter Ullmann offer additions to Esmein's study: "Reflections on Medieval Torture," *Juridical Review* 56 (1944), pp. 123-37, and "Some Medieval Principles of Criminal Procedure," *Juridical Review* 59 (1947), pp. 1-28. The most useful recent studies on the law of proof in general, with much information upon the ordeal and torture are included in *La Preuve*, Recueils de la Société Jean Bodin, Vol. XVII (Brussels, 1965). Particularly important are the studies of F. L. Ganshof (pp. 71-98), Jean Gaudemet (pp. 99-136), J. Ph. Lévy (pp. 137-68), and R. C. van Caenegem (pp. 691-754).

The most recent study of the principles of political violence is that of E. V. Walter, *Terror and Resistance: A Study of Political Violence* (New York, 1969).

There is extensive treatment of the history of torture in particular regions in the works of Pertile, Dahm, His, and Cauzons (cited above in Chapter 6). The recent studies of Jeffrey Russell and Norman Cohn properly place great emphasis upon the role of judicial torture in shaping the persecution of heresy, magic, and witchcraft. For heresy and the Inquisition, see especially Henri Maisonneuve, *Etudes sur les origines de l'inquisition* (Paris, 1960) and Siegfried Leutenbauer, *Hexerei- und Zaubereidelikt in der Literatur von 1450 bis 1550* (Berlin, 1972). L. Tanon, *Histoire des tribunaux de l'Inquisition en France* (Paris, 1893), offers additional substantial data for France. Three studies by Hans Fehr have contributed substantially to the history of torture: "Gottesurteil und Folter: eine Studie zur Dämonologie des Mittelalters und der neuren Zeit," *Festgabe für Rudolf Stammler* (Berlin and Leipzig, 1926); "Zur Erklärung von Folter und Hexenprozess," *Zeitschrift für schweizerische Geschichte* 24 (1944): 581-85; "Zur Lehre vom Folterprozess," *Zeitschrift der Savigny-Stiftung für Rechtsgeschichte. Germanistische Abteilung* 53 (1933), p. 317 ff. Eberhard Schmidt, *Inquisitionsprozesse und Rezepten. Studien zur Geschichte des Strafverfahrens in Deutschland vom 13. bis 16. Jahrhundert* (Leipzig, 1940), focuses upon the question of torture in greater detail than His. See now John H. Langbein, *Torture and the Law of Proof* (Chicago, 1978).

Appendix 2

Nicholas Eymeric:
On Heresy, Magic, and
the Inquisitor

Throughout the fourteenth century, manuals for inquisitors grew more detailed and systematic. Between the *Practica officii inquisitoris heretice pravitatis* of Bernard Gui, written in 1323/24, and the *Directorium inquisitorum* of Nicholas Eymeric, written in 1376, the question of the magician as heretic was extensively explored. Eymeric's work, especially, became the most widely circulated and widely read manual for inquisitors between the late fourteenth and the seventeenth centuries. It was printed in 1578 in a careful edition with many additions, by Francisco Peña, a learned jurist at the papal court; other editions and printings soon followed in 1585, 1587, 1591, 1597, and 1607. Thus, Eymeric's remarks upon the topic of the magician as heretic are especially important because they formed the basis of most later inquisitorial approaches to the topic. His treatment of heretical magic occurs in part 2 of the *Directorium,* in *Quaestiones* 42 (*De Sortilegiis et divinatoribus*), and 43 (*De Invocantibus Daemones*). The translations of the two questions follow:[1]

The forty-second question asks whether magicians and diviners are to be considered heretics or as those suspected of heresy and whether they are to be subjected to the judgment of the Inquisitor of heretics. To this we answer that there are two things to be seen here, just as there are really two things asked in this question. The first is, whether magicians and diviners are subject to the judgment of the Inquisitor of heretics. The second, posed thusly, is whether they are to be considered as heretics or as those suspected of heresy.

1.   The first thing to be considered, just as in the last *Quaestio* different kinds of blasphemers were distinguished, is that diviners and magicians must be distinguished; that is, there are two kinds of diviners and magicians.

2.   Some are to be considered magicians and diviners just as are those who act purely according to the technique of chiromancy, who divine things from the lineaments of the hand and judge natural effects and the condition of men from this. . . .

3.   Some others, however, are magicians and diviners who are not pure chiromantics, but are contracted to heretics, as are those who show the honor of *latria*[2] or *dulia*[3] to the demons, who rebaptize children and do other similar things. And they do these things in order to foresee the future or penetrate to the innermost secrets of the heart. These people are guilty of manifest heresy. And such magicians and diviners do not evade the judgment of the Inquisitor, but are punished according to the laws pertaining to heretics.

The Forty-third question asks whether those who invoke demons, either magicians or heretics or those suspected of heresy, are subject to the judgment of the Inquisitor of heretics. . . .

2.   It appears to the Inquisitors from the above-mentioned books and from other books that certain invokers of demons manifestly show the honor of *latria* to the demons they invoke, inasmuch as they sacrifice to them, adore them, offer up horrible prayers to them, vow themselves to the service of the demons, promise them their obedience, and otherwise commit themselves to the demons, swearing by the name of some superior demon whom they invoke. They willingly celebrate the praises of the demon or sing songs in his honor and genuflect or prostrate themselves before him. They observe chastity out of reverence for the demon or abstain upon his instructions or they lacerate their own flesh. Out of reverence for the demon or by his instructions they wear white or black vestments. They worship him by signs and characters and unknown names. They burn candles or incense to him or aromatic spices. They sacrifice animals and birds, catching their blood as a curative agent, or they burn them, throwing salt in the fire and making a holocaust in this manner. All of these things and many more evil things are found in consulting and desiring things from demons, in all of which and in whichever the honor of *latria*, if the above things are considered intelligently, is clearly shown to the demons. If, note well, the sacrifices to God according to the old and

the new law are considered, it is found there that these acts are true sacrifices only when exhibited to God, and not to the demons. This, then, is the case with the first category of those who invoke or speak on behalf of demons. . . . And by this manner the priests used to invoke Baal, offering their own blood and that of animals, as one reads in 4 *Kings*, 18.

3. Certain other invokers of demons show to the demons they invoke not the honor of *latria*, but that of *dulia*, in that they insert in their wicked prayers the names of demons along with those of the Blessed or the Saints, making them mediators in their prayers heard by God. They bow down before images of wax, worshipping God by their names or qualities. These things and many other wretched things are found described in the aforementioned books in which the honor of *dulia* is shown to demons. If, indeed, the means of praying to the Saints which the Church has diligently instituted are considered, it will clearly be seen that these prayers are to be said, not to demons, but only to the Saints and the Blessed. This, then, is the case of the second category of those who invoke demons. And in this manner the Saracens invoke Mohammed as well as God and the Saints and certain Beghards invoke Petrus Johannis and others condemned by the Church.

4. Yet certain other invokers of demons make a certain kind of invocation in which it does not appear clearly that the honor either of *latria* or *dulia* is shown to the demons invoked, as, in tracing a circle on the ground, placing a child in the circle, setting a mirror, a sword, an amphora, or something else in the way before the boy, holding their book of necromancy, reading it, and invoking the demon and other suchlike, as is taught by that art and proved by the confessions of many. This, then, is the third way of invoking demons. And by this means Saul invoked the spirit of the python through the Pythoness. In Saul's invocation, it is seen, no honor was done, neither *dulia* nor *latria*, as one reads in 1 *Kings*, 26.

It seems, therefore, that the means of invoking demons vary in three ways. These conclusions pose in turn three cases or conclusions according to which the invokers of demons ought to be distinguished from one another in three ways.

5. First, the case or conclusion is that if the invokers of demons show to the demons they invoke the honor of *latria* by whatever means and if they are clearly and judicially convicted of this, or if they confess, then they are to be held by the judgment of the Church not as magicians, but as heretics, and if they recant and abjure heresy they are to be perpetually immured as penitent heretics. If, however, they do not wish to desist or if they say they wish to desist and repent but do not wish to abjure, or if they do abjure and afterwards relapse, they are to be relinquished to the secular arm, punished by the ultimate torture according to all the canonical sanctions which judge other heretics.

This conclusion may be deduced in three ways: first from the sayings of the saints and doctors of theology, second from the sayings of the doctors of canon law, and third from the decisions of the Church.

First, from the sayings of the theologians, Blessed St. Augustine in Book 10 of *The City of God*, speaking of sacrifices shown only to God and not to Demons, says this: "We see that it is observed in each republic that men honor the highest leader by a singular sign which, if it is offered to someone else, would be the hateful crime of *lèse-majesté*. And thus it is written in the divine law under pain of death to those who offer divine honors to others. Exterior deeds are signs of interior deeds, just as spoken words are the signs of things; we direct our voices signifying prayers or praises to him, to whom we offer the same things in our hearts which we say, so we know that in sacrificing a visible sacrifice is to be offered to him to whom in our hearts we ought to offer ourselves as an invisible sacrifice. . . ."

By these words Augustine shows clearly that such sacrifice ought to be offered to God alone, and when it is offered to another than God, then by that deed one shows oneself to believe that that person is higher than God, which is heresy. Whoever, therefore, offers sacrifice to demons considers the demon as God and shows himself to believe the demon to be the true God by offering external signs. By which deeds they are to be considered heretics. . . .

Superstition is a vice opposed to the Christian religion or Christian worship. Therefore, it is heresy in a Christian, and as a consequence those who sacrifice to demons are to be considered heretics.

6. St. Thomas, in a commentary on Isaiah (1 *Isaiah*, 3) . . . poses the question whether it is illicit to seek the future through augury, and at the end of his commentary says, concerning demonology and what the demons are able to know, that it is always a sin to inquire of them as well as an apostasy from faith. As says Augustine, so says blessed Thomas.

The same St. Thomas [in his commentary to Peter Lombard's] *Sentences*, in Book 2, *distinctio* 7, asks whether it is a sin to use the aid of a demon and answers . . . that that which is beyond the faculties of human nature is to be asked only of God, and, just as they gravely sin who, through the cult of *latria* to an idol, impute that which is only God's to a creature of God, so indeed do they gravely sin who implore the aid of a demon in those things which are only to be asked of God. And in this way is seeing into the future [to be considered]. . . .

7. Indeed, the same is to be said of other magical works in which the accomplishment of the task is anticipated by the aid of the devil. In all these there is apostasy from the faith because of the compact made with the demon or because of a promise if the compact is already in existence or by any other deed, even if sacrifice is not performed. Man may not

serve two masters, as says St. Matthew in Chapter 8, and St. Thomas. From these things it is shown clearly that to invoke and consult demons, even without making sacrifice to them, is apostasy from the faith and, as a consequence, heresy. It is much worse if a sacrifice is involved. . . .

Peter of Tarentaise, who later was Pope Innocent V, holds . . . that although a man may be asked about a book which is lost, a demon may not, because the demon, when asked about such things, will not respond unless a pact is made with him, or illicit veneration, adjuration, or invocation. . . .

8. Our conclusion is also proved by the sayings of the Canon lawyers. . . .

Thirdly, our conclusion is also proved by the decisions of the Church. Indeed, Causa XXVI q.5 c.[12] *Episcopi* says this: "Bishops and their officials should labor with all their strength. . . ."[4]

And from this it appears that those who share and exercise the magical art are to be considered heretics and avoided. . . .

And from this it appears that the said evil women, persevering in their wickedness, have departed from the right way and the faith and the devils delude them. If, therefore, these same women, concerning whom it is not contested that they offer sacrifices to the demons they invoke, are perfidious and faithless and deviate from the right way as the said canon from the Council of Ancyra makes clear, then, as a consequence, if they have been baptized they are to be considered heretics; since for a Christian to deviate from the right way and faith and to embrace infidelity is properly to hereticize. How much more, then, are Christians, who show the honor of *latria* to demons and sacrifice to the demons they invoke, to be said and considered to be perfidious, deviants from the right way, and faithless in the love of Christians, which is heresy—and by consequence to be considered heretics? . . .

Indeed, the further a creature is separated from divine perfection, the greater the fault it is to show him the honor of *latria*. And since the demons (not on account of their nature, but on account of their guilt) are the most separated from God of all creatures, so much the worse is it to adore them. And to number them among the Angels is wicked heresy. Those who count Angels among the heretics show manifest heresy by so counting them, adoring them, or by any way sacrificing to them. And as a consequence, those who perpetuate this kind of wickedness are to be judged as heretics by the Church.

9. The Constitution of Pope John XXII against magicians and magical superstitions. . . .[5]

10. . . . Whoever invokes the aid of Mohammed, even if he does nothing else, falls into manifest heresy. So does anyone who in his honor constructs an altar to him. In similar cases the same thing may be said of

invoking any demon, building him an altar, sacrificing to him, etc. These are the acts of *latria*, which ought to be given only to God. . . .

11.   In the second case the conclusion is that if those who invoke the demons do not show to the demons they invoke the honor of *latria*, but do show them the honor of *hyperdulia* or that of *dulia* in the manner described before and have clearly confessed to this judicially or have been convicted of it, such are to be considered by the judgment of the Church not magicians, but heretics, and as a consequence if they recant and abjure heresy they are to be perpetually immured as penitent heretics. If, however, they do not recant, they are to be treated as impenitent heretics; likewise if they abjure and then relapse, they are to suffer punishment like other heretics.

12.   . . . *Dulia* may be expressed in two ways, or rather in two kinds of case. The first is as a sign of sanctity. This is the case of Abraham, Lot [and others]. . . . This case is that of Angels and saints who are in the heavenly fatherland and are adored by us and celebrated by the honor of *dulia*.

13.   The second case is a sign of governance, jurisdiction, and power. This is the case with the prophet Nathan, and *Bersabee* the mother of Solomon who adored David the King, as it says in 3 *Kings*, 1. This is also the case with Popes, Kings, and others who lawfully wield power, as vicegerents of God in authority and rule. If, therefore, anyone should show to them the honor of *dulia* then he shows himself to believe that person to whom he displays the honor of *dulia* to be a saint and a friend of God, or a governor or a rector duly constituted by God, and thus that God ought to be honored in him, his vicar. Now when the honor of *dulia* is shown to a saint, God is principally adored by the honor of *latria* through the saint. And when a Pope, King, or any other person who wields power is revered by the honor of *dulia*, God is venerated by the honor of *latria* through his Vicar. And thus by these kinds of honors which are shown to the saints and to the rectors of the Church and to the princes of this world, it is not themselves, but God in them who is principally venerated. Therefore, showing the honor of *dulia* to a demon who has been invoked by these means and by exterior actions, is to reveal oneself in heart and mind as believing inwardly that the demon is above the saints and the friend of God and is to be venerated as if saintly, or that he is above the rectors of this world and the governors duly constituted by God and therefore is to be revered as having jurisdiction and power. In both senses this is heretical and perverse, since it is contrary to the holy scriptures and against the decisions of the Church. The Demon is neither a saint nor the friend of God, chiefly since he is obstinate in his sin and wickedness. Nor is he one of God's governors in this world duly constituted, but he is the captured slave, the falsifier and deceiver, as the sacred canons and all that we have

said above clearly shows. Therefore, those who are convicted of showing the demon the honor of *dulia* are to be treated not as magicians, but as heretics. . . .

NOTES

1. The edition of the *Directorium inquisitorum* translated here is: Rome, 1587, pp. 235-36; 338-43. On Eymeric's work and the genre of inquisitors' manuals generally, see my article "Editing Inquisitors' Manuals in the Sixteenth Century: Francisco Peña and the *Directorium Inquisitorum* of Nicholas Eymeric," *The Library Chronicle* 40 (1975): *Bibliographical Essays in Honor of Rudolf Hirsch*: 95-107. The standard study is A. Dondaine, "Le Manuel de l'inquisiteur (1230–1330)," *Archivum Fratrum Praedicatorum* 17 (1947): 85-194. On the question of *latria and dulia,* see Nicholas M. Haring," "*Liber de dulia et latria* of Master Michael, Papal Notary," *Medieval Studies* 33 (1971): 188-200. I hope to write a longer study of *latria* and *dulia* in medieval thought.

2. *Latria* is that form of adoration which must be shown only to God; hence, *idolatria* is worship shown to idols which ought to be shown only to God.

3. *Dulia* is a form of veneration to be shown only to saints, holy men, and to God's vicars on earth.

4. Eymeric here gives the *Canon Episcopi* (above, p. 73).

5. Eymeric here gives the constitution of Pope John XXII (above, p. 132).

Appendix 3

The Magician
the Witch
and the Historians

The first century of the modern study of early European witchcraft opened in 1843 with the publication of W. G. Soldan's *Geschichte der Hexenprozess* and J. G. T. Grässe's *Bibliotheca Magia et Pneumatica*. Its principal landmarks are the works of Heinrich Heppe (Soldan's editor and son-in-law), Jules Michelet, Henry Charles Lea, and Joseph Hansen. Besides the great histories and source collections assembled by these scholars, there appeared a host of specialized studies, so that by 1900 Robert Yve-Plessis's *Essai d'un bibliographie française méthodique et raisonée de la sorcellerie et possession démoniaque* faced a vast amount of material. That material has increased throughout the twentieth, at a particularly rapid rate during the past ten years. Two recent scholars, H. C. Erik Midelfort and E. William Monter, have both written studies of the literature produced in recent years in the hope of coordinating its major themes and suggesting further research and new directions.[1]

Besides the great scholarly histories of the nineteenth century, to which may be added the mork of Julies Garinet and others, the subject of witchcraft interested other, less scholarly and more excitable writers. The confessional debates of the Reformation and the rationalist debates of the seventeenth and eighteenth centuries gave the topic wide currency among both learned and unlearned publics. The Romantic passion for occultism and folk-wisdom only increased general interest, even as it attacked Enlightenment attitudes. Within this mass of learned and unlearned interest, William Monter has discerned two distinct attitudes toward witchcraft, the rationalist and the romantic. The rationalist attitude argued that witchcraft never existed, that a misunderstanding of scripture, the flowering (or debasement) of scholastic exegesis and ontology, and the murderous cynicism of the Inquisition had concocted witchcraft, and that ecclesiastical ignorance, rapacity, and fanaticism had sustained it until the devastating and purifying arrival of the Age of Reason. The romantic attitude, represented by Michelet and several more recent writers, identified witchcraft either with the survival of non-Christian beliefs or, somewhat later, with institutionalized dissent and resistance to authority in late medieval society. To this group there may be added those (mostly clerical) scholars who believed that the witches did what they were accused of doing, or worse, that they posed a real danger, and that the medieval Church acted with prudence and legitimate authority against them. The rationalist attitude has tended to remain strong in scholarly circles. Perhaps the enduring attraction of one variety or another of the romantic attitude may be explained by twentieth-century interest in social history, anthropology, and religious dissent.

In some ways, each of these two attitudes reinforced the other. The nineteenth-century liberal rationalist approach was strengthened by an age of political and ecclesiastical reaction, the romantic fascination with the occult, and an increasingly articulate and professional scholarly approach by Catholic historians who wrote with an eye toward the criticism they knew they would receive for their learned defenses of Church policy. Thus, during the nineteenth century, as much scholarly energy, talent, and labor on this subject was expended in the service of confessional or epistemological conflicts as by disinterested curiosity, and these differences usually dominated the reception of individual works and the reputations in one set of circles of writers belonging to others. Catholic historians regarded such writers as White and Lea warily; rationalist historians often regarded their critics with as much contempt as they did the subjects of their studies, the engineers of the witchcraft persecutions and the literary demonologists who taught them.

Confessional and epistemological polarization was one aspect that governed nineteenth-century scholarship. Another was the state of disciplines that might have (and since have) clarified problems that plagued both sides. The following developments might have lifted studies in the history and character of the witchcraft persecutions out of the confessional and epistemological tracks on which they had generally run since the eighteenth century: a reliable and field-tested social anthropology; extensive studies in the history and nature of mental outlooks, mental illness and medicine in general; the expansion of new models of social theory and sociology; and a disciplined approach to folklore. However, few of these were available, particularly to rationalist historians, whose work suffers precisely from an excessive reliance on individual texts divorced from their literary or social context and from a lack of contact with social and anthropological theory. When new disciplines such as those discussed above did become available from the early twentieth century on, they usually avoided the controversial area of confessional argumentative scholarship and turned toward the analysis of non-European societies, on the one hand, or to problems of social and economic history and demography, on the other. In spite of the promise and great intellectual power of the work of Gabriel Le Bras, Marc Bloch, and Lucien Febvre, the investigation of the cultural context of medieval and early modern religion had acquired an unfashionable, almost unpleasantly exotic character which still lingers in most general histories of the early European Church and society. The rationalist model, perhaps best represented by the work of George Lincoln Burr and by Henry Charles Lea's fragmentary and unfinished *Materials toward a History of Witchcraft*, painstakingly compiled and edited by Arthur Howland and published in 1938, became virtually sealed off from the new social history by its fundamental premises. However Lea might have finished it if he had lived, it would have never become the authoritative masterpiece that his *History of the Inquisition in the Middle Ages* became and remains. It is impossible to write an institutional history of witchcraft, and Lea's great failing in the *Materials* was his inability to connect the materials from vastly diffuse sources into a coherent historical explanation.

It was precisely in other disciplines that the most influential work began to be done. The work of Bloch, Febvre, and many other historians opened up the life of small early-European communities and their mental outlook as dramatically as history has ever opened up anything. In 1937, the year before Howland published Lea's *Materials*, the anthropologist E. E. Evans-Pritchard published his own seminal study, *Witchcraft, Magic, and Oracles among the Azande*, and from that date the results of anthropological study have been incorporated into many studies of early European witchcraft, notably those of Alan MacFarlane, Keith Thomas, and Jeffrey Russell.[2] The dialogue between historians and anthropologists has been only one of several useful cross-disciplinary links that have offered the historian of witchcraft new avenues to explore. Peter Brown's use of Evans-Pritchard's approach has even cast new light on the problem of sorcery in late imperial Rome.[3] The study of social deviance and nonconformity, the confessional frontiers of Reformation and Counter-Reformation Europe, the psychology and the life mechanisms of small traditional societies, all have been brought forth and offered as explanatory strategies to account for what has become a complex and often maddeningly vague subject.

Indeed, from the impoverished rigidity and narrowness of the early rationalist approach and the devout vagueness of the romantic approach, the field may now be said to suffer from a surfeit of explanatory strategies, each of which runs the risk of excessive generalization based upon a relatively slender or specialized data base and a limited methodology.[4] In contrast to studies purporting to deal with what their authors designate as a craze, delusion, mania, obsession, or aberration (with their implicit echoes of a monkish, scholastic, popish, or heretical theodicy), the recent studies of witchcraft have, at their best, focused upon the social and psychological reality of the practice of magic and witchcraft. Their authors have properly assumed that such beliefs reflect, preserve, and reinforce a society's larger beliefs about the world, and they must be examined in the context of a society's view of the world. Perhaps the greatest achievement of the scholarship of the last forty years is its refusal to isolate the study of sorcery and related practices and beliefs from other beliefs and social practices.

Although some of the particular generalizations offered by anthropologists concerning the universality of societal concerns with sorcery and witchcraft have come under recent criticism, the anthropologists' injunction that these topics must be studied in the context of a society's whole existence has been perhaps the single most influential theme in recent witchcraft research. A second theme, dealt with in an increasing number of studies, is the small community and the place of witchcraft in its whole life. The works of H. C. Erik Midelfort, Alan MacFarlane, and Emmanuel LeRoy LaDurie are models of this kind of study.

In the light of these influences, not only have the older rationalist and romantic approaches lost much of their intellectual attractiveness, but other, less scholarly theories of witchcraft have been utterly confounded. The fabrications and confections of Montague Summers and Margaret Murray, however often even anthropologists have tried to touch up the work of the latter, simply do not stand up to serious criticism. The denunciation of Murray's work, by C. L'Estrange Ewen and others, began when she first began to publish it and has been echoed by Eliot Rose and virtually every other modern scholar in the field. The work of Murray and Summers now seems as remote as the rationalist and romantic works of a century ago. So too is the hasty theory, invented by Joseph Hansen and pursued recently by no less sensible a historian than H. R. Trevor-Roper, that witchcraft as it was conceived and prosecuted in the sixteenth and seventeenth centuries originated in the mountainous regions of Europe and was based upon inquisitors' and theologians' misunderstandings of peasant lore and custom. There is no evidence to suggest a particularly mountainous origin for the idea of witchcraft; in fact, there is considerable evidence that witchcraft was as much an urban as a rural phenomenon.

One of the great advantages of H. R. Trevor-Roper's essay, the "European Witch-Craze of the Sixteenth and Seventeenth Centuries," was that it forced the historians of the sixteenth and seventeenth centuries to look at the whole of the periods they worked with, rather than neglecting the witchcraft beliefs and prosecutions of men whom they admired for their contributions to rationality. Although Trevor-Roper's essay is not particularly reliable when it deals with the period before 1550, it effectively and eloquently forced witchcraft prosecutions upon the attentions of many historians who otherwise might have continued to ignore them. In addition to Trevor-Roper's work, the great Spanish scholar Julio Caro Baroja's studies *The World of the Witches* and *Vidas magias y inquisición*, and the massive, immensely learned, but idiosyncratic *Encyclopedia of Magic and Witchcraft* by Rossell Hope Robbins all contributed to raising the consciousness of historians to the point of being willing to treat witchcraft beliefs and prosecutions as legitimate objects of historical study. The work of Robert Mandrou in France, a pupil of Febvre, and Raoul Manselli in Italy also contributed to this new interest.

The first results of this new and serious concern with witchcraft were the publications of Keith Thomas and Alan MacFarlane. The former deals with the cultural world of sixteenth-century England; and the latter, with a series of specific trial records of that time. H. C. Erik Midelfort's *Witch-Hunting in Southwestern Germany*, published in 1975, is also a masterful study of a particular region, guided by a sound knowledge of anthropological principles and an extensive historical familiarity with the whole society studied. Indeed, Mac Farlane's and Midelfort's studies of case records and individual centers of persecution utilize what is perhaps the most promising method for future scholarship in the social history of witchcraft: the consideration of specific regional crises on the basis of a close study of archival resources and a social analysis of victims and accusers.

Besides the kind of acute and revealing social history produced by the disciplined study of local records and societies, a second important influence has been the study of religious sentiment and its relation to dissent and heterodoxy in the medieval and early-modern worlds. The work of Herbert Grundmann, *Die religiöse Bewegungen im Mittelalter*, published in 1935 and revised in 1961, has been perhaps the single most influential book in this area. It lies behind some of the most exciting historical work of the past thirty years. Its influence can be seen in Christopher Brooke's brilliant study "Heresy and Religious Sentiment" and in Jeffrey Russell's encyclopedic history *Witchcraft in the Middle Ages*, which makes the strongest case yet for the role of heresy in the shaping of the witchcraft persecutions.

One of the problems recognized by all historians of witchcraft from 1843 on is that of the relationship between the literary, learned clerical class that described and recorded witchcraft beliefs and practices, and the content of those beliefs in the minds of those who allegedly held them. It is the problem of the relation between high and low culture that has vexed historians working on many other topics besides witchcraft. One of the most successful attempts to resolve some aspects of this divergency of sources is Richard Kieckhefer's fine short study *European Witch Trials: Their Foundation in Popular and Learned Culture, 1300–1500,* published in 1976.

The study of local persecutions, including several very recent studies of the witches of Old Salem (now Danvers), Massachusetts in the 1690s, do not lend themselves to an understanding of the mental world of the learned judges and demonologists. Studies of the learned tradition, on the other hand, often fail to illuminate the unsophisticated, rough world of the town and village. The bar separating accusers and their victims, on the one hand, from the judges and the learned demonologists, on the other, is literally as real in scholarship as it was in the sixteenth-century courtrooms. One of the virtues of Kieckhefer's work is that it attempts successfully to find a means of connecting the world of the participants in the persecutions with the learned world of the theoreticians of witchcraft.

In modern studies of witchcraft different disciplines offer different perspectives. Anthropology, for example, helps to explain local societies and regional persecutions, but it is unable to deal with the passage of time, with the specific historicity of European witch-beliefs, and with the role of learned culture in these beliefs. The history of religion can, as Thomas and others point out, explain the parallelisms and relationships between sacramental magic and forbidden magic in traditional European culture. The selective analysis of texts, especially in their relation to traditional genres and their provenance, can overcome some of the generalizing tendencies that some historians of witchcraft still reveal when discussing generally vague categories, such as "ecclesiastical documents"; medieval documents, like modern ones, came from different sources, many of them indeed "ecclesiastical," but very different from one another. A canon lawyer and a theologian addressed problems with very different aims and resources, albeit within a generally agreed-upon Christian tradition. An instructor of monastic novices wrote with a different purpose, using different materials, for a specific audience different from those of a pope, an author of inquisitors' manuals, or a moral theologian. In all, the works of Midelfort and MacFarlane, Thomas and Russell, Kieckhefer and Caro Baroja have helped the field of witchcraft scholarship (and social, intellectual, and religious history, generally) to begin a new synthesis to replace the older rationalist or romantic ones that for so long have dominated learned and popular histories.

Another problem that has faced historians of witchcraft, that of the enormous chronology demanded by the nature and history of ideas of witchcraft, in many respects has not been solved. Few historians, including Trevor-Roper, are able to work comfortably in a period that stretches from Roman antiquity to the mid-eighteenth century. The diversity of regions in which trials were held also militates against synthesis. Usually, the generalist is forced by the sheer bulk of his materials to adopt a single explanation and focus all his energy upon it alone. Thus, Jeffrey Russell's able and intelligent study argues a single thesis: that witchcraft derived from heresy, not only in the forms of trial and accusation, but from actual heretical sects and their devices for rebelling against ecclesiastical authoritarianism. Such explanations, however valuable they are for an author, as well as for providing a focus for very diverse data studied over a long period, tend to distort the historical picture by the very nature of their tendency toward an exclusive focus. Thus, in what is probably the most important general history so far, Norman Cohn's *Europe's Inner Demons,* published in 1975, such theses as Russell's are attacked and criticized on precisely these grounds. Although Russell's book is more exhaustive, Cohn's criticism is sharp and usually effective.

Cohn's own thesis is extremely impressive. First, Cohn disproves the authenticity of several documents that had always been regarded as key pieces in the history of the development of witchcraft. By critically denying the authenticity of some fourteenth century trial records (which Kieckhefer had also done, quite independently), Cohn forces the historian to look, not at the "anticipation" of the later sixteenth-century portrait of the witch, but at what the sources actually discuss—magic. For Cohn, the motifs of most of the later witchcraft literature are already found in antiquity, in the Roman traditional invective against enemies of the state, Jews, and Christians. He next traces the process whereby heresy was associated with worship of and association with demons. Finally, he traces the process whereby the magician, rather than the heretic, turned into the witch of the late fifteenth, sixteenth, and seventeenth centuries. The greatest virtue of Cohn's study is its point of view. Critically and effectively working on specific incidents and texts, Cohn nevertheless manages to keep a sense of continuity over long periods of time and a diversity of sources. His views on the destruction of the Templars, the importance of magic, and the legal and social attitudes toward heresy are exemplary. His book is a required piece of reading with the works of Russell, Kieckhefer, and Thomas. These general studies, along with the local studies of MacFarlane, Midelfort, Carlo Guinzburg, and LeRoy Ladurie, constitute an important and extremely informative body of scholarly literature, devoid of cant, confessionalism, ideology, or *idées fixes.* They exactly and dramatically describe the state of the field, by constituting the best of it.

Aside from the study of Robert-Leon Wagner, *"Sorcier" et "magicien"*:

Contribution à l'histoire du vocabulaire de la magie (Paris, 1939), an important work primarily concerned with literature, there has been no systematic analysis of the actual terminology in Latin and the European vernacular languages used to describe and label magicians and witches. In my own work with the sources, *maleficium* and the *maleficus* (or *malefica*) are the most commonly used terms, and such terms as *sortilegium* and *divinatio* and others are specific subcategories of the broader designation for occult offenses of any kind. Having found "witchcraft" and "sorcery" linked semantically in the sources, I have worked with condemnations of magic not usually associated with the medieval history of witchcraft. I have drawn heavily upon Lynn Thorndike's monumental and magisterial *History of Magic and Experimental Science*, more than most recent writers on the history of witchcraft, because the figures of the sorcerer and the witch—although set apart semantically and, by anthropologists, functionally—were once very close. Thorndike wrote his great history of magic because he would have had no adequate framework for a discussion of medieval scientific ideas and their place in the organization of knowledge without considering magic. I have attempted to take some of Torndike's materials and juxtapose them, not to experimental science, but to the *ars magica* as that subject was viewed by medieval moralists, theologians, lawyers, and inquisitors. Thorndike's *History* and Joseph Hansen's great anthology of original documents, *Quellen und Untersuchungen zur Geschichte des Hexenwahns und der Hexenverfolgung im Mittelalter* (Bonn, 1901), are cited throughout the notes to this book. The other standard histories and references to texts—Lea's *Materials*, Hansen's own *Zauberwahn, Inquisition und Hexenprozess* (Munich, 1900), Robbins' *Encyclopedia*, Russell's *Witchcraft*, and Cohn's study— all bear upon most of this book and offer bibliographical guidance. I have only cited their discussions of points on which there is disagreement.

The pioneering work of Lea and Hansen, both rationalist historians, has strongly influenced all subsequent twentieth-century study of the history of witchcraft. The modern works discussed above, although most of them transcend the limits of rationalist historical thought, all take a similar approach. Among the most novel recent approaches, however, three deserve to be particularly singled out because they suggest important new directions for research. Keith Thomas, *Religion and the Decline of Magic* (New York, 1971), is a monumental study of sixteenth-century English popular beliefs based upon the anthropologist's techniques and the historian's command of different kinds of data. This work has greatly illuminated large areas of sixteenth-century thought and custom hitherto either lightly treated (as in C. Grant Loomis, *White Magic* [Cambridge, Mass., 1948] or C. MacCulloch, *Medieval Faith and Fable* [Oxford, 1936]) or explored only in part. Raoul Manselli, *I Fenomeni di devianze nel medio evo* (Turin, 1975), pp. 85-99, constructs a typology of ecclesiastical deviance that includes *"magia e stregoneria."* In some respects Manselli shares Russell's interest in social deviance as a means of understanding such phenomena as the heretic and the magician. Finally, Gerhart Ladner, *"Homo viator:* Medieval Views on Alienation and Order," *Speculum* 42 (1967), pp. 233-59, deals with the larger question of medieval theodicy, regarding magic and witchcraft as one aspect of a new kind of alienation that appeared in late twelfth- and early thirteenth-century European society. These three approaches suggest some of the range of the most recent modern scholarship and the long road from rationalist historiographical presuppositions that most of it has travelled.

Historians, fortunately, keep working. It is a pleasure to end this bibliographical appendix by citing three recent and very helpful works that have appeared in fields touched by this book. Raoul Manselli's *La religion populaire au moyen age* (Montreal-Paris, 1975) is a useful and illuminating methodological approach to the problem of popular religion in medieval Europe. *The Damned Art: Essays in the Literature of Witchcraft* (London, 1977), edited by Sydney Anglo, contains ten studies of some of the most important treatises on demonology and witchcraft produced between the late fifteenth and the early eighteenth centuries. This fresh approach to often ignored literary texts is particularly welcome. Finally, the great collection of witchcraft materials at Cornell University has now been catalogued: Martha J. Crowe, ed., *Witchcraft: Catalogue of the Witchcraft Collection in Cornell University Library* (Millwood, N.Y., 1977). Not only is the catalogue itself a superb guide to one of the world's greatest collections, but the introduction, by Rossell Hope Robbins, is a fine contribution to the history of witchcraft, to the history of the rationalist school of witchcraft historians, and to the role of penology and the courts in the witchcraft prosecutions. With the bibliographical studies of Midelfort, Russell, and Monter, these works suggest important new directions, not only for historians of spirituality and ecclesiology, but for scholars of social history and intellectual history. It is to these diverse fields that the present book is offered.

NOTES

1. H. C. Erik Midelfort, "Recent Witch-Hunting Research, or Where Do We go from Here?" *Papers of the Bibliographical Society of America* 62 (1968): 373-420; E. William Monter, "The Historiography of European Witchcraft: Progress and Prospects," *The Journal of Interdisciplinary History* 11

(1972): 435-52. See also Jeffrey Burton Russell, *Witchcraft in the Middle Ages* (Ithaca, 1972), pp. 345-77.

2. Alan MacFarlane, *Witchcraft in Tudor and Stuart England* (New York, 1970); Keith Thomas, *Religion and the Decline of Magic* (New York, 1971); Jeffrey Russell, *Witchcraft in the Middle Ages* (Ithaca, N.Y., 1972).

3. Peter Brown, "Sorcery, Demons and the Rise of Christianity: from Late Antiquity to the Middle Ages," in Peter Brown, *Religion and Society in the Age of St. Augustine* (New York, 1972), pp. 119-46.

4. See the remarks of the anonymous reviewer in *The Times Literary Supplement*, No. 3583 (October 1970), "Witches and the Community: An Anthropological Approach to the History of Witchcraft," and Lawrence Stone, "The Disenchantment of the World," *New York Review of Books*, 2 December 1971. A good anthology of anthropological approaches is Max Marwick, ed., *Witchcraft and Sorcery* (Baltimore, 1970).

Index

Individuals born before 1600 are listed under the first name. Those born after 1600 are listed by the last name.

Acts of Peter, 8

Adam Stratton, 119

Adso, *Libellus de Antichristo,* 7

Agrippa von Nettesheim. *See* Henry Cornelius

Alain de la Roche, 146–47

Alain de Lille, 78–79

Albertus Magnus, 95

Alexander III, Pope, 99–100, 117

Alexander IV, Pope, 99–100, 131–33, 152

Alfonso Testado, 147

Alice Perrers, 124n

d'Alverney, Marie-Thérèse, 25, 86

Anselm of Besate, 21–28, 32–34, 45, 50, 56, 67, 89

Antichrist, 7n, 18

Apuleius, 7n, 56

Aristotle, 91n

Arnald of Villanova, xi, 66, 106, 112, 117, 118

Augustine, St., 4, 10, 15, 41–43, 47, 53, 56, 69, 73, 76, 85, 97; *De civitate Dei,* 6, 8, 72, 75, 127, 134, 198; *De doctrina christiana,* 4–5, 50, 72, 75; *Quaest. in Hept.,* 68

Baldwinus, 77–78

Bartholomew of Exeter, 78

Benedict IX, Pope, 28

Benedict XIII, Pope, 143

Bernard Delicieux, 130n

Bernard Gui, 41, 131–32, 133–34, 160, 189, 194

Bernard, St., 45

Bible: Exodus 7–11, 68; Exodus 7:8, 3, 148; Exodus 22:18, 17–18, 68–69, 70, 139–40, 148; Leviticus 19–20, 69, 148; Deut. 18, 69; 1 Samuel 18, 69; John 8:44, 12; Acts 13: 6–12, 3; Revelations 2:9; 3:9, 12

Bodin, Jean. *See* Jean Bodin

Boniface VIII, Pope, 98, 120n, 124–27, 128

Brown, Peter, 9, 114, 117–18
Burchard of Worms, 14, 71, 73, 80, 99

Caesarius of Heisterbach, 92–93, 112
Canon episcopi, 15, 72n, 101, 134,
  141, 150
Cathar, xiv
Cecco d'Ascoli, 105–6, 118
Charlemagne, 16
Cicero, *Rhetorica*, 22, 28
Cohn, Norman, xiv, xvi, xviii, 7, 11–
  12, 41, 124–27
controversiae, 23–24, 26
court, 49, 111n
Cowdrey, H. E. J., 22, 27, 28
crimen exceptum, 152
crimen magiae, xiii, xvi, 124, 176
curiositas, xiv, 2, 16, 90
Curtius, E. R., 23

Dante, 34, 86, 102–6, 112
demimonde, 10, 123, 133
dulia, xiv, xv, 196–200

Edric Wild, 51
Eleanor Cobham, 125
Elymas, 3–5, 8, 12–13
Enguerrand de Marigny, 121, 128
Etienne Tempier, 89
Eudo, 51
Eugenius IV, Pope, 146, 149
exemplum, 32, 41

Faust, xii, 13
folklore, 14, 24

Galeazzo Visconti, 131n
Gerbert of Aurillac. *See* Sylvester II,
  Pope
Gervais of Tilbury, 35, 37, 41, 45, 53–
  57, 67, 102
Gianfrancesco Pico, 163–64, 166
goes, goetia, 2
Gratian, 16, 71–78, 91, 100–1, 117
Gregory VI, Pope, 28, 30
Gregory VII, Pope, 28

Gregory IX, Pope, 79, 86, 98, 156–57
Griffolino d'Arezzo, 103–5
Guibert de Nogent, 41–42, 44, 75
Guichard of Troyes, 120
Guido Bonatti, 102–4
Gundissalinus, 65, 67

heresy, xvi, 10, 33–45
Herla, 51
Hincmar of Reims, 15–16, 75
Honorius III, Pope, 99
Hopkin, Charles E., 95n
Hrabanus Maurus, 15–16, 47, 53, 66
Hubert de Burgh, 119
Hugh of St. Victor, 13, 53, 56, 65–67,
  70, 79, 85, 91
Huizinga, Johann, 145–46
humanism, xi–xii
Hugues Geraud, 130n

impotence, 76n
Indiculi superstitionum, 14, 24
Innocent IV, Pope, 140–41, 152, 190
Innocent VIII, Pope, 170–73
Inquisition, 150–61
Isidore of Seville, 13n, 47, 53, 56, 66,
  72, 87
Ivo of Chartres, 72–73

Jean Bodin, xv, 164
Jews and magic, 3, 11–13; as sorcerers,
  13, 31, 48, 94
Joan of Navarre, 125
Johann von Frankfurt, 146–47
Johannes Andreae, 100
Johannes de Turrecremata, 149–50
John XXII, Pope, 99, 129–35, 149
John Bromyard, 142–43
John of Freiburg, 140–42
John of Salisbury, xvii, 45–50, 52, 55,
  64, 70, 73, 78, 85, 89, 112, 114,
  115, 123
Jones, William R., 122–23
Jordanes de Bergamo, 147
Justin Martyr, 6–8, 43

Kelly, H. A., 91
Kennan, Elizabeth, 93
Kieckhefer, Richard, 167
Konrad von Marburg, 156–57
Kors, Alan C., xiii

Law, Germanic, 14; Roman, 8, 75, 135, 150–55, 185–87; *Theodosian Code*, 14; Canon, 71–78, 98–102, 148–61
Latria, xiv, xv, 196–200
Lea, H. C., 14, 55, 92, 182–85
Leo I, Pope, 11
Liber iuratus, 111–12, 117, 119, 124
Louis the Pious, 16

Macfarlane, Alan, xviii
Mahaut d'Artois, 121n
Malleus maleficarum, 147, 153, 160, 170–75
Manitius, Karl, 23
Marsilio Ficino, 162
Merlin, xii
Michael Scot, 86–89, 102–5
Midelfort, H. C. Erik, xviii, 163–64
Moore, R. I., 41

narratio fabulosa, 33
Nicholas Eymeric, 132–33, 160, 189, 194–201
Nock, A. D., 2

Oldradus da Ponte, 133–34

Palumbus, 31
pastourelle, 37
Paucapalea, 76
Paul, St., 3–5, 8, 12–13, 72
Pedro Alfonso, 64–65, 67
Peter the Chanter, 70, 89
Peter Comestor, 70
Peter Lombard, 70, 89, 91, 95–96
Peter the Venerable, 43
Philip IV, 119–29
Picatrix, 110–12, 117, 119, 124, 165
Pico della Mirandola, xi, 161
Pierre de Latilly, 121n, 128

Plato, 1–2, 56, 162
porphyry, 8
praestigium, 74n
prisca magia, xii
Prospero, xii
Psellos, 42, 162

Ralph of Coggeshall, 35–44
Raymond of Peñafort, 78–79, 80, 98–101, 140
Regino of Prüm, 17, 72
Richard Fishacre, 88
Richard Ledrede, 119n
Robbins, R. H., 166n
Robert of Flamborough, 78–80
Robert Grosseteste, 85–86
Robert Kilwardby, 66, 89
Robert Pullen, 70
Roger Bacon, 66, 88, 98, 118
Rolandus, 76
Rufinus, 77–78
Russell, J. B., xiv, xviii, 14, 43, 45, 94, 154, 169–70

Saul 5, 68–69
Simon Magus, xii, 7n, 86
Southern, R. W., 94
Stephen of Tournai, 76–77
Summa Parisiensis, 76–78
Sylvester II, Pope (Gerbert), 28, 31, 48, 51, 65, 87

Templars, 54, 125–29
Tertullian, 4
Thomas Aquinas, 50, 75, 91, 95–98, 103
Thomas of Chobham, 78–80
Thomas, Keith, xv, 166
Trachtenberg, Joshua, 13

Ugolino Zanchini, 134–35
University of Paris, 91, 143–44

Venus, 31
Vergil, 53–54, 55, 102n
Vilgard of Ravenna, 22

Walter Langton, 119

Walter Map, 39, 40, 45, 50–53, 55,
    56, 67
William of Auvergne, 66, 85, 86, 89–
    91, 95, 101, 112, 139n
William of Conches, 64

William of Reims, 35–36, 53
William of Malmesbury, 28–33, 49,
    51, 56, 57, 142
William of Santa Sabina, 131
Witch of Berkeley, 28n

The Middle Ages

EDWARD PETERS, *General Editor*

Christian Society and the Crusades, 1198–1229. Sources in Translation, including The Capture of Damietta by Oliver of Paderborn. Edited by Edward Peters

The First Crusade: The Chronicle of Fulcher of Chartres and Other Source Materials. Edited by Edward Peters

The Burgundian Code: The Book of Constitutions or Law of Gundobad and Additional Enactments. Translated by Katherine Fischer Drew

The Lombard Laws. Translated, with an Introduction, by Katherine Fischer Drew

Ulrich Zwingli (1484–1531). Selected Works. Edited by Samuel Macauley Jackson. Introduction by Edward Peters

From St. Francis to Dante: Translations from the Chronicle of the Franciscan Salimbene (1221–1288). G. G. Coulton. Introduction by Edward Peters

The Duel and the Oath. Part I and II of Superstition and Force, Henry Charles Lea. Introduction by Edward Peters

The Ordeal. Part III of Superstition and Force, Henry Charles Lea. Introduction by Edward Peters

Torture. Part IV of Superstition and Force, Henry Charles Lea. Introduction by Edward Peters

Witchcraft in Europe, 1100–1700: A Documentary History. Edited by Alan C. Kors and Edward Peters

The Scientific Achievement of the Middle Ages. Richard C. Dales. Introduction by Edward Peters

History of the Lombards. Paul the Deacon. Translated by William Dudley Foulke. Introduction by Edward Peters

Monks, Bishops and Pagans: Christian Culture in Gaul and Italy, 500–700.
    Edited, with an Introduction, by Edward Peters

The World of Piers Plowman. Edited and translated by Jeanne Krochalis and
    Edward Peters

Felony and Misdemeanor: A Study in the History of Criminal Law. Julius
    Goebel, Jr. Introduction by Edward Peters

Women in Medieval Society. Edited by Susan Mosher Stuard

The Expansion of Europe: The First Phase. Edited by James Muldoon

Laws of the Alamans and Bavarians. Translated, with an Introduction, by
    Theodore John Rivers

Law, Church, and Society: Essays in Honor of Stephan Kuttner. Edited by
    Robert Somerville and Kenneth Pennington

The Fourth Crusade: The Conquest of Constantinople, 1201–1204. Donald E.
    Queller